# Game Design Deep Dive

This entry in the *Game Design Deep Dive* series takes a look at the shooter genre: one that has grown with the times and whose influence can be felt from indie teams to major studios. Joshua Bycer breaks down the 30-plus-year history of one of the most popular genres of the games industry to educate readers on how to design their own. This book is suitable for students and designers to learn about one of the most popular genres on the market.

Key features:

- Discusses reflex-driven design and the challenges and balances that go into single and multiplayer gameplay.
- Provides a breakdown of what gunplay is and how to make your FPS design pop.
- Draws from examples across the industry.
- Examines the design and philosophies that went into many of the best shooters released in the past 30 years.

**Joshua Bycer** is a Game Design Critic with more than 7 years of experience critically analyzing game design and the industry itself. In that time, through Game-Wisdom.com, he has interviewed hundreds of game developers and members of the industry about what it means to design video games.

# Game Design Deep Dive
## Shooters

Joshua Bycer

**CRC Press**
Taylor & Francis Group
Boca Raton  London  New York

CRC Press is an imprint of the
Taylor & Francis Group, an **informa** business

Cover Art: Peggy Shu. Title Graphic: Kenneth Oum.

First edition published 2025
by CRC Press
2385 NW Executive Center Drive, Suite 320, Boca Raton FL 33431

and by CRC Press
4 Park Square, Milton Park, Abingdon, Oxon, OX14 4RN

*CRC Press is an imprint of Taylor & Francis Group, LLC*

© 2025 Joshua Bycer

ISBN: 9781032584102 (hbk)
ISBN: 9781032581163 (pbk)
ISBN: 9781003449959 (ebk)

DOI: 10.1201/9781003449959

Typeset in Minion
by codeMantra

Developer Quote:
"I ain't reading all that but you should"
- Dave Oshry, CEO of New Blood

# Contents

# Preface

Despite my background focusing on reflex-driven design, it's been a long time since I could dedicate a deep dive to a genre like this. I'm excited to be able to talk about shooters, as the genre itself has seen several different periods of design, and as I'm writing this book at the end of 2023, there has been a new trend in the last few years of more indie developers putting together some fantastic takes on the genre. I hope you enjoy this entry as I believe it's my longest to date.

# Acknowledgments

For each *Game Design Deep Dive*, I run a donation incentive for people to donate to earn an acknowledgment in each one of my upcoming books through patreon. com/gwbycer. I would like to thank the following people for supporting my work while I was writing this book:

- Michael Berthaud
- Ben Bishop
- D.S.
- Jason Ellis
- Jake Everitt
- Thorn Falconeye
- Puppy Games
- Luke Hughes
- Adriaan Jansen
- Jonathan Ku
- Aron Linde
- Josh Mull
- N.W.D.D.
- Rey Obomsawin
- Janet Oblinger
- Onslaught
- David Pittman

## Social Media

Social Media Contacts

- Email: gamewisdombusiness@gmail.com
- My YouTube channel where I post daily design videos and developer interviews: youtube.com/c/game-wisdom
- Main site: Game-Wisdom.com
- Twitter and Bluesky: GWBycer

## Additional Books

If you enjoyed this entry and want to learn more about design, you can read my other works:

*20 Essential Games to Study*: A high-level look at 20 unique games that are worth studying their design to be inspired by or for a historical look at the game industry.

*Game Design Deep Dive: Platformers*: The first entry in the "Game Design Deep Dive" series focusing on 2D and 3D platformer designs. A top to bottom discussion of the history, mechanics, and design of the game industry's most recognizable and long-lasting genre.

*Game Design Deep Dive: Roguelikes*: The second entry in the "Game Design Deep Dive" series focusing on the rise and design of roguelike games. A look back at how the genre started, what makes the design unique, and an across-the-board discussion on how it has become the basis for new designs by modern developers.

*Game Design Deep Dive: Horror*: The third entry in the "Game Design Deep Dive" series examining the philosophy and psychology behind horror. Looking at the history of the genre, I explored what it means to create a scary game or use horror elements in any genre.

*Game Design Deep Dive: F2P*: The fourth entry in the "Game Design Deep Dive" series, focusing on the mobile and live service genre. Besides looking at the history and design of these games, I also talked about the ethical ramifications of their monetization systems.

*Game Design Deep Dive: Trading and Collectible Card Games*: The fifth entry in the "Game Design Deep Dive" series, which looks at the deck building genre along with Collectible Card Games (CCGs) and Trading Card Game (TCG) design, as well as covering the balancing that goes into designing cards and sets.

*Game Design Deep Dive: Role Playing Games*: This entry focuses on the role-playing game genre to look at the history of Computer Role-playing game (CRPG) and Japanese Role-playing game (JRPG) design, and lessons on abstract-based design.

*Game Design Deep Dive: Soulslikes*: The first entry to focus on a specific sub-genre of design, this book tackles soulslike design as well as a discussion on difficulty in games.

All my books are available from major retailers and from Taylor & Francis directly.

# Foreword

Now more than ever game design needs to be studied. Because the blueprints for great games lie in the history of great games! Especially first person shooters. The devil is in the details as they say and what Josh aims to do here is get into those details. So sit back, dig in and Get Psyched... or *BLOW IT OUT YOUR ASS*. Oh, and enjoy.

**Dave Oshry**

# 1

# Introduction

## 1.1 What Is the Goal of *Game Design Deep Dive: Shooters?*

My last book on soulslikes was one that covered a brief history of the game industry, but now it's time to talk about one of the major genres that has always dominated the market in some capacity (Figure 1.1). Shooters, consisting of the first and third persons, is one of the most reflex-driven genres in the industry today. It is something that can be played on any platform now, with examples ranging from fan games and *mods* to massive games with their own *eSports* following. In this entry, I'm going to cover the history of shooters and how the genre's focus has changed dramatically. This is the second time in the Deep Dive series to date where the genre's design is built heavily on level design, and I will be focusing on how this is different from other reflex-driven genres.

By the end of this book, you will understand where the genre has come from and why it is so popular. You should be able to take the lessons and principles here and apply them to making either a single player-based or a multiplayer-based game.

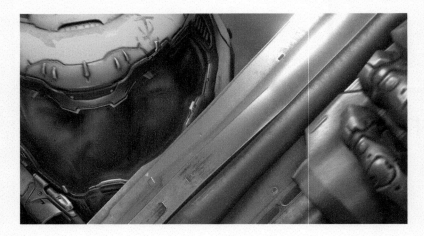

Figure 1.1

A perfect screenshot to begin a book all about shooting and gunplay.

## 1.2 The Feel of It

When I talk about reflex-driven games, it is important to discuss how the feel of the game is in the player's hands. This is a complete 180 from discussing role-playing games (RPGs) – where the abstraction at the heart of the design is the focus (Figure 1.2).

Figure 1.2

Feel is not something that is discussed a lot in role-playing games (RPGs) and abstracted design, but it can add a lot to the experience when done right, such as in the *Darkest Dungeon* series by Redhook Games.

1. Introduction

For any designer who has built abstracted games, it is very easy to miss how the feel of the game is often the difference between someone sticking with a reflex-driven game or becoming disappointed and quitting it. In this book, I will be talking about the concept of "gunplay" and what it means to design a weapon that can feel good to use. If you try to design a shooter without understanding feel and gunplay, I can guarantee you that your game is going to fail. With these lessons, this will help you when it comes to understanding what it feels like for someone to play your game and interact with the tools you've provided for them. Getting this right is what separates good shooters from legendary ones.

# 2

# The Beginning of "Boomer Shooters"

## 2.1 Early Shooters and the Rise of id Software

A common theme of discussing "the first" of a genre is that it can be hard to officially cite it for the older ones. With first-person shooters (or FPSs), the examples that have become most synonymous with the genre didn't appear until the 90s and are now colloquially referred to as "boomer shooters," and I'll talk more about that design in the next section.

Early examples of first-person shooting would be seen as far back as the 70s. What is considered the very first example of first-person shooting as a game mechanic would be *Maze War* first made available in 1973, created by Steve Colley, Howard Palmer, and Greg Thompson. In it, players would hunt each other down in a maze to try and shoot one another for points. The game originally could only be played using Advanced Research Projects Agency Network (ARPANET) or connecting two computers together. It would eventually be ported to other platforms and its design would go on to inspire many games.

In 1980, the game *Battlezone* released by Atari would become the first commercial arcade game to be made in first person. Using vector graphics to simulate 3D, players would roam a battlefield as a tank trying to take out enemies before they were attacked.

4

DOI: 10.1201/9781003449959-2

Figure 2.1

*Wolfenstein 3D* would be the game that not only popularized the *Wolfenstein* brand for fans in the 90s, but would set the stage for shooters going forward.

There were other examples of games played in first person; but for the design that this book is focusing on, that specific design would first appear in 1992. In my book on role-playing games (RPGs), I brought up *Ultima Underworld: The Stygian Abyss* developed by Blue Sky Productions that, while it wasn't a pure FPS, was in fact the first major game of the 90s to be played in first person.

As for the genre itself, in the same year, the game *Wolfenstein 3D* was released by id Software, and would be the first FPS by the company and the first example of what would become the FPS genre (Figure 2.1). *Wolfenstein 3D* was originally conceived as a sequel to *Castle Wolfenstein* (released in 1981 by Muse Software). *Castle Wolfenstein* was a stealth game that tasked players to escape castle Wolfenstein to help the allies win the war against the Nazis. Part of the original founders of id, John Carmack, John Romero, and Tom Hall, enjoyed the first game and wanted to do their own take using 3D. Instead of being a stealth game, the team focused more on combat and high-speed movement to deliver the start of the FPS genre.

In *Wolfenstein 3D*, players controlled BJ Blazkowicz who would be the central character in each game going forward. After being captured by Nazi soldiers, he must break out of castle Wolfenstein and stop their plans. Besides being the first FPS, the game is also remembered for the final boss of Hitler in a giant mech suit that the player must kill to win.

Just like with a lot of the genres discussed in this series, it's often the second game of a genre that goes on to cement its legacy, and this trend holds up with FPS and the release of *Doom* in 1993. Here, players controlled a space marine who would become known by fans as "Doom Guy." In a base on Mars, the Union Aerospace Corporation (UAC) conducted teleportation research which opened a portal to hell. When the Doom Guy became the only remaining human left after everyone has been wiped out, he goes on a one-man mission to push the demons back and end the invasion from inside hell itself.

*Doom* was a major step up from *Wolfenstein 3D* – featuring more weapons, enemy types, and an expanded focus on level design. Much like how *Super Mario Bros. 1's* (released in 1985 by Nintendo) first level, World 1-1, would become a historical point for platformers and their design, *Doom's* first level "E1M1" holds that distinction for FPS (Figure 2.2). The flow of the level, enemy and item placements, and the use of secrets would become the benchmark for countless levels not only created by id, but also by fans and *modders*. The success and reach of *Doom* cemented id Software at the time as the ones who ushered in the era of FPS games in the 90s. This is also one of the games that would infamously be talked about by politicians and conservative groups as games going too far with violent actions and would lead to the formation of the Entertainment Service Ratings Board or ESRB.

The success of *Doom* led id to work on *Doom 2* and release it in 1994 – featuring larger levels, more weapons, including the now famous "super shotgun," and the easter egg of putting John Romero's head as the weak point for the final boss. Both games also had multiplayer functionality with dial-up modems and would also be the progenitor for playing FPS against other players. Both *Doom* and *Doom 2* have been ported to multiple platforms, with both *Doom* and *Wolfenstein 3D* even ported to the Super Nintendo Entertainment System (SNES). The legacy of both

Figure 2.2

One of the most iconic levels and weapons in shooter design, *Doom* still inspires developers to this day. (This was captured using GZDoom and may look different from the retail version.)

2. The Beginning of "Boomer Shooters"

*Dooms* still remains to this day thanks to GZDoom, an editor software that was first conceived by fans to make custom levels and has since expanded into its own free engine that people have been releasing complete games with for years. There is a lot to talk about in terms of the basic design and structure that I will be saving for the next section and later chapters in this book.

The other major FPS franchise from id during this decade was *Quake*, released in 1996. Where *Doom* went for the theme of fighting demons and hell itself, *Quake* was first conceived to focus more on cosmic horror with Lovecraftian elements. The player had to explore various dimensions and deal with an invading army from Quake and fight elder Gods to save the Earth. *Quake* featured even more interesting and maze-like levels, alongside an original cast of enemies for the player to fight.

From a development standpoint, *Quake* did not have an easy one, and issues and lack of leadership according to stories led to many original members of the company leaving, including John Romero. Part of the problem was trying to figure out what they wanted the game to be and how it could stand out from *Doom*. This is a very big point for developers today – there are now a countless number of FPS of all sizes available to play, and that means the consumer is going to be far pickier regarding the ones they're going to check out. One of the points I try to stress in this series is that just copying a big name does not mean your game is going to succeed the same way.

The lack of a defining element for *Quake* did in the long run come to help it stand out. *Quake* would become more famous for its multiplayer component thanks to the advances in the engine and weapon variety (Figure 2.3). In 1996,

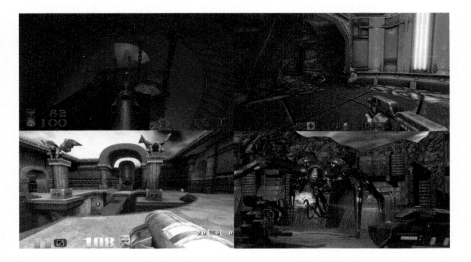

Figure 2.3

*Quake* as a franchise went through many revisions in terms of style and tone, but ultimately became more known for its multiplayer gameplay.

id released *QuakeWorld*, a standalone multiplayer version of *Quake* with its own networking code. With it, people were able to set up online games and there are still tournaments played to this day with it. *Quake 2* featured a completely different setting and structure when it was released in 1997. Interviews and stories stated that the plan was to create an entirely new franchise, but in the end, it was decided to call the game a sequel to *Quake* to help it with name recognition in the market.

id's final game for the 90s was *Quake 3 Arena* released in 1999 and would be the first commercial game from the studio that focused solely on multiplayer. While this could have been viewed as odd back then, having shooters designed only for multiplayer or with multiplayer-specific content would become a major aspect of the genre in the 2000s and to this day. Over the years, the founders and original members of id are no longer with the company, but their legacy is still strong, and I'll be talking more about their later games as they come up in this book. For more about the early history of id Software, you can read *Doom Guy: Life in First Person* by John Romero.

## 2.2 The PC Boom of the 90s

The FPS genre during the 90s, much like other genres that came about during this decade, quickly received multiple entries and franchises that all had the goal to take the crown away from *Doom* and id Software. While the designs of these games stayed the same, and I'll talk more about the design of this decade of shooting in Section 3.2, many games stood out thanks to different *aesthetics* and tone.

The spectrum of tone for FPSs could go all over the place – from very serious to scary, comical, or as bombastic as 80's action movies, and this would play into the changing of the genre in the 2000s that I'll come back to in Chapter 4 (Figure 2.4). For this section, I'm going to focus on the famous, and infamous, games that use FPS gameplay. There are plenty of games that use the first-person perspective for other gameplay loops that I will not be covering here.

As an interesting point about FPS games, not only did the games become famous, but so did the engines they were built in, with many games released after licensing the game engine from another studio. This also became another incentive for studios to create their own game engine – as a successful game with a new engine would not only earn money from consumers buying the game, but also licensing fees to studios interested in using the engine for their own games.

The *Doom* engine has been a part of countless games and custom levels thanks to the modding community, and that I'll be returning to in Section 6.2. Following the success of *Doom* and *Doom 2*, the engine was licensed to Raven Software who worked on both the *Heretic* and the *Hexen* series (released in 1994 and 1995, respectively). Both series took place in fantasy worlds with a focus on larger levels and game spaces. *Hexen* is also famous for implementing a light RPG system where players could earn experience and build one of several different classes as their main character throughout the game. There would be plenty more games

Figure 2.4

Shooter aesthetics went all over the place in the 90s and would also establish the different kinds of first-person gameplay we would see in the future.

throughout the years that would recontextualize first-person shooting and the use of guns for other designs. Both games did receive sequels in 1997 for *Hexen* and 1998 for *Heretic*. Raven would be purchased by Activision in 1997 and in recent years are one of several studios working on the *Call of Duty* franchise.

The second major game engine at the time was the Build engine, created by 3D Realms and Ken Silverman, and it would be responsible for several major franchises during the 90s as well. One of the most famous shooters in the 90s was *Duke Nukem 3D* released in 1996 (Figure 2.5). The first two games were platformers with 3D being the first one in the series to go first person. When aliens invade the Earth, it's up to Duke Nukem to save the planet. Duke was the first of what would become many FPS to feature a main character who would talk and provide wise cracks and commentary about what's going on. Voiced by Jon St. John, Duke embodied the kind of over-the-top musclehead hero of the 80s. The game boosted a variety of weapons, had different locations and levels, and was controversial at the time for allowing players to visit strip clubs to see various women in very pixelated nudity. The game went on to have multiple expansions both by 3D Realms and by other studios. While there have been several sequels over the years, *Duke Nukem* is most remembered for the failure of *Duke Nukem Forever* which took over 14 years to be released due to constant problems and frequent changes to the design. When the game was released in 2011, it was considered one of the worst games of the year. Part of the reason was the constant need to keep adding more to *Duke Nukem Forever*. Instead of trying to build one game that was a cohesive whole, the design kept changing to try and make "the" shooter of

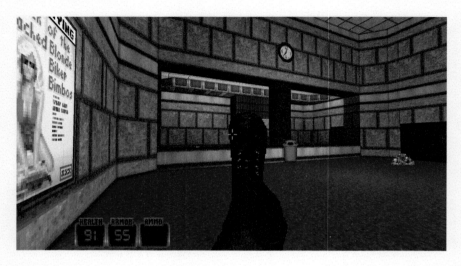

Figure 2.5

The complete opposite of tone and aesthetics from id's games, *Duke Nukem 3D* succeeded thanks to being considered not politically correct for the time and the over-the-top action style.

that year – changing engines, adding, or removing game systems. By the time the game was released, it felt like someone who tried to combine as many popular trends of FPS design over the 2000s as one could fit. In 2022, a leaked version of the 2001 build of *Duke Nukem Forever* was revealed and a lot of people enjoyed what they saw in it.

In 1997, *Blood* was released by Monolith Productions and was built using the Build engine. Here, players were Caleb, who after being betrayed by the god Tchernobog goes on a one-man rampage around the world to take revenge. This is one of the harder shooters released due to the focus on hit-scan attacks that I'll be discussing more in the next chapter. Caleb, voiced by Stephan Weyte provided dry commentary and became a fan favorite thanks to his gravelly voice. The level design stands out at the time for both its variety of stages, and the focus on exploring and interacting with the environment. The levels both had a sense of place to them, trying to evoke the environment they take in, while still providing multiple secrets, enemy fights, and keys to find. Monolith would go on to make even more shooters that will show up later in this book. One of their most famous was the spy thriller *No One Lives Forever* released in 2000. However, due to licensing issues the game is not available legally in any store at the time of writing this.

In the same year *Shadow Warrior* by 3D Realms was released. The game sparked controversy for its humor and main character "Lo Wang." Like *Blood*, there was variety in terms of levels and interaction with the environment, but the game still played like a lot of the FPS released during this decade. This point is going to come back when I talk more about shooter design later in this book and the challenges designers face with iterating on it.

One of the most famous, at the time, game failures was *Daikatana* released in 2000 by Ion Storm. The game was heavily promoted as the next game from John Romero after leaving id Software. It was shipped with numerous problems and, due to the publicity surrounding John, it was seen as his fault for them. Reporting after the fact found issues with the development of the game that led to the game being shipped in that state. Since then, modders have worked on the game and there have been unofficial patches released to improve the game.

Even though this section is meant for games released in the 90s, there is one entry that came out in 2001, but was clearly inspired by the decade. *Serious Sam* was developed by Croteam who were unknown at the time (Figure 2.6). Instead of licensing a preexisting game engine like other studios did, they used an engine they created for a game project that was canceled and redubbed it the "serious engine," as they couldn't afford the licensing for a major engine. To secure funding, the plan was to license the engine out and use one of the test levels they built for it as the vertical slice to show people the potential of it.

People enjoyed what they saw in the demo and the scope of the level and number of enemies that were attacking the player, and the demo and the studio started to get word of mouth. An interview with the website Old Man Murray started to spread awareness and the studio received a publishing deal with Gathering of

Figure 2.6

*Serious Sam* may not have done anything revolutionary with its gunplay or tone, but it was the first of its kind to go for the sheer spectacle of arena fights – far more than any other game before it.

Developers or G.O.D. *Serious Sam* told the story of Sam "Serious" Stone, who had to travel back in time to defeat an alien force before they could invade and destroy the Earth in the present. Sam had the same over-the-top personality as a lot of 90s FPS heroes with Duke Nukem being an obvious comparison. The game landed more on the side of comedy rather than seriousness, despite the name of the character. One of the most famous enemies were the kamikazes who screamed at the player despite not having a head and would chase after them to explode and cause massive damage. Weaponry included the usual mix of shotguns and machine guns, but then there was a literal cannon that shot giant cannonballs at enemies.

The most famous aspect of *Serious Sam* were the arena fights that would pit the player against dozens, or even hundreds, of enemies in a single encounter. Even though *Serious Sam* didn't do anything in terms of gameplay that was different from other shooters, it came out just as the industry was moving to more grounded shooters and attracted a following thanks to the scale of combat. Since its success, Croteam has put out more games in the series and has updated the Serious Engine over the years, with the current version at the time of writing this book at 4. *Serious Sam* has also been used in other games from smaller studios and the original games have been remastered and re-released on Steam. Besides *Serious Sam*, they have also worked on the puzzle series *The Talos Principle* and have switched to the unreal engine for the sequel released in 2023.

During this time, we also saw the release and invention of immersive sims (or immsim) games. These titles are designed to simulate the world and setting and are an advanced form of game design. While many of them did have shooting as part of their gameplay, they are not defined as boomer shooters and offer more, and different game design and *mechanics*, compared to the games mentioned so far. One of the biggest was *Deus Ex* released in 2000 by Ion Storm. The level design was set up to allow and encourage players to find different routes and solutions. By leveling up their character, it was possible to play the game avoiding combat, getting into every fight, and everything in between. Due to their scope and difference in game design, I won't be focusing on them in this book and possibly come back to them in a future Deep Dive.

As a final point for this section, here are the copies shipped for the major games mentioned, but this period of the game industry was not the best for finding accurate sale numbers.[1]

| Game Name | Copies Sold |
| --- | --- |
| Blood | Can't find |
| Daikatana | Can't find |
| Deus Ex | Can't find |
| Doom | 3.5 million |
| Doom 2 | 3.6 million |
| | (*Continued*) |

| Game Name | Copies Sold |
| --- | --- |
| Duke Nukem | 3.5 million |
| Heretic | Can't find |
| Heretic 2 | Can't find |
| Hexen | Can't find |
| Hexen 2 | Can't find |
| No One Lives Forever | 350k |
| Serious Sam 1 (Remaster) | 1.02 million |
| Shadow Warrior | Can't find |
| Star Wars: Dark Forces | 1.95 million |
| Quake | 1.4 million |
| Quake 2 | Can't find |
| Quake 3 Arena | 1 million |

There are two more major games that were released at this time that also represented the shift that happened to the genre, which I will come back to later in this book. The 90s boomer shooter period provided designers with an easily accessible blueprint of design that has been copied, iterated, and enhanced over the years. The focus on reflex-driven design allows the gameplay to shine. For this book, it's why there is going to be a lot of discussion on moment-to-moment gameplay and level design.

## 2.3 The Early Console Shooters

The 90s was a period of the game industry where the divide between Personal Computer (PC) and console audiences was at their peak. This was the same time that the arcade was still around and produced some of the best-looking games. During the 8-bit period with the Nintendo Entertainment System (NES), it was not possible to create an FPS that could run on the platform; at most, there were first-person adventure games.

A major limitation of trying to get consoles to play nice with FPS design was the inability to easily move and aim at the same time (Figure 2.7). It wouldn't be until the Dreamcast in 1999 that a console shipped with a controller that had two analog sticks as the default. The Nintendo 64 found a workaround by having the C-buttons, but that wasn't a good fit. For the PC, it has been definitively proven that a keyboard and mouse is the best way to play a shooter thanks to the fidelity of fine control provided by a mouse. In Section 7.3, I will go into detail about how designers have made console shooting more approachable to try and narrow the gap between the two audiences.

What this meant for FPS fans was that, to play the best FPS, you needed a PC, but that didn't stop designers from attempting to create a console FPS market. In 1994, *Wolfenstein 3D* was ported to the SNES, and *Doom* was released a year later. Due to Nintendo's rules for content allowed, both games were censored in

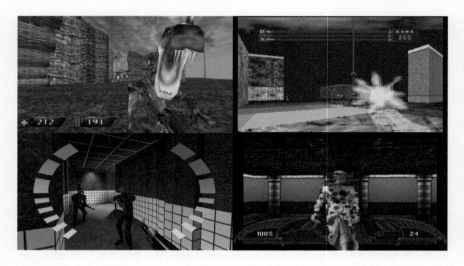

Figure 2.7

Console shooters were severely limited in the 90s due to the hardware at the time, and even the ones featured here had PC ports or remasters over the years.

various aspects as per Nintendo's stipulations. This would not be the first time that these games were ported, and they would appear on later platforms with less censorship.

The real push for shooters on the consoles came during the mid-90s. This was a period where everyone saw the success of the SNES and the console war between Sega and Nintendo and wanted to get in – a far cry from the modern market that is dominated by Nintendo, Sony, and Microsoft. With the PlayStation released in 1994, many popular FPSs were ported to it including *Doom*, and with less censorship compared to the SNES port. Exclusive console shooters were rare during this decade, due to the as-for-mentioned technical limitations at the time, but there were a few that did set the stage for the console market to accept shooters in the coming decade.

To stand out, other console makers had games of all genres made exclusively for their platform, and the FPS was no exception. The Atari Jaguar came out in 1993, and it had the exclusive game *Alien vs. Predator* released in 1994. This is not to be confused with the *Alien vs. Predator* PC game released in 1999; both were created by the same studio Rebellion Developments. The Atari version was original and exclusive to the platform. There were different campaigns for the marine, alien, and predator characters – each with their own weapons and strengths and weaknesses. The game was considered the killer app for the Jaguar, but it was not enough to save it from going under in 1996. The 1999 version was its own game and built off the designs Rebellion did for the Jaguar version.

The Panasonic 3DO also, released in 1993, had its fair share of ports and original games. In 1995, *Immercenary* was released by Five Miles Out. This would be one of the early examples of a **roguelite** FPS. Players had to infiltrate a digital world in the future to destroy the artificial intelligence (AI) keeping everyone held hostage. By killing enemies, the player could absorb their data and enhance their stats. Exploring the world, they could find additional shot types and items they could use and what would aid them during the boss fights. At this time, it has not been ported to any other platforms.

As a strange point about this period, while many FPSs were released on both console and PC during the mid-90s, there were also several FPSs that were altered from their PC versions to the point that some could be considered entirely different games based on the platform in question. *Killing Time* (developed originally by Studio 3DO) first released in 1995 for the 3DO combined shooting with exploring a massive estate. The game was praised at the time for its use of digitized actors who would talk to the player at specific points. The PC version released a year later played faster, altered levels, but removed some of the quality of the graphics. A far bigger change was with the game *Powerslave* which was released in 1996 by Lobotomy Software for the different consoles had elements of **Metroidvania** design – allowing the player to find upgrades that gave their character new ability and return to levels. There were also differences between the different console versions. The PC version that came out around the same time played as more of a traditional FPS with no upgrades or the ability to return to levels. It would be the console versions that were remade and re-released in 2022 by Nightdive Studios under the name *Powerslave: Exhumed*.

Censoring violent content in the past, did not stop Nintendo from getting their own exclusive version of *Doom*: titled *Doom 64* released in 1997 (Figure 2.8). This was created by Midway Games under supervision from id Software. While it did feature the same gameplay of the series, this was an entirely original game set in the franchise and not available on PC at the time. It wouldn't be until 2020 that the game was ported to modern platforms and consoles for everyone to experience it.

Even though the PlayStation did have more power than the Nintendo 64 and received numerous ports of popular shooters, the Nintendo 64 received one of the most famous console shooters for the decade with *GoldenEye 007* released in 1997 by Rare. Based on the movie of the same name, *GoldenEye 007* was one of the few shooters released this decade that did not focus entirely on run-and-gun gameplay. As James Bond, missions involved performing various objectives based on the difficulty that the player selected. Some levels required the player to be stealthy, while others were about getting into fire fights. The game also set the foundation for multiplayer content for console shooters – featuring up to four-player matches, different gameplay modes, characters to play as, and more. Not only did *GoldenEye 007* become one of the best games for the Nintendo 64, but it also broke the curse of licensed games being uniformly bad, which

Figure 2.8

*Doom 64* is not as famous as the original two *Dooms* but it has gone on to be another source of inspiration for modders and still holds up with its PC port remaster.

was the trend at the time. They also made a third-person shooter with *Jet Force Gemini* released in 1999. In 2000, they released *Perfect Dark* which was a spiritual follow-up to *GoldenEye* 64, but in their own original property. The game featured more content and was popular for multiplayer despite not having access to online functionality.

The importance of Rare's offering of shooters was that they worked within the confines of the console and using a gamepad. While it wasn't perfect, the gameplay was good enough that people could enjoy these games without the need for mouse look functionality. What they did to get around not having a mouse was to use the analog stick for general movement, the c-buttons for looking and strafing, and holding L or R brought up a crosshair for aiming. While the player could move and shoot at the same time, they could only accurately aim while standing still. As a funny point, this style for reviewers and consumers was considered the standard for shooters on consoles; and when Sony unveiled the DualShock 1 that provided two analog sticks, it initially confused people about using this for FPS gameplay with a famous review for *Alien Resurrection* released in 2000, but in the next chapter, this would become the accepted standard for console shooters. Rare would put out other memorable games on the Nintendo 64 until they were purchased by Microsoft in 2002.

1997 also saw the release of *Turok: Dinosaur Hunter* by Iguana Entertainment. Based on the comic book of the same name, players controlled Turok who had to explore the Lost Land where dinosaurs still roamed. Besides fighting enemies, the player could explore to find pieces of an ultimate weapon and there was a good variety of enemies and locations. The success would lead to four main games in the series with the first three available on PC now as remastered versions.

The popularity of evolving shooter design would also find its way to the PlayStation with the *Syphon Filter* series first released in 1999 by Bend Studio. The story involved agent Gabe Logan who must travel the globe trying to stop a terrorist from unleashing a bioweapon attack. The game combined action and stealth gameplay through its level design. The game would feature a lock-on system instead of requiring the player to aim manually at enemies. Making use of lock-on targeting is often used in games that have shooting as part of the gameplay loop, but the focus is often on movement and positioning instead of gunplay. This is also an important user experience (UX) feature that will be talked about later in the book.

The same year, the first *Medal of Honor* was released by DreamWorks Interactive, with a story penned by Steven Spielberg following the success of *Saving Private Ryan*. The original concept was to create a shooter that would focus on various parts of being a soldier in World War II (Figure 2.9). Unlike the other shooters at the same time, the series focused on a slower pace and provided a variety of scenarios based on the mission the player was in. Despite starting on the consoles, future entries would be released on PC as well, with the last entry at this time released in 2020 with *Medal of Honor: Above and Beyond*. While the game stood out in 1999, part of the reason for its decline was the sheer number of

Figure 2.9

*Medal of Honor* as a series would begin the rush of World War II-based games over the 2000s, and incidentally would also lead the way of just about every one of these games featuring one level taking place during D-Day. (All screenshots are from *Medal of Honor: Allied Assault*.)

multiplayer-based shooters released starting in the 2000s, and the rise in popularity of the *Call of Duty* brand as the premier military shooter.

During the 90s, arcades popularized light gun shooters – games in which players could use a light gun to shoot at all manner of enemies. While these games were shooters, they could also be defined as "on rails shooting" – where the player has little to no control over where they're going, and the entire point of the game is the shooting. Many of the bigger names did make their way to consoles, and some have even been ported to PC over the 2010s. However, their design is not the focus for this book and I'm just including them here to be complete about the history at the time. Once again, trying to find accurate numbers for copies sold during this decade proved to be difficult.[2]

| Game Name | Copies Sold |
| --- | --- |
| Alien: Resurrection | 250,000 |
| Alien vs. Predator | 52,223 (can't confirm) |
| Doom 64 | 470,000 (can't confirm) |
| GoldenEye 007 | 8 million (lifetime) |
| Immercenary | Unknown |
| Jet Force Gemini | 1.16 million (lifetime) |
| Killing Time | Unknown |
| Medal of Honor | 2.67 million |
| Perfect Dark | 3.2 million (lifetime) |
| Powerslave | Unknown |
| Syphon Filter | 2.88 million (lifetime) |
| Turok: Dinosaur Hunter | 1.5 million |

Between the console and PC markets, the shooter genre thrived with many other games released. And these successes would set the stage for how the market shifted in the 2000s and how the design changed.

## 2.4 The Unreal Arrival of *Half-Life*

Throughout the 90s, what was considered the norm for boomer shooters and the FPS market stayed the same on PCs. While consoles were seeing more original takes on the design, the popularity of *Doom* and *Quake* was still the standard for what people expected out of shooters on the PC. For people who wanted other gameplay with first-person combat, the growing stealth and immsim genres were available.

But in 1998, two games were released that would change the entire industry: not just the shooter genre. In November of that year, *Half-Life* was released by Valve Software (Figure 2.10). Valve was founded in 1996 by Mike Harrington and Gabe Newell. After talking with id Software who gave them advice and a copy of the Quake engine, they decided to make a shooter for their first game.

2. The Beginning of "Boomer Shooters"

Figure 2.10

The original *Half-Life* (a) would define the changes that shooters would have in the 2000s but doesn't quite hold up as well by modern standards compared to the likes of *Doom*, and why there were attempts to modernize and remake it with the biggest example being *Black Mesa* (b).

*Half-Life* told the story of Gordon Freeman – a scientist for the Black Mesa Research Facility. When an experiment goes horribly wrong, he finds himself caught between invading aliens and special government forces sent to clean up the incident. Unlike the other shooters during this period, *Half-Life* would focus on interactivity and world design far beyond anything else. Instead of using cutscenes that would take the player out of the game space, all interactions and conversations were done within the game itself – making sure that the player was always amid something.

The level design would break the FPS tradition at the time of designing each level as a one-time "block" of content that would disappear when it's over. The goal was to move through the facility to try and find a way out. The levels were broken up by different sections that would be announced via a title card. A new level would come with a new enemy type, come with a new obstacle, or take the player to a new environment within the facility itself. Depending on where the player was at, it was possible to return to earlier areas to collect any spare resources they might have missed.

The gunplay was still on the arcade side but was built to be a bit slower paced compared to the other shooters. Players would find an assortment of weapons that they were free to carry them all. Recovering health and armor was done by finding them in boxes or strewn about, or by going to specific terminals that would fill them up to a point. The game featured a wide variety of enemies consisting of humans and aliens including the now famous "headcrabs" who would jump at the player. The different behaviors of the enemies had to be considered while fighting them, as the special forces would try and draw the player out using grenades.

*Half-Life* would set a new standard for storytelling as well as being a new foundation for mods, with both *Counter-Strike* and *Team Fortress* originating here and will be discussed later in the book. There were two expansions released for the original game, and *Half-Life 1* was re-released in 2004 using Valve's own game engine: the Source Engine, which would be used for all future games developed by Valve.

What would cement Valve's and *Half-Life*'s legacy would come with *Half-Life 2* released in 2004. The sequel saw Gordon Freeman return to the Earth that has been conquered by the aliens from the first game and must lead a revolution to free humanity and uncover what happened after the end of the first game.

The amount of variety in terms of level and environmental design grew in the sequel, as the player explored the mysterious City 17, a prison, took a dune buggy out to explore the desert, and more differing level designs (Figure 2.11). Like the first one, the game doesn't take the player out of the world to introduce a new level and would still use title cards to designate the next stage. While the basic gunplay didn't change that much from the original, the number of things the player did and could do in the world did.

*Half-Life 2* was one of the first FPSs to introduce a weapon/utility device that wasn't just about shooting in the form of the gravity gun. With it, the player could lift most small to heavy objects and use them for setting up platforms, blocking

Figure 2.11

*Half-Life 2* was ahead of its time at the release – both for having a variety of gameplay beyond just shooting, and for introducing PC audiences to Steam which has forever changed the game industry and market.

enemy shots, or flinging at other characters to do damage. Like the first game, a lot of the level design was created to attempt to mirror a realistic-looking place at the start but would get more and more alien-like near the end when the player had to assault the citadel.

*Half-Life 2* became an industry-defining game of the decade and would receive two expansions, a "lost episode," and have left fans clamoring for a sequel ever since. The closest that was released was the virtual reality (VR) game *Half-Life: Alyx* in 2020. The Source Engine has since been used for a variety of mods and other games, but the major contribution to the industry that *Half-Life 2* heralded was the introduction of Steam as the first major digital client and storefront. To talk about the importance and legacy of Steam now is beyond the scope of this design book, but it is not hyperbole to say that it did change the growth and future of the industry forever. Because Valve is a privately owned company, finding exact sales numbers is difficult. In 2008, Valve did report sales numbers for its games at the time.[3] However, given sales and just the growth of consumers using Steam, that value is most likely not accurate as of writing this book.

For the other major game of that year, it's time to turn to *Unreal* developed by Epic Games (Figure 2.12) The *Unreal* franchise itself is split between two different styles – the story-driven and single player-focused *Unreal* 1 and 2 and the multiplayer-focused arena shooters of the *Unreal Tournament* series. The first game had players control a prisoner aboard a spaceship that crashes into an alien world and must fight their way to find the means to escape. While the shooting

Figure 2.12

Even though *Unreal* started as a single player franchise, it has become more famous for the utility of its game engine and its multiplayer design. Sadly, finding the means to play the original games has proven harder since Epic has delisted them from all stores.

itself didn't do anything new at the time, the technical achievements of the Unreal Engine did. The engine was the most powerful in terms of features and graphical fidelity for shooters at the time – enabling designers to create large maps with both indoor and outdoor sections. The game also came with a level editor called UnrealED which made it easier to develop and play custom mods and maps.

In 1999, Epic released *Unreal Tournament* which would compete with *Quake 3 Arena* as the other standalone multiplayer-focused game that year. While the game did have a single player campaign, it was just about fighting against AI opponents or bots. The tournament series did overtake the single player-focused games to be the more popular aspect of the franchise. While the single player games were similar in pacing and structure to *Half-Life*, the tournament games were faster-paced, and *Unreal Tournament* and *Quake 3 Arena* were the first major multiplayer shooters released during this period. *Unreal Tournament* would have a total of five games released on PC with the last one out in 2014. Estimates online have *Unreal* as a series selling 8 million copies worldwide,[4] but this is another game where it's hard to find accurate numbers for.

The real impact *Unreal* had on the industry was outsourcing the engine thanks to its popularity and power. Besides being used by Epic for a variety of games, including *Fortnite* that will be mentioned later in the book, the different iterations of the engine have been used in countless games over the years – from major studios to indie teams, with the latest iteration Unreal Engine 5 released in 2022. Epic has done a lot to make their engine popular for everyone, including having the lowest royalty rates on selling games with it, and making it completely free to download and use.

Both Epic and Valve would go on to become major names in the game industry in the 2000s – thanks to Steam by Valve and the Unreal Engine by Epic, and both couldn't have had their start if not for their opening games.

By the end of the 90s and into the 2000s, the FPS design would begin to change and evolve with the evolution of technology, consoles, and the market, and that will be discussed more in Chapter 4.

## 2.5 The Limits of 90s Multiplayer Shooters

Online multiplayer will become a huge aspect of shooter design and releases but, for most of the 90s, the architecture was not set up for multiplayer in the same way that it is now. Computers were not always online back then and had to rely on dial-up modems for connecting to the internet. For console games, it wouldn't be until the Sega Dreamcast in 1999 that a console came pre-built with access to the internet through a dial-up, and the Xbox released in 2001 that had a cable connection by default (Figure 2.13). Cable modems didn't start to become adopted by home consumers until the end of the 90s, and it would take far longer for most households to have access to it. As a quick tangent, this also had an impact on the fighting game genre in the 2000s after the arcades died and limited their reach and multiplayer.

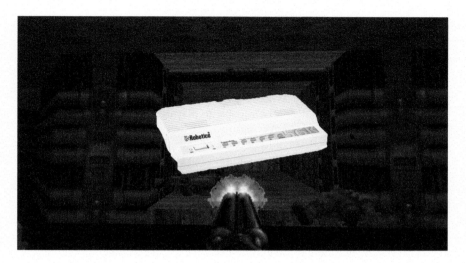

Figure 2.13

Truly the greatest monster of shooters in the 90s was the dreaded dial-up modem.

Shooters didn't have this problem on the PC as most of them were designed first and foremost as single player experiences. But many shooters had multiplayer modes, and they were severely limited by the times. Without servers and cable connections, players had to use direct Internet Protocol (IP) connections to set up multiplayer with a limited number of people at the time, a far cry from today's market. Another option was to connect to a third-party server that would handle the multiplayer component of the game, such as GameSpy. As I mentioned earlier in the chapter, *QuakeWorld* was the first to be built exclusively as multiplayer first experiences. For the console games, they did feature multiplayer modes as discussed, but they were limited to local only.

One of the most popular games to come out of this time was *Starsiege: Tribes* released in 1998 by Dynamix. Teams of players would compete on a variety of maps with different game modes, with the twist being that everyone was equipped with jetpacks that they could use for offensive and defensive maneuvers. Adding movement tech to shooters at the time was unheard of and would be something that was adopted by more games in the 2010s. The series would have several sequels released, with a remake of *Tribes 3* expected in 2024 at the time of writing this. I could not find official copies sold for the original game.

In terms of design, at this point in the industry, there was no real thought given to having exclusive features or balancing between the single and multiplayer components. Instead, the main unique factors were the different kinds of modes people could play in or building a game as a uniquely multiplayer experience. The most popular ones included were deathmatch – two players or teams fight each other for the most kills and capture the flag – teams try to capture the flag of the opposing team first. At this point in terms of gameplay, there were no persistent elements or unlocks that would form the basis for online shooters and progression in the 2010s. At most, multiplayer games would have some kind of ranking system based on the number of kills/wins for each player.

Multiplayer, even limited as it was, still boasted the unique element it had over single player experiences – being able to play against another player is different from playing against the AI (Figure 2.14). Being able to find people to play against and meet those that could become friends would evolve over the 2000s to where it is today. And while discussions about balancing weapons and content weren't really thought of here, it will become a major point that I will be talking more about in Section 8.4. As the popularity of game engines grew, along with being able to mod games, modders would go on to create custom maps and game modes for their favorite multiplayer games. Several genres that would go on to become huge over the next 20 years originally had their start as a custom game mode created by modders in various games.

Looking back at this period for multiplayer design, it's interesting to examine how these games hooked people with just the simple notion of being able to play against other people. For today's market, however, your game must be built around a live service model regardless of the genre you are working in, and this will be discussed later in the book.

Figure 2.14

Multiplayer design may have changed over the years, but one thing has remained the same: the thrill of playing against other players and hopefully winning.

## Notes

1 Source: VGchartz.com
2 Sources: VGChartz.com and news articles online
3 https://arstechnica.com/gaming/2008/12/valve-divulges-life-time-retail-sales/
4 https://www.vgchartz.com/game/226139/unreal/sales

# 3

# Basic Shooter Design

## 3.1 Reflex-Driven Design

It's finally time to start delving into some game design and gameplay for this book. To understand shooters, or any kind of action game design, you need to learn about reflex-driven gameplay. There are two broad categories of gameplay featured in any video game released – reflex-driven and abstracted. Abstracted design is when there are elements within the game that dictate, or abstract, the results of the player's actions. This is the most seen in RPGs and was the basis for my Deep Dive on the RPG genre.

Reflex-driven gameplay focuses on the players themselves as the deciding factor in whether they win or lose (Figure 3.1). Hand-eye coordination is at the center of this kind of design, and why many action games of the 90s through to the 2000s had a high *skill floor* for simply trying to play them.

Part of the reason why the keyboard and mouse became the go-to control for shooters was how the mouse provides better fidelity of control compared to a gamepad. When someone uses an analog stick to move a character or reticule, all force and direction on the stick is factored into the control. With a mouse,

DOI: 10.1201/9781003449959-3

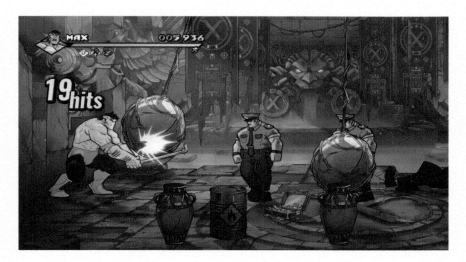

Figure 3.1

Reflex-driven design focuses entirely on the player and was the standard of action games and best-em-ups for more than 20 years. Beat-em-ups are also seeing a revival lately with notable examples like *Streets of Rage 4* (released in 2020 by DotEmu).

it is 1:1 – how the player moves the mouse, the camera/reticule moves accordingly. As I'll come back to in Section 7.3, part of the evolution of shooters and video games in the 2010s was to focus on accessibility and approachability.

Reflex-driven design also impacts the difficulty of your game. With RPGs, a game can be made easier or harder simply by adjusting stats and attributes of the player and enemy characters. For reflex-driven design, you have the challenge of balancing a game that is dependent on the user's hand-eye reflexes. Changing attributes won't help someone who is struggling with aiming or moving, likewise making enemies do more damage only matters if the player is not able to dodge them. As a designer, you need to be more aware of how difficulty is balanced in your game, as it is very easy to break your game by making it too easy or too hard.

What would eventually happen with the reflex-driven design in the 2010s, which will be discussed in Chapter 6, was integrating abstracted elements to both engage players longer and to provide another way of making progress. For you reading this, the more your game is built on reflex-driven design, it will attract a hardcore following, but this will always come at the expense of some approachability. There are methods to try and soften the edge of your game, which will be discussed in Section 8.2, but designing a shooter is always about delivering on its gameplay.

## 3.2 What Are Boomer Shooters?

The term boomer shooter has become a way to reference FPSs from the 90s or those that were inspired by them. What these games share, and what distinguishes them from modern shooters, is focusing on surrealism rather than a grounded take that would take hold of mainstream shooters in the 2000s and I'll be talking more about modern shooter design in Chapter 4. This is an era where elements like a normal movement speed, inventory, or trying to make any real sense to the physics of the world are ignored (Figure 3.2). However, due to the enormity of the genre, there are exceptions to these rules, and we've seen them from indie developers over the 2010s that I'll come back to later in this book.

Boomer shooters mostly keep the same core gameplay loop from beginning to end, except for having sections or levels that may break the norm, such as having to use a jetpack or drive a vehicle. During this period, enemy AI was kept basic depending on the game played. Enemy behaviors either focused on charging the player's character to do damage in close range or attack them from afar with a ranged weapon or attack. *Quake* was one of the first shooters to feature a very diverse selection of enemies with different behaviors. The most notable were the ogres and the shamblers – with the ogres, they could launch grenades and, thanks to their AI, could bounce them around corners to hit the player. The shamblers would move around the environment and, if the player was too close, they would attack in melee, but if they were far away they would use a lightning attack that could only be dodged by hiding around an object.

Figure 3.2

Boomer shooters could care less about realism in terms of gunplay, world design, and the enemies the player fights – as long as someone is having a good time, that's all that matters.

3. Basic Shooter Design

Due to the player character's speed, the two best defensive options from this time were to either use cover to avoid damage, or strafe around enemies. Strafing is the act of moving left or right without changing where you are aiming. By holding in one direction, players could circle strafe around enemies to attack them while avoiding damage. As the FPS genre evolved, designers would find means of weakening the effectiveness of strafing, usually by making enemies more aggressive and better at tracking the player.

Before I talk about level design, it's important to begin discussing what gunplay is and how it started with boomer shooters.

## 3.3 Examining Gunplay

A concept unique to shooter design is "gunplay," and it stands for the overall feel of a weapon in a game. The reason why this is something that comes in shooters is that part of the gameplay experience is how the weapons behave in the player's hands, and with shooters focusing on guns or ranged weapons, gunplay as a term stuck.

To put this another way, gunplay is part of the aesthetic of your weapons and something as a designer you cannot ignore. Since attacking is part of the core gameplay loop, if the player is not enjoying using weapons in your game, they're not going to want to keep playing (Figure 3.3).

The first element you need to understand is the difference between a projectile and a hitscan weapon. In all video games, every character has a *hitbox* – this

Figure 3.3

Gunplay can refer to any and all weapons in a shooter. A hallmark of many boomer shooters is to feature unusual or different weapons that don't necessarily fit as guns, such as throwing dynamic in *Blood*.

invisible frame around a character is what the game's engine uses to determine if someone is attacked or not. Projectiles in games also have a hitbox: if the hitbox of an attack collides with a character hitbox, then that character will take damage. For guns in games that shoot a projectile, that's how the game determines if the player scores a hit. Some weapons, such as explosives, will do damage in a large area; if any character is in that area when the attack goes off, they'll take damage in relation to how close they are to it. This is also referred to as splash damage, or damage that comes with an area of effect (AOE). With projectile-based weapons, it is possible to dodge them by moving out of the way of the incoming projectile.

A hitscan weapon is when there is no physical projectile within the game space. Instead, when the player or enemy attacks, the weapon sends out a hitscan function from the reticule or the enemy's weapon. If this detects a hitbox of an opposing character, the attack is considered true, and the character will be damaged. Hitscan weapons are used for several situations – the first is when you want to have a weapon that is far easier for the player to use and one that is easier to program. With a hitscan, there is no need to worry about physics or animating and rendering a projectile in your game. Many shooters will have their default or weaker weapons as hitscan-based attacks. From the player's point of view, all they need to do is worry about getting the reticule on the enemy's model to score a hit (Figure 3.4). The other reason why hitscan weapons are used is that they require less work by the engine in a multiplayer setting. In a single player game, the game only must worry about projectiles and attacks from enemies and just one player. If we're looking at a multiplayer game with multiple people moving around on a

Figure 3.4

Hitscan weapons provide the player with the easiest kind of weapon to process – if the cursor is on an enemy when they fire, it's going to hit, period. But other factors can impact how easy it is to land said hit.

3. Basic Shooter Design

map generating projectiles all over the place, that can cause issues when dealing with online play and lag. You can have situations where a projectile looks like it hits someone or they dodged it, but the server is having lag problems, and the opposite may happen. Another point, playing a multiplayer game with eight or more players all firing different physical projectiles can easily turn into a confusing mess to look at, let alone figure out what's going on.

I'll be covering weapon design and balance throughout this book, as the concept changes based on the type of shooter discussed. For all the different aesthetics and games available, most weapons in shooters fall into one of the following categories:

1. Single-shot fast hitscan: Typically, a pistol or rifle for more damage.
2. Rapid-fire hitscan: An assault rifle or machine gun-styled weapon.
3. Medium-speed hitscan: A shotgun-styled weapon designed for close to short-ranged combat.
4. Heavy single-shot projectile: A rocket launcher or some other big attack that can also do splash damage.
5. Medium rapid-fire projectile: A rapid series of projectiles that do more damage than the hitscan variety.
6. Throwable explosives: Grenades or some other form of an AOE attack.

While those examples are considered the basic ones, designers over the decades have made their own unique takes and exceptions to these rules. A major one is the high-damage single-shot hitscan, aka the sniper rifle. While sniping became more of a popular addition in later shooters and in the 2000s, the use of a "sniper class" weapon can be seen in some older boomer shooters and the newer ones. One of the first examples of this would be the rail gun in *Quake 2* that would then be adopted as one of the major multiplayer weapons in later iterations. This kind of weapon has the slowest rate of fire (or ROF) but makes up for it by doing the most damage and being a hit scan attack means that the hit is instant. Its weakness is that the reticule for it is often the smallest and requires a skilled player to properly aim and hit the enemy, and the slow ROF makes it bad to use in close to mid-range combat. When later shooters introduced locational damage (more on that at the end of this chapter), so did we see the implementation of "headshots": hitting an enemy with a sniper round in the head is often an instant kill.

There are no agreed upon rules for balancing weapons other than the harder it is to hit someone with a weapon, the more damage it should do to compensate for it. Over the course of this book, there will be far more diverse examples of weapons and how games were balanced around them, with many of the best ones designed to be as different from contemporary weapons as one can.

As a quick point, due to how weapons in shooters are limited by their ammo (more on this in Section 7.1 on balancing), it is possible for the player to run out of rounds and become unable to attack enemies. Because of this situation, designers will often put in a melee weapon or attack as the last-ditch option for doing

Figure 3.5

Good gunplay is about making sure every weapon or weapon type in your game is 100% distinctive – *Gunfire Reborn* pictured here is a great example of making each weapon look and feel different to use.

damage. Expert players have used melee attacks as a means of killing enemies and saving rounds, and you should always have a weapon that does not need ammunition to work.

Moving on to the next detail about gunplay, as I said further up about the aesthetics of the weapon, how the weapon feels during combat is also a factor (Figure 3.5). In the last chapter, I mentioned how the shotgun in *Doom* became one of the most iconic weapons in a FPS for the decade, and the sound effects and reload animations were a part of it. When the player uses it, they hear the loud sound of the shotgun going off, followed by the reloading sound of the character loading another shell in. When enemies are struck by it, smaller enemies are often killed outright, while middle to larger ones may get slightly stunned for a few milliseconds.

How the enemy responds to being attacked is also a part of gunplay. If the player fires a massive rocket at something and their only response is "ow," that's going to take them out of the gameplay. As hardware and fidelity improved, so has the option to show all kinds of impacts on enemies – having limbs come off, body deformation, electrocuted, burned, frozen, etc. For games that recontextualized shooting into something else, you could have a character clean up, turn into a chicken, anything that you can think of. But there must be some kind of visible impact from using the weapon on them to go with the visual and sound design of the weapon itself.

The look of your weapon is also important, and I will be talking more about what this means in Chapter 8, but it's still vital to bring it up here. Another part of making an iconic weapon for a shooter is that it needs to look and animate differently than anything else in your game. This includes how the gun is fired, what the projectiles (if it's projectile-based) look like, and how it looks to reload.

There is more to weapon designs that go with the evolution of shooters that I will talk about in later chapters. To wrap up this section, gunplay is one area where I see a lot of novice designers, or those not familiar with shooters, mess up on. For the genre, messing up on the gunplay is as much of a sin as not working on the overall aesthetics and style of your game. From a marketing point of view, good gunplay can be used in advertising your game, and has been the basis for the marketing success of many indie shooters over the years. Just having one Graphics Interchange Format (GIF) showing off an original weapon, even without having enemies, can get the ball rolling.

If you are reading this book now and have never heard of the term gunplay before, then you are not ready to start creating any kind of shooter. Being able to analyze the feel of a weapon is essential if you want to create an effective reflex-driven design.

## 3.4 Basic Level Design

Level design is another concept that appears in every Deep Dive book, as every genre has its own philosophy and style of design. Building your game is also about creating the level and environmental design of it, and we can define them as the following:

Level design: The layout of the level along with any environmental obstacles, enemy placements, resources, and goals for the player to reach.
Environmental design: The aesthetics of the level, building the style of the environment, and how it relates to the story of the game.

Level design has seen the most change as shooters evolved, because the pacing and speed in which someone can play the game directly impact how the levels are designed and their overall size. Many of the early shooters focused on the level design – constructing elaborate mazes, secret areas, and traps for the player to avoid. Due to the focus on reflex-driven design, the flow and arrangement of the levels are the most important details when combined with the enemy designs and weapons available (Figure 3.6).

Imagine building a level where the player is in a long corridor with no cover, and there are hitscan sniper enemies at one end of it and the player only has a shotgun, this would be very annoying to fight. Part of building the levels of your games is considering what weapons the player has access to at that time. For boomer shooters that also rely on resource placement, which must also be factored into the level design – how many health packs are there, ammo supplies, different kind of ammos, can the player find different weapons and their respective ammos? Regarding supplies, there should be enough available so that, if someone does mess up, they can still recoup and make it through. Many makers

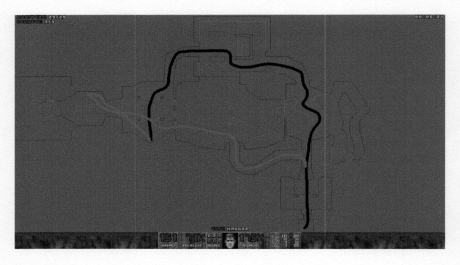

Figure 3.6

This is E1:M1 from *Doom* in all its level design glory. The black line marks the general path through the level, while the green one is a faster route using a secret to skip two rooms of enemies and head straight to the exit marked by the red line on the bottom-right.

of custom levels in FPS have introduced expert challenges or build their levels around the highest skill level of play – such as fighting the hardest enemies in the game with the starting weapons.

As far back as *Wolfenstein 3D*, designers have placed secret areas in their levels. They could be behind a false wall, hidden out of normal view, and can have anything in them from more resources, better weapons, or even the route to a bonus stage. Another mainstay of shooters, which has only gotten bigger over the years, is having "arenas" in stages. An arena is an area that the player is locked in until they defeat every enemy. Enemies can appear either all at once, or "spawn" in waves of different groups and difficulties. Some games allow the player to leave an arena if they can find a switch or button that will open the door, but this can be very difficult to find when the arena is full of enemies.

Level design can fill its own book for every genre out there, and there are numerous concepts, themes, and designs you can use. Some designers like to build their levels as gauntlets – challenging the player with enemies in every corner, difficult arenas, where survival comes down to the use of every bullet. And there are designers who build their levels as puzzles – where enemies are there, but the focus is figuring out how to get to the exit or complete the objective, and everything in-between. When more custom mods and fan games were made for shooters, the variety got even wider.

How you build levels is going to be based on what kind of game you want to make and the style of your game. There are some universal tips to a good level

Figure 3.7

The theme of your level is the all-encompassing mission statement for what you want the player to get out of it. Good level design creates interesting fights and areas to explore; great level design also creates a sense of place within the environment, such as with *HROT* pictured here (released in 2023 by Spytihněv).

design that can apply to any reflex-driven genre. Going into a level, you want to figure out what your "theme" is going to be (Figure 3.7). The theme is the central concept or mission statement of your level; here are a few examples of what I mean:

1. A spooky graveyard where the player must explore various crypts to find the keys needed to enter the mausoleum to find a portal to hell. Enemies can pop out of coffins or rise from the ground to attack in mass.
2. Aboard a space station that is slowly crashing into the planet, and gravity is not working right. Using the enhanced jumps, the player must avoid exposed electrical wires and fight their way through enemies to reach the remaining escape pod.

It is always better to design one focused level than try to fit two or more concepts into a single level. Once the theme is figured out, you need to start working on the structure of your level. What separates novice level designers from experts is how they can create a sense of pacing and flow in the level. It is not about the player fighting dozens of enemies every second or walking from arena to arena but guiding them from beginning to end. Your environmental design is factored here – as creating interesting or unique landmarks can guide the player's attention to specific areas you want them to go. Resources can also be used to guide the player or lead them into a trap. There must be a beginning, a middle, and an end to your level – each designated by specific and unique challenges that are indicative of the theme you set up.

In my book on platformers, I said that a good level knows when to end, and that is when the designer has run out of ways to introduce new elements to the theme. With shooters and the fact that combat is the focus, you need to be mindful of level length and how it relates to difficulty. Due to the player having limited resources in terms of health and ammo for weapons, longer levels can see players running out of them. A major point about older shooters vs. newer ones that comes up not only with User Interface (UI)/UX, but also with level design, is having checkpoints or the ability to save in the middle of the level.

Older shooters were balanced under the assumption that someone could just quicksave their game at any time, and often why these games were far harder. Modern shooters may give the option for quicksaving, but they will also auto save after major events in a level to prevent the player from losing too much progress when they die.

Creating and balancing the individualized sections of your level and putting them together will be discussed more in Section 7.3. One final point before moving on, your level design is going to be dependent on the overall gameplay of your game. One of the hallmarks of newer shooters today is to create unique mechanics and abilities that aren't just about shooting – increased mobility on the ground and the air are popular examples. Anytime you create a new ability, your levels must then be designed to accommodate it going forward (Figure 3.8). Just like with platformers and defining your jumping angles, any changes to how the player moves, how the player attacks, or what the enemy can do will have an

Figure 3.8

*Ultrakill* introduces new mechanics and abilities for the player over the course of the game. In this level, the player is given more use of the recently unlocked whiplash, with the water provides them the means of testing it out in direct combat without worrying about its downsides.

3. Basic Shooter Design

impact on your level design and must be changed accordingly. Good level design is an art in itself: mastering it as a custom mod either for a game, or in your own game, can help build your reputation.

For developers working on making their own boomer shooters today, even if you are dealing with a limited number of mechanics and systems, you must be able to use them in different ways when designing your levels. A fantastic example of this that's worth studying are the numerous total conversion mods for *Doom 1* and *2* released over the years that I will talk about in Section 6.3. Just like how platformer fans have been building original levels and games out of the classic *Mario* series for years, so has there been an infinite number of custom levels made for these games.

However, making a good shooter requires more than just having memorable levels, and all that will be explained further into this book.

## 3.5 The Limitations and Evolutions of Early FPS Design

Before I move on to the next period of shooter design, I wanted to talk about how the FPS gameplay evolved over the 90s as new engines and hardware pushed the design further. When designers work on longstanding genres, there is a tendency to look at a classic game as the exact model to follow to the very letter, but just making a game with the exact limitations of the design is not how you can stand out in the market today. Some of the best games of any genre are never happy with just repeating what someone else did but refining or iterating on those ideas to create something new.

Despite its prestige, both *Doom 1* and *2* came out before the integration of "mouse look" also known as free look in FPS design. Mouse look is the ability to use the mouse to look up or down while in first person. In the original FPS, while the player could turn left and right, it was not possible to change the elevation of the camera (Figure 3.9). This also meant it was impossible to aim at enemies beyond just pointing the gun in the general direction. For enemies set up on different elevations or parts of the environment, the game would automatically aim the attack at the enemy without changing the orientation of the camera. The first recorded example of mouse look in an FPS would go to *Marathon* by Bungie released in 1994.[1]

Being able to look and aim with your gun would lead to the next innovation with locational damage. In the early FPS, there was nothing differentiating a headshot from a body shot, or any other part of the body. The first noted example of this came with the mod *Quake Team Fortress* released in 1996[2] for its sniper class. Locational damage would lead to designers rewarding good aiming on the player's part by letting them do more damage with headshots. This would evolve over the years to introduce enemies that had other weak spots or would behave differently if certain parts of their bodies were attacked.

In the last chapter, I discussed how console shooters began to evolve in the mid-90s, and this also brought with it the innovation of "aim assist" or "auto

Figure 3.9

In this screenshot from *Doom 2*, these enemies at a higher elevation could still be hit by the player even if the gun wasn't aimed directly at them. When the *Dooms* were made playable in GZDoom, they now feature mouse look by default.

lock-on." As previously discussed, analog sticks are not as accurate in terms of aiming compared to a mouse and, to make the FPS design work for gamepads and people who had trouble aiming, aim assist was created. Finding the first version of this was a bit harder, but the consensus credits *GoldenEye 007* as the first console FPS to feature it. Aim assist works by having the reticle stay on an enemy's hitbox by varying degrees based on the design. This way, someone doesn't need to worry about constantly adjusting the reticle once it is on an enemy. Consequently, it did make it harder to aim at specific parts of an enemy with the reticle moving on its own. Aim assist would become a feature for many console shooters and its role would change depending on the design itself. In games where the greater focus is on moving and avoiding damage, aim assist would turn into a hard lock-on – once a character is locked on, all bullets and projectiles would automatically be aimed at that hitbox while the player focused on dodging. Locking on to enemies became essential for action games as a means of allowing players to target and engage with multiple enemies in close range. Due to the nature of aim assist, it would also lead to one of the most popular cheating options in shooters: the aim bot. Frowned upon by designers, and can lead to someone's account being banned, aim bots allow someone to let the game automatically target the weakest point on any player character they are looking at. This can track through walls and provide 100% accurate firing regardless of the player's skill.

The next innovation was with the use of secondary attack modes or "alt fire" for weapons. The first game credited is once again *Marathon*. Instead of every

3. Basic Shooter Design

Figure 3.10

Alt fires can greatly add to the depth of your gunplay and was one of the standout features in *Painkiller*.

weapon only having one primary use, alt fires provided them with a secondary way of attacking enemies. There are no rules for what this can mean an alt fire could mean just switching between semi auto to full auto attacks, to literally a complete change in the gun's functionality – like turning your pistol into a rocket launcher, grenades out of your shotgun, and many more (Figure 3.10). In terms of balancing, some games require another ammo source on top of the gun's primary to use the secondary, and others may just require a different amount of the ammo to use the secondary vs. the primary. This radically changed the gunplay and the variety of weapons in shooters, doubling the number of ways the player could attack at one time.

To return to *Hexen/Heretic*, besides immsims and before other FPS would integrate RPG progression into their games, these were one of the first to do that and provide a form of progression that wasn't just tied to finding new weapons. The reach of this can be seen with the rise of role-playing shooters and integrating RPG progression into many action-driven games in the 2010s; and for more on this point, you can find it in *Game Design Deep Dive: Role Playing Games*.

Not so much an innovation intended by designers, but something that did come about during this period was the introduction of additional movement techniques, or movement tech for short. The game that popularized this at the time was *Quake* with the now famous maneuver known as "rocket jumping." Because rockets in the game create a force emanating from the explosion, if someone jumped at the same time they were looking at their feet and firing a rocket, it would propel them up several times higher than they would have been able to with a normal jump. This would soon be used to skip areas in the main game or get to harder to reach spots to attack other players in multiplayer. To this day, rocket jumping's utility will greatly depend on the physics engine and design of a shooter. There have been games built entirely on rocket jumping.

Another classic example was "crouch jumping." Based on how the character model works, when a character crouches in a shooter, their hitbox shrinks down along with a change in the camera perspective. By crouching while in the air, it was possible to leap up small platforms. This is a maneuver that, while many older fans know about, has fallen out of popularity for games today, as it was a bit counter-intuitive if you didn't grow up with it. In today's market, movement tech is another marketing and design point for any reflex-driven game, and there would be more innovations introduced in the 2000s and 2010s.

A popular form of shooter that would come about in the early 2000s was cover shooting – where the act of hiding behind cover became a mechanic beyond just standing behind something. *Winback* released in 1999 by Omega Force is the earliest example I could find of cover-based shooting. In most shooters, cover is simply hiding behind whatever object is nearby to reduce your hitbox and make it harder for the enemy to hit you. With cover shooting, the player could hide behind a corner or chest-high wall and then "stick" there and can attack enemies while remaining in cover (Figure 3.11). In these games, being outside of cover while enemies were attacking was a death sentence, and this will be discussed a lot more in the next chapter when more games integrated cover shooting.

Figure 3.11

Cover-based shooting and hiding would become major parts of stealth and third-person shooters in the 2000s, such as with *Uncharted 2* (released by Naughty Dog in 2009). While this style dominated the market during the 2000s, it also led to level design being massively altered to accommodate it.

3. Basic Shooter Design

For the last innovation in this section, I want to touch on the introduction of class-based shooters. While this form of FPS gameplay would become huge in the 2000s and 2010s, it did get its start with *Quake Team Fortress*. The concept is that, instead of everyone playing as the same generic character with the same attributes, players could choose from different classes that were distinguished by their health, movement speed, and weapons and utility. Teams had to coordinate who would play as what class based on the needs of the match at the time. This kind of design will be discussed more when we get to live service shooters like *Team Fortress 2*. Another name for this kind of design is "hero shooters," where the class is now distinguished by having unique individual characters who, even if they belonged to the same base class, had completely different skills and utility for combat.

The 90s era of shooters still holds many of the most memorable examples of the genre, and why this kind of design would come back to the mainstream by the end of the 2010s.

## Notes

1 https://www.guinnessworldrecords.com/world-records/first-use-of-freelook-in-a-fps#:~:text=The%20first%20commercial%20FPS%20to,or%20down%20using%20the%20keyboard
2 https://www.guinnessworldrecords.com/world-records/421751-first-first-person-shooter-videogame-fps-to-feature-a-sniper-rifle

# 4 The Cinematic Era of Shooting

## 4.1 The Rise of *Halo* and Xbox

The 2000s was an important decade for the game industry. This is when video games "grew up" – control schemes and peripherals became standardized, there were agreed upon mechanics for genres and UI design, and the console market that we know today consisting of Nintendo, Sony, and Microsoft became set in stone.

Sega left the console market in 2001 after the Dreamcast did not do well enough for the company to keep investing in it. And there was a brief window where Nintendo and Sony were the only two companies in the console market. But in November of that year, Microsoft would enter the fray with the original Xbox. At the time, it was the largest and heaviest system and was promoted as both the future of console games and what would kill the PC market. Microsoft, with the obvious experience of PCs with the Windows platform, wanted to make a console more powerful than anything else available, and would use PC hardware as part of the design of it.

During the late 90s, Bungie created the universe for *Halo* originally as a real-time strategy game, before changing it to a shooter (Figure 4.1). At the time,

DOI: 10.1201/9781003449959-4

Figure 4.1

*Halo* and Master Chief become the biggest franchises of the 2000s and one of the best shooters on consoles for this decade. The impact it had on the industry led me to include it in my list of games from *20 Essential Games to Study.*

the studio was having financial difficulties due to a problem with their game *Myth 2* released in 1998 that had to be recalled for having a bug that uninstalled the entire directory it was in. The original plan was to release the shooter version of *Halo* on PC, but when the studio was purchased by Microsoft in 2000, they wanted to make *Halo* the launch game for the Xbox, much to the dismay of fans who wanted the next Bungie shooter on a computer.

*Halo* told the story of a war between humanity and a group known as the Covenant – an alien force made up of various species with players controlling the character Master Chief who is a genetically enhanced super soldier. The conflict takes place on a ring world where Chief and the Covenant are looking for a supposed long-lost piece of technology that could turn the tide of the war.

From a gameplay perspective, *Halo* would stand out from other shooters, especially on the console side, with a variety of gameplay and changes to traditional FPS design – the most notable being the introduction of regenerating health. Players had two health bars – their normal health and a recharging shield. If anyone who has taken damage avoids being hit for a few seconds, their shield would recharge; taking health damage could only be recovered by finding med kits placed throughout the level. For multiplayer, players had to be more aggressive as they couldn't leave a character near death anymore. This could be seen as the first step toward push-forward combat that I'll return to in Section 6.1. From a combat perspective, it guaranteed that a player would enter any fight or arena without having to worry about one stray bullet killing them at low health. *Halo*

Figure 4.2

Vehicle combat of this kind was unheard of before *Halo*, and had the added benefit of letting players work together in coop.

also limited the number of weapons the player could carry to two and featured a mix of standard military guns like the pistol and sniper rifle, to weapons carried by the Covenant forces.

The game also featured vehicle combat and being able to explore larger areas in both human and Covenant vehicles. The game would shift into a third-person perspective while someone was driving or riding in a vehicle (Figure 4.2).

*Halo*'s single player campaign with cinematics would pull fans into the story of Master Chief across many games, but what gave *Halo* its staying power was the multiplayer. When the game first came out, it was possible to connect Xboxes together for up to 16-player multiplayer across its different game modes and play the campaign in coop. Having 16 players on a console shooter was the first done by the *Halo* series. The game featured a variety of multiplayer modes beyond just deathmatch and capture the flag to add more variety.

*Halo*'s popularity would only grow, and this would be tied to Microsoft's other major innovation – Xbox Live. The early 2000s saw the point in which online connectivity was being integrated to consoles. In 2002, (Special Operations Command) *SOCOM*, which was a military shooter, was released on the PlayStation 2 by Zipper Interactive and made use of the recently released online adapter for the console. Multiplayer functionality was not yet a standardized feature, with each studio having to use their own online architecture and servers if they wanted their games to have it. What Xbox Live offered was a centralized online architecture that could handle the multiplayer connectivity and servers for titles instead of the developers having to create and support it themselves.

To pay for it, consumers had to subscribe which one subscription granted them access to online multiplayer of any game they owned and was available on the service. This kind of bundled subscription would eventually be adopted by Sony for their Massively Multiplayer Online Games (*MMOGs*) as a way of consolidating the price to access them and make them more appealing to consumers and then to the other consoles with their own respective services.

What this meant for *Halo* and other shooters on Xbox was that, for a subscription fee, it was possible to play against other people from all around the world. This not only provided more value to Xbox games, but we would begin to see a greater push for multiplayer modes in shooters – sometimes over their single player campaigns (Figure 4.3).

The success of *Halo* would ignite a new market for console shooters and elevated Bungie as a studio. They would continue to work on the series up until *Halo: Reach* released in 2010. *Halo 4* was created by the studio 343 Industries who would take over the franchise with its release in 2012 from that point on. During this period, Bungie became independent while Microsoft kept the rights to the *Halo* franchise and formed 343 as the new studio to work on the franchise. The latest *Halo* was *Halo Infinite* released in 2021 and had its multiplayer and single player sides split, allowing someone to play the mode they were interested in without needing to download and keep both on their systems. The series in recent years has also had its back catalog ported to PC, with their multiplayer

Figure 4.3

*Halo* multiplayer, and multiplayer design in itself, would become a selling point for any worthwhile shooter for years to come – providing players with more games to play after finishing the story. But many shooters today now offer the single and multiplayer content as separate entities for people who prefer one over the other such as with *Halo Infinite* pictured here.

systems intact. For Bungie, they would go on to produce their own shooter: *Destiny*, which is a live service game that I'll return to later in this book.

As of this time, *Halo* as a franchise has sold an estimated 81 million copies lifetime[1] and, with its connection to Xbox Live, it's impossible to find the exact profit the series has brought in. *Halo's* importance to the game industry and FPS design cannot be understated. The innovations in its gameplay and multiplayer would change console shooters and provided Microsoft a way to secure their spot as one of the top three console makers. The notion that shooters could only work on PC was shattered. The integration of multiplayer and online connectivity would set a new standard for any multiplayer game released on a console and forced Nintendo and Sony to catch up with their own versions.

*Halo* is a game that came out at the right time on the right platform, and it's in my opinion that, if the game was just released on PC as originally planned, it would have been competing with the other shooters at the time and not be able to stand out on its own.

For the rest of the decade, we would see a change in FPS design from the boomer shooter era to focus on different kinds of first-person gameplay.

## 4.2 Set Piece/Modern Shooting

Before I go into talking more about the shooters of the 2000s, it's important to note how the level and gameplay structure changed during this period. When I talked about boomer shooter designs, specifically how levels were built, they were designed as a singular entity – the player is exploring the entire level as one complete experience from beginning to end. In the 2000s, more shooters embraced a focus on storytelling within the levels themselves, and this gave way to the idea of "set pieces" (Figure 4.4).

A set piece in this respect is like the arenas of the boomer shooter era, but, instead of a level being built as one complete area, this segments the level into noticeable smaller sections divided by checkpoints. For those unfamiliar, to prevent progress lost in a game, many titles now will save the player's progress in a level at specific points, aka checkpointing. A set piece could be anything from an in-game cutscene where the player listens to other characters talk, a stealth section, a shootout, a driving segment, and anything else. Once the player is finished with a set piece and it is checkpointed, they will not return to that specific area again.

This provides a few advantages to the designers in terms of balancing and level design. By designing each area as a self-contained one-off, it lets them be far more creative with each individualized set piece as there is no worry about the state of the player's character at any given time, nor do they have to worry about what happened in set piece 1 impacting set piece 2. Thanks to the change to regenerating health, it means there's no need to place consumables in the level and, if the player needs more ammo or weapons, they could be conveniently placed at the start of a set piece.

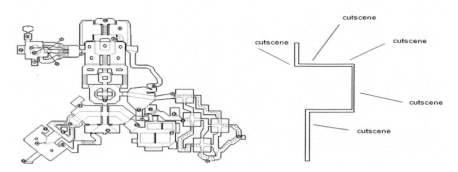

Figure 4.4

This meme has been circulating for years now and does a good job of presenting what consumers felt the change from the 90s to 2000s era of shooting represented.

In a way, this kind of structure is a simplified take on the design presented in *Half-Life 1* and *2*, where each level was a kind of one-off, with general elements of the gameplay loop (mainly shooting) a part of each level (Figure 4.5). The downside of this approach is that it robs the level design of the ability to feel like a cohesive whole. Due to the nature of the checkpoints, the player is never returning to a previous point in the level, and they are only moving forward from a set piece to a set piece. Many fans of shooters have talked about how linear the focus on set piece design makes a level. While there is certainly room to create unique set pieces, many designers opt for repeating the same style throughout their game. The player knows, that if they enter a huge room with chest-high walls, more than likely enemies are going to spawn around them and they will have to take cover. The act of spawning enemies also became more used during this period. Many older shooters would have enemies wandering around corridors or already being active in the level, and set piece games had a larger division between the combat and exploration sections. While exploring, the player would not find any enemies whatsoever or just those as a part of the story or specific scene. Once they get to combat, enemies can appear from off screen or some other narrative device for how they arrived. There is no room to go off the beaten path; many games may not even let the player out of the specific route through the level.

To return to *Half-Life*, the reason why their approach worked so well was that they didn't change things up for a single section, but for the entirety of the level. That way, the player was able to see the unique aspect of the level in all its utility, to then move on to the next with something new and different. It would hurt the

Figure 4.5

Returning to *Half Life 2*, what the developers did was design levels as unique elements, instead of trying to segment a level into multiple sections. This had the effect of making the levels unique from one another and keep the player guessing, as the game did not repeat its set pieces throughout the game.

game's pacing if Valve repeated entire sections in each new level. The open world genre would become another example of heavily relying on set pieces and fixed content types to pad out their worlds and gameplay. When the gameplay turns into a checklist of activities, it can make the experience feel hollow – that the player's only job isn't to explore the world, but complete tasks X, Y, and Z.

The changes to shooter design during this decade would solidify the 90s era as the boomer shooter period; even though that term didn't start to be discussed until the end of the 2010s. Consumers could tell that something was different with the shooter designs that were coming out, and there would be a whole lot of them for the next decade.

## 4.3 Grounding the Guns and the Gameplay

In the 2000s era of shooters, besides the system of regenerating health, there were two other trends that would be adopted by most shooters of this era. This was a period where designers were trying to make their games "grow up" or feel more grounded compared to the 90s, and shooters went very far in this respect. The idea was to try and create a more realistic approach to shooting to go with the storytelling that many developers focused on. For shooters, this led to limiting how many weapons the player could have access to at one point. The most popular number was two – letting the players have a gun that they liked and one as a backup if they ran out of ammo (Figure 4.6).

4. The Cinematic Era of Shooting

Figure 4.6

Removing unique weapons in favor of a generic pool became the norm for the 2000s era of shooting, especially with any military shooters, and there were a lot of them.

Instead of featuring unique weapons, the player's arsenal would come from the enemies they killed. Battlefields would often turn into a small depot of guns to go through to find the weapons they want to take into the next area. The stronger the weapon, the fewer bullets the player could store for it to prevent them from just relying on one weapon throughout the entire game. Although, that didn't stop people from hoarding a powerful weapon for boss fights or harder arenas.

The other trend that went well with set piece design was fully adopting cover-based shooting for console and third-person shooters. Where boomer shooters focused on high-speed play and movement, many shooters in the 2000s slowed things down. Pairing cover with designing fixed set pieces and encounters worked well for a lot of series. One of the biggest that came out at this time was *Gears of War* by Epic Games (released in 2006) (Figure 4.7). The game's story is about humanity trying to fight back against a force known as the Locust who live deep underground. There was an emphasis on creating heft or weight to the characters and the gameplay, with everyone being very muscular and moving and turning slowly. Weapons were designed to be over-the-top, including attaching a chainsaw to the stock assault rifle. Being out of cover was a death sentence, and players had to navigate fighting enemies while moving between cover to get the best shooting angle. *Gears of War* would go on to popularize a mechanic known as the "active reload." During the reloading animation, a bar starts to fill up on screen; pressing the reload button at the sweet spot would automatically reload the gun and let the player start shooting immediately; miss it, and the gun would take a little longer to finish reloading. Besides having a competitive versus mode,

Figure 4.7

*Gears of War* would become the other major console shooter franchise exclusive to Microsoft for some time to blow up. Where *Halo* went sci-fi, *Gears* went more gritty and brutal, and surprisingly both series would eventually be moved off the Xbox to PC in the 2010s.

*Gears of War* would also popularize the concept of a "horde mode." In it, players teamed up to survive escalating waves of enemies with high scores and rewards for the teams that could survive until the very end.

*Gears of War* would eventually grow to five main entries with several spin-offs including a tactical strategy take, *Gears Tactics*, released in 2020 and a new entry subtitled "E-Day" was announced in 2024.

At the end of the 90s and into the 2000s, part of the grounded era that was occurring came with the rise of tactical shooters. These are FPSs that remove all the arcade/nonrealistic elements, in favor of making something that relies on high skill beyond just shooting a gun. In 1998, the first *Tom Clancy's Rainbow Six* was released, developed by Red Storm Entertainment. Based on the book series, the early *Rainbow Six* games focused on performing special operations around the globe. Players had to plan how to engage an area with different squads of operatives to take out the bad guys, minimize casualties, and do it as efficiently as possible. While the series over time has removed the planning elements, the focus on grounded and challenging shooting has remained.

The growing popularity of military shooters also led to a series focusing on being a police officer, and one of the most popular ones was *SWAT 3* released in 1999 by Sierra Entertainment. The first two games in the series were done more in the style of a point and click or choose your own adventure format, with the third and future games switching to first person. Like *Rainbow Six*, your mission isn't to run in and start shooting everyone, but to plan out operations, try to arrest when possible, and minimize any civilian deaths. The developers did research about Special Weapons And Tactics (SWAT), and it earned a fanbase much like *Rainbow Six* for being a more realistic and challenging take on shooters.

Another game that would grow big, thanks to its focus on more challenging shooting, was *Counter-Strike*. The original mod was released in 1999 for *Half-Life 1*, by Minh Lee and Jess Cliffe; and following the popularity of it, they were hired by Valve who took ownership of the property and released it as a stand-alone game in 2000 (Figure 4.8). Two teams take turns playing as a terrorist force and a counterterrorist group with the terrorists trying to set off a bomb while the opposing group must stop them. After enough rounds have passed, the teams switch, and whichever side succeeds the most will win the match. The depth of *Counter-Strike* was about how quickly firefights would end thanks to extremely low health pools for every character. It's more important to hit vital parts of the opponent rather than just spray a lot of bullets in a direction. In-between rounds, teams can spend money earned through play to buy new equipment, armor, and of course guns. Every gun handled differently and was better at specific ranges. A sniper rifle would kill in one shot but missing it in close range and that player will not be able to reload before they are taken out. Both *Counter-Strike* and *Rainbow Six* continued to be popular to this day, and I'll talk more about them in Chapter 5.

One of the first games to highlight a shift toward grounded and more serious shooting and storytelling was *Max Payne*, released in 2000 by Remedy. Billed as a stylized noir story, players controlled detective Max Payne – framed for the

Figure 4.8

*Counter-Strike* is now one of the longest running eSports in the entire industry. While the mechanics haven't really changed, the engine and updates made with each new iteration continue to keep people playing.

Figure 4.9

*Max Payne* brought a more stylized test to its gameplay that hadn't been seen before. The use of the graphic novel and narration helped to sell the story, and this wouldn't be the last time that Remedy would stand out from other studios with their games.

murder of his partner while investigating the murder of his wife and child, he goes on a one-man rampage through New York to discover the conspiracy that led to everything (Figure 4.9). Each chapter of the game was highlighted by a comic book-styled cutscene with narration done by Max. While the story tried to be grounded, the gameplay was not – as Max could hold multiple weapons, could heal himself by taking painkillers, and had the power of slow-mo or "bullet time." With the press of a button, the entire world around Max slowed down: enabling players to see incoming bullets and dodge them while getting the drop on any opponents. Heavily inspired by *The Matrix*, this would not be the last game to make use of bullet time. As an interesting point, giving the player abilities or powers to help them along with shooting would become a major aspect of how shooters would evolve in the 2010s.

This is also the decade where *Call of Duty* would first come out in 2003 by Infinity Ward. The original concept for the game was to make a shooter that would follow different soldiers throughout World War II who would either participate in major battles or take part in their own fictionalized story set during the war. I will be returning to the franchise when it transformed into the multiplayer behemoth that is very well known today in Section 5.2.

You may be wondering what became of *Doom* during this period. In 2004, id Software released *Doom 3*. Designed as a soft reboot of the original game, *Doom 3's* tone was built entirely on action horror design. Players controlled a nondescript marine who arrives at the UAC base on Mars just as an experimental mishap causes portals to hell happens. Now the only one alive, they must make their way through the base and into hell itself to save the day. *Doom 3*'s structure was designed to be slower paced than the previous games. Instead of wide environments with a variety of rooms, the developers tried to keep the player on their toes by hiding enemies behind multiple walls or teleporting behind them (Figure 4.10). The term "monster closet" has been popularized to describe areas where monsters are hiding behind a fake wall or as a trap waiting to get the player, and *Doom 3* was full of them.

While the player wasn't limited to two guns, they had a far more debilitating factor in the form of lighting. The entire base loses power after the portal mishap and, for the player to see more than a foot in front of them, they need to keep a flashlight out. The dynamic here was that the player could use their gun, or light their way, but not at the same time. This, along with the weaker gunplay of the weapons, caused fans to declare it one of the worst games of the time. The game would be re-released in 2012 under the BFG: Edition moniker. This edition also integrated the "duct tape mod" into the game – putting the flashlight on whatever weapon the player was holding instead of having them swap between the two.

As for the legacy of *Doom 3* it has aged better than people expected it to at the time. While it is not considered a classic compared to the first two, people today appreciate the difference in tone and structure that id Software was trying to achieve. The lesson learned is that you need to be careful with how you position games in a franchise. Consumers have different expectations when playing a gamethat is a spin-off vs. the next main entry in the series. If people come to

Figure 4.10

When compared to the other *Dooms*, *Doom 3* did not work for fans at the time and was viewed as a poor shooter. It does succeed as an action horror game and remains the black sleep of the *Doom* franchise.

a game expecting X, and your next main game doesn't deliver it, then it can be viewed as an act of betrayal by the fans.

Part of the 2000s was trying to emulate Hollywood, and shooters and action movies went together. In 2007, *Uncharted* by Naughty Dog was released to critical and commercial success. The series starred Nathan Drake – a treasure hunter and charismatic rogue who would explore the world looking for long-lost treasure and getting into loads of trouble. Featuring a mix of third-person cover shooting, platforming, and solving puzzles, the series blew up thanks to its outrageous set pieces and witty dialogue of Nathan voiced by Nolan North. One of the most iconic aspect was Nathan having to climb up a rail car of a train hanging off the ledge of a cliff in the second game.

With any genre, there are always exceptions to major trends with some that became famous, and a few that were infamous. In 2000, Raven Software released *Soldier of Fortune* – a shooter based on the magazine of the same name, which gained a lot of notoriety for its body deformation system thanks to the GHOUL engine. This was a game where it was possible to shoot the limbs and heads off your enemies with different guns creating a different impact on the enemy's model. While the graphics are dated today, the depiction of humans being killed in graphic ways led to the game being banned in some countries and requiring Raven to put out censored versions to sell it, but they also released an optional patch to enable the violence.

The other famous example of a game going against social norms and becoming infamous for it was *Postal 2* released in 2003 by Running with Scissors. Here, players controlled the "postal dude," a man who is trying to have a normal week but is constantly put into situations that can lead to mass violence and destruction. The game is famous at this point for being as non-politically correct as a game could be with examples a bit too graphic to mention in this book.

Like *Serious Sam* with designing an arena-focused shooter, *Painkiller* was released in 2004 by People Can Fly. The two selling points were fighting massive waves of normal enemies with boss fights against giant ones, and the variety of weapons – each one with a unique alt fire.

There are games that try to have it both ways – be more grounded while still having the nonrealistic elements. *S.T.A.L.K.E.R.: Shadows of Chernobyl* was released in 2007 by GSC Game World (Figure 4.11). The player explores an alternate setting in Chernobyl following a second nuclear meltdown that has transformed the area into "the zone." Creatures have mutated, objects have taken on strange properties, and everyone is fighting each other to try and survive and/or become rich. The world itself featured massive game spaces where the different groups of Non Playable Characters (NPCs) would fight and interact with one another separate from the player's involvement. This also coined a phrase "AI Life" to describe games where the NPCs would interact with one another and the world on their own. Gunplay and progression were about completing missions and exploring the world to acquire better equipment – from suits that offered better protection, different guns, and different ammo types. While exploring,

Figure 4.11

*S.T.A.L.K.E.R.* is a game that does a little bit of everything – it's open world, with grounded shooting and progression, and can give way to becoming a horror game every time the player goes underground and explore. The game has also aged well thanks to the modding community and fan-made patches.

players could find anomalies that posed various degrees of threats and they could find artifacts that could be worn for unique benefits. While the original release was very buggy, fans have worked on mods to fix certain elements, completely change the game, and everything in-between. There is currently a sequel in development for 2024 at the time of writing this.

The *Metro* series also fits this kind of style and has dabbled with being level-based and open world. First released in 2010 by 4A Games, the series is based on a book of the same name by Dmitry Glukhovsky and follows survivors in Russia following a nuclear war. The series is up to three now and has been praised for its world design and evolving the gameplay to go open world in the latest one: *Metro Exodus* released in 2019.

There were plenty more shooters that were released and franchises that came and went, and here is a quick snapshot of some of the more notable ones and how well they did.[2]

| Name | Sales Numbers |
| --- | --- |
| Counter-Strike | Free to play, no sales numbers |
| Doom 3 | 3.5 million |
| Gears of War series | 41 million |
| Max Payne series | 11.5 million |
| Metro series | 14.7 million |

*(Continued)*

4.3 Grounding the Guns and the Gameplay

| Name | Sales Numbers |
|---|---|
| Postal 2 | 1.91 million |
| Rainbow Six series | 36 million |
| Soldier of Fortune | Cannot find |
| S.T.A.L.K.E.R. series | 4 million |
| SWAT 3 | Cannot find |
| Uncharted series | 44.33 million |

While the shooter market was changing in the 2000s, there were other trends that would go on to shape the genre and give gamers very different offerings in first person.

## 4.4 Hyperrealistic Shooting

The 2000s came with the biggest jump the game industry saw in terms of hardware and software. By this point, 3D became the standard for AAA releases, and studios were trying to capitalize on this increased power, and both the Xbox and PlayStation 3 were trying to compete to be considered the best and most powerful console.

A trend that would start here, and weirdly enough, would become a focus by indie studios in the 2010s, was trying to make the depiction and act of shooting as realistic as possible. This meant not only making games that look like they took place in a realistic setting, but also focusing a lot on the gunplay and feel of weapons to make them behave as they would in reality, or in an action movie (Figure 4.12).

Figure 4.12

Hyperrealism like in *F.E.A.R.* and other games may have looked great in screenshots, but this style of shooting was rarely integrated into the gameplay and tactics by the player in most games unfortunately.

4. The Cinematic Era of Shooting

While not specific to shooting, a unique tangent in this respect was *Red Faction* released in 2001 by Volition. Instead of making guns realistic, they would make the environment fully destructible. Using their "geomod" technology, it was possible to dynamically blow up the environment and terrain using heavy weapons and explosives. Games for years at this point have had destructible environments in them, but those were scripted events laid out by the designer. Here, it was possible to make tunnels around enemies, open entrenched areas, and more. Surprisingly, no other studio after this would try something similar for years. The only examples I could think of are *Red Faction Guerrilla* (released in 2009 by Volition), and *Rainbow Six: Siege* that will be discussed later.

In 2005, Monolith Productions released First Encounter Assault Recon (*F.E.A.R.*), a first-person shooter that attempted to combine Japanese horror with challenging shootouts and gunplay. Players controlled the character simply known as "point man" who is the latest member of F.E.A.R., an organization that specializes in supernatural events. When a psychic armed with an army of cloned soldiers attacks Armacham Technology Corporation, it's up to point man to be the one-man army to stop the situation. All the while, a ghost by the name of Alma stalks point man and indicates there's far more going on here. Like *Max Payne*, *F.E.A.R.* features its own form of bullet time in the form of reflex time – allowing the player to slow down time and the enemies around them to make it easier to fight them.

The gunplay is famous for not only providing destructibility to the environments, but also fighting clones, or as they are called replicas. To this day, *F.E.A.R.* still has one of the best enemy behaviors and AI seen in a shooter. This point will come back when I talk about enemy design in Section 7.2, but most enemy behaviors in shooters are very basic. Here, enemies were designed to actively engage the player – moving around the room to flank them, throwing grenades to flush the player out, and communicating with the other enemies in the room. Even though the player had the power of reflex time, they were always outgunned and at a disadvantage against a squad of enemies. While the player couldn't regenerate health, they still had a limited weapon inventory.

The series would end up with three main games, two expansions for the first, and an attempt at making an online shooter that never got out of beta. The last main game *F.E.A.R. 3* released in 2011 had the added component of building the campaign about coop play with one character playing as point man and one as the ghost of the psychic from the first game (Figure 4.13). Despite this system, the game was viewed as the weakest of the three due to frustrating combat and controls.

While AAA studios would focus more on the bombastic side of shooting in the 2010s, the appeal of making shooters, and handling weapons more realistically, would spawn their own niche among indie and smaller studios. The *Red Orchestra* series by Tripwire Interactive, and first released in 2006, was a World War II shooter where players fought as different armies in various conflicts throughout the war. The weaponry was all modeled to be realistic to their real-world versions, and so was the damage. No one could take more than a bullet

Figure 4.13

*F.E.A.R.* tone was always inconsistent between military shooting combat and the spooky ghost sections, but this went into overdrive in the third game featuring more monsters to fight and an overall downgrade to the enemy AI.

of two from most weapons, and proper positioning and aiming were key to keep yourself from taking a stray bullet.

That same year, *Arma* by Bohemia Interactive was released. The focus was not only on simulating using weapons but also on driving and handling military vehicles in various environments. As far away from a run-and-gun or boomer shooter a game could get, the series has grown a following thanks to the variety of mods for it, and the degree of difficulty and skill needed to play it. One of the most famous mods was *DayZ* – taking the complexity of the *Arma* series and turning it into an open world survival game in a world where zombies and other players are your biggest threats. *DayZ* became so popular that the mod was turned into its own standalone game and released in 2018. Another mod that sprung out of *Arma* and *DayZ* was *Player Unknown's Battlegrounds* or *PUBG* for short (officially released in 2017), and I will talk more about it and battle royale games in Section 5.3. The latest entry was *Arma 3* released in 2013, but it has been supported with numerous expansions since.

The *Receiver* series started out as part of an FPS game jam and was then turned into a franchise starting in 2013 by Wolfire Games. These games are all about simulating the actual firearms themselves with the challenge of the game is understanding how to properly load, maintain, and use them, while being attacked by enemies.

What attracts people to realistic-focused FPSs is that they typically reward aiming and a slower pace compared to other shooters (Figure 4.14). When you

Figure 4.14

Taking shooting and gunplay as far to the realism side as possible can lead to incredibly tense matches and moments in games, but this level of detail can be very difficult to learn for new players and has always led to unique, but niche, experiences.

can only fire one bullet every few seconds compared to dozens, you need to make sure that one bullet is going to hit. That said, these shooters are on the niche side and are not as popular compared to the more run-and-gun and over-the-top styles.

Realism has always been a highly touted goal for designers from both a gameplay and a graphical standpoint. As we have seen from genre to genre, realism for the sake of being realistic doesn't end up with games that are that interesting to play or look at. During this period of the game industry, many AAA games started to look alike using the same dull browns and grays for most of the environments. In the 2010s, developers had to find a middle ground between making a slower-paced, more challenging shooter and something that was still appealing to the greater market. This also came with redesigning the UI/ Graphical User Interface (**GUI**) to reduce the number of key presses needed to play. The tactical management layer of *Rainbow Six* and *SWAT* fell out of popularity – consumers still wanted to play a challenging shooter, but they didn't want to spend so much time on the pre-planning stages. And in the 2020s as I'm writing this, outside of a few longstanding franchises, many games now put looking awesome over being realistic.

That doesn't mean that there isn't an audience for realism with shooting but making it engaging outside of the hardcore niche is a different story. When you are making your shooter realistic, a lot of the design decisions and balancing has already been decided for you by the real-world specs of those weapons. But the consumer who is going to play a game like *Arma* vs. *Call of Duty* or vice versa is like having two different universes. The appeal of the gunplay is less about making the player feel powerful and unstoppable, but the challenge of taking out another player when both have weapons where a single missed shot could mean death.

Finally, here is a quick snapshot of how these games did in terms of copies sold[3]:

| Game Name | Units Sold |
|---|---|
| Arma series | 13 million |
| DayZ | 5.8 million |
| F.E.A.R. series | Can't find |
| Receiver series | 700,000–1.5 million (estimate) |
| Red Orchestra series | 2.5–6 million (estimate) |

## 4.5 Interacting in First Person

Creating first-person viewpoints in other genres became more popular in the 2000s, and this would continue to grow with the return of VR in the 2010s. Being able to do other things than just shooting in first person would lead to new designs and popular franchises (Figure 4.15). It is important to remember that the *Elder Scrolls* series by Bethesda has always been in first person and did allow players to fight, but they were built more as action RPGs rather than FPSs, but Bethesda will be mentioned again when they took over the *Fallout* series.

*Breakdown* released in 2004 by Namco is the first example I could find of a game that was in first person, but also played like an action game. In it, the main character was Derrick Cole. He is trapped with no memory in a facility that was set up to study a strange race of beings known as the T'lan who are immune to conventional weaponry. Derrick, thanks to an injection of a substance from the T'lan, now has the power to fight them at the cost of his memory. The game would alternate between first-person shooting and first-person beat-em-up based on the enemies at hand, by getting into gunfights with humans and fist fights with the T'lan.

*Star Wars* as a license would go on to be a part of multiple fan-favorite series over the 90s to today. The original *Dark Forces* (released in 1995 by Lucas Arts) was a boomer shooter with the aesthetic of *Star Wars*. As the franchise grew, it would then turn into the *Jedi Knight* series which introduced the ability for the player to use force powers and lightsabers along with blasters and other ranged weapons. By the final game in the series, *Star Wars Jedi Knight: Jedi Academy* in 2003, Raven Software who developed it at the time fully embraced third-person lightsaber combat as the core gameplay loop. Players could design different lightsabers and use powers in both single player missions and multiplayer fights against other players.

4. The Cinematic Era of Shooting

Figure 4.15

First person has always been a popular perspective for melee combat in RPGs, but the 2000s era gave us games where first person could also be used for real-time combat to deliver a more visceral feeling.

In 2005, Monolith Productions also released *Condemned: Criminal Origins* which was an Xbox exclusive at the time. Playing as special agent Ethan Thomas, he is on the hunt for a serial killer who has framed him for murder and must explore a decrepit and crime-ridden city to find the truth.

Unlike the other games I've mentioned until now, *Condemned* was a first-person action horror game with a focus on close range combat. As Ethan, players could pick up various implements and tools to use as weapons. Each one was rated in terms of different attributes like reach, damage, and attack speed. While there were guns, they were heavily downplayed due to having limited ammunition and were only used in specific situations. Fighting in first person provided a visceral feel to combat thanks to seeing directly through Ethan's eyes while deranged murderers were attacking. This also helped with the horror, as players never knew what enemies were around the corner, or if someone was sneaking up behind to deliver an attack. The game did get a sequel in 2007. That added more to the exploration and combat but has not been re-released since.

Creating first-person horror games became a huge aspect of the genre's continued existence among indie studios in the 2010s. It is far creepier to see a monster or something coming at you when you are looking through the eyes of the character as opposed to being in third person. This also helped with building the game, as the designers didn't need to worry about rendering or animating a main character, when they could just use the viewpoint of the camera to handle everything. For more information about the horror genre and design, be sure to read *Game Design Deep Dive: Horror*.

The idea of using the environment and the physics of the world to help the player has always been a part of FPS design – going back to the likes of *Doom* with exploding barrels. In 2006, *Dark Messiah of Might and Magic* from Arkane Studios was released. Another game that focused on close range combat in first person, the game became famous thanks to the interaction of the physics of the world and using the environment to fight enemies. While players could fight enemies using their sword and bow in traditional combat, they could just kick them into a spike pit, or off a ledge, or into any other environmental hazard in the area. Finding creative ways of dealing with enemies would be explored more in the 2010s and as FPS design evolved again.

With regard to shooters, one of the most popular examples built on the basic concepts of first-person shooting was *Portal*, released in 2007 and part of Valve's "Orange Box" collection. Players controlled Chell who was trapped in a testing facility run by an AI named Genetic Lifeform and Disk Operating System (GlaDOS) and forced to go through various tests using a portal gun. With the portal gun, the players could create two portals and move themselves or objects between the two with simulated physics impacting velocity of anything that goes through them (Figure 4.16). This kickstarted an entire trend of designers building first-person puzzle games of exploring places with some kind of weird or unusual technology. The sequel released in 2011 also added an entire campaign that could be played with a friend with original puzzles. However, because these

Figure 4.16

*Portal* has become famous at this point for clever designs, well-written characters, and an amazing sense of place with its level and environmental design. And while there have been many games that have used a similar style over the 2010s, *Portal* 1 and 2 still reign supreme.

4. The Cinematic Era of Shooting

games are more focused on puzzle design rather than shooting, I won't be talking about them with the design chapters.

In 2008, *Mirror's Edge* by DICE was released to acclaim by combining first-person fighting, platforming, and shooting together. The story focused on Faith, a courier in a futuristic city where information is controlled by the government. To get around, she must parkour around the world to deliver messages and get away for the city forces. *Mirror's Edge* did have combat in it, but it was a game that focused more on platforming and moving around. There were guns, but the player could not reload them and had to discard them when they were emptied. The sequel released in 2016 expanded the design to be more open world.

A trend that I will be talking about more later in this book is the notion of combining action game mechanics with first-person shooting and combat. One of the most popular takes of this would be *Zeno Clash* released in 2009 by Ace Team. Taking place in a strange world, the player controlled Ghat who was on the run and had to fight his way through the inhabitants of the world. The art style and aesthetic of the game are still unique and part of the charm of Ace Team's games. While there were weapons to use, guns had limited ammo and melee weapons would break after a few hits. The focus was on fighting enemies using dodges, punches, and grabs to succeed in combat. Here are some estimates for sales numbers of these games provided by Steam Spy, as I couldn't find accurate reports elsewhere.

| Game Name | Copies Sold |
| --- | --- |
| Condemned 1 | 200–500k |
| Dark Forces series | 2.5–5 million |
| Dark Messiah of Might and Magic | 1–2 million |
| Mirror's Edge series | 2.5–6 million |
| Portal series | 20–40 million |
| Zeno Clash | 400k to 1 million |

Being able to interact with objects in first person with simulated physics would also create another sub-genre of first-person games – first-person puzzle/adventure games. This led to many escape room-styled adventure games and would grow in popularity with VR. Another incredibly popular sub-genre that I won't be focusing on in this book is the "simulator" genre – where the game is played in first person and tasks the player to do some kind of real-world work in first person. Interacting with the environment in first person would also become a staple of indie horror in the 2010s, as players could interact with doors, closets, drawers, and many other objects to try and solve puzzles, hide from monsters, and much more.

Recontextualizing first-person shooting mechanics into something else will be discussed more in Section 8.5 and represents how designers could take the basic mechanics of a shooter and do something else with them – both to stand out from other games and to tell a different kind of story. This would open the design to gamers who aren't interested in shooter mechanics when they are attached to violence and attacking.

## Notes

1 https://www.vgchartz.com/game/226032/halo/sales
2 Source: VGChartz.com
3 Sources: VGChartz.com and estimates provided by Steam Spy.

# 5

# The Live Service Shooter Era

## 5.1 The Time of *Team Fortress 2*

A monumental aspect of how shooters and game design evolved over the past 20 years has been the gradual and complete adoption of online and multiplayer design. The rise of the internet transformed the world and daily life, and the game industry is no exception. By the early 2000s, the use of cable modems to allow for internet access without the use of a phone line was starting to be adopted. According to Statisa,[1] 42% of households in 2000 had internet access; by 2010, it was 71% to about 91% in 2022.

As I talked about earlier in the book, shooters were played online using either a dial-up or Local Area Network (LAN) connection in the 90s. In 2007, two games that would set very different standards for online shooters came out, *Team Fortress 2* and *Call of Duty: Modern Warfare* (I'll talk about COD in the next section).

*Team Fortress 2* was in development by Valve for a long time and was the sequel to the mod *Team Fortress* that was developed for *Half-Life 1* (Figure 5.1). This was a class-based team shooter that was developed by the same team who created *Quake Team Fortress*: Robin Walker, John Cook, and Ian Caughley. They were hired by Valve to create the first *Team Fortress* built off the Source engine.

DOI: 10.1201/9781003449959-5

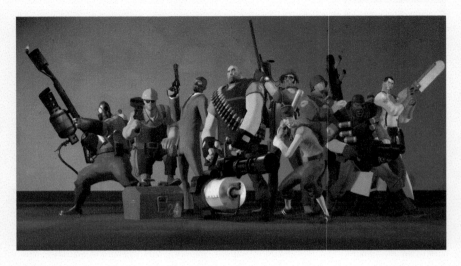

Figure 5.1

*Team Fortress 2* is a lesson in how a strong aesthetic and identity can make a game look and feel timeless. The marketing and characterizations still hold up to this day, and only a few live service games have managed to beat it in terms of growth and changing the gameplay over the years.

For the sequel, Valve invested heavily into aesthetic and would forgo a realistic military-themed shooter, for one that was more animated and cartoony. Each class from the first game was reimagined as a character with their own backstory and personality. Part of the marketing for *Team Fortress 2* was the "meet the team" videos, where Valve created fake interviews and introductions of the character using the Source engine. The creativity and writing earned a lot of praise, and these videos would go on to be one of the best forms of marketing for the game, and something many developers would copy for their own games.

The gameplay at first was an extension of the original concept – two teams of players would fight against each other picking the different classes as their controlled character. There were no rules for how many of each class could be on a team. What made *Team Fortress*'s gameplay work was how each class played differently – giving the player nine different forms of gameplay and gunplay. The Soldier's rocket launcher was a projectile-based weapon that required good aiming, which is different from the Pyro's close-range flamethrower that was all about getting in close and burning the enemy team. There were specialty classes like the Engineer who could build turrets and support structures, or the Spy who could disguise themselves as the enemy team and cause trouble behind the frontlines.

To keep growing the game, Valve would implement what we now call both as a live service game and as "games as a service." Traditionally, multiplayer games outside of the MMOG genre had a limited window of player interest and development

5. The Live Service Shooter Era

**THE SANDMAN**
HOME FRICKIN' RUN!

You Scouts are gonna love this highly collectible bat that smacks baseballs at the other team, stunning the living crap outta anybody dumb, slow, drunk, mute or Australian enough to get in the way. The farther the ball flies before ricocheting offa some chucklehead's skull, the longer he's gonna be stunned. And guys who think they're tough because they're invulnerable? *It works on them too.* Now the bad news: You can't double jump when you're carrying this little beauty. On the other hand, double jumping never put anybody in a coma.

**A.** Hit a guy with the ball to stun him. The farther the ball travels, the longer he's gonna be out.

**B.** Now laugh at the guy because he ain't doin' nothin for a while but gettin' beat on.

**C.** Get in there and take some cheap shots! You deserve it. So does he. Batter SWING!

Figure 5.2

*Team Fortress 2* had some of the best writing for a game, not in the game itself. The updates would all be written within the universe and present items, locations, events, from the point of view (POV) of the various characters.

after release. What ended up happening in most cases was that the general consumers would move on from a multiplayer game, leaving only the hardcore to play against each other. Developers would release some support patches here and there, maybe one expansion, but then they would go to their next game project. Multiplayer for these older games would just be left to the hardcore players as there wasn't anything keeping casual and core audiences coming back to play. Valve wanted to keep working on *Team Fortress 2* and first put out an update with a new game mode and maps to play on. Their biggest change that would affect the game for years to come was adding in equipment that players could put on the different classes (Figure 5.2). Starting with the medic in 2008, and would eventually go to everyone else, this would add customization to the game.

The idea behind the equipment, and what would figure into their overall design balance, was creating "sidegrades" – an item that would boost one aspect of the class but would negatively affect something else. This could be having a gun that does more damage, but is less accurate, to something that completely changes the utility at the expense of the original function. For example, the Sniper could forgo his close-range submachine gun for a shield to protect them from spies.

2009 introduced personalization with hats that players could unlock to give an added touch of flair to their characters. Personalization for live service and online games has become one of the defining aspects of monetization and something I went on at length about in *Game Design Deep Dive: Free to Play*, and I also talked about *Team Fortress 2* from a live service perspective.

The game would go free to play in 2011 and would become one of the bestselling and profitable games around. Even though Valve has stopped focusing on it, *Team Fortress 2*, from its design, marketing, and live service support, would become the blueprint for many shooters and online games released in the 2010s that I'll return to in Section 5.4.

As a shooter, the game still holds up thanks to the focus on class-based design that would be translated to hero shooters in the 2010s. There are people who learned to play as all nine classes, just as there are those who only played one, and both forms of play were acceptable. All the different game modes were added, and special holiday events were built with the game's gunplay in mind.

Map design was about providing ways for each class to shine – straightaways where the Heavy could cut loose, lookouts for the Sniper, places to hide Engineer support items, and more. One area that is unique to *Team Fortress 2* compared to other shooters was adding far more game modes or ways of playing over the years. Throughout the years, Valve allowed the community to create items, maps, and even new game modes that could be played and officially adopted into *Team Fortress 2*. This is also on top of people having their own custom servers where they could add their own unique elements that people could play with.

Here is a quick list of the main game modes that would all be integrated into the game not counting specific themed versions of certain modes:

- Arena: Teams fight each other with a single life per player each round.
- Attack/defend: Teams take turns trying to take control of a map from one another.
- Capture the flag: Teams fight to take a briefcase from the opposing team's base back to their own.
- Competitive mode: Ranked play where kills and losses are factored in for each player.
- Control point: Teams compete to take over nodes on the map to score points.
- King of the hill: Teams compete for a singular point to capture it and start their countdown. The team that finishes their countdown first wins.
- Mann vs. machine: A coop mode where a team of players must fight against waves of invading robots.
- MannPower: A capture the flag mode that focused on moving around using grappling hooks and more with melee weapons.
- PASS time: Teams compete in a sporting event to deliver a ball to the goal to earn points.
- Payload: Teams take turns pushing a cart to the opposing team's base; whichever team gets the cart the fastest (or furthest if no one makes it) wins.
- Player destruction: Players must deliver pickups earned by killing opposing team members to a specific point to score, and the team with the most points wins.

- Special delivery: Teams compete to transport a briefcase to a specific point. If the briefcase is dropped, it can be picked up again by the same team, while the opposing team must stop that from happening for 45 seconds to make it neutral again.
- Territorial control: Teams fight to take over randomly chosen territories on maps with one side attacking and one side defending and then the roles are switched.
- Vs. Saxton Hale: A one vs. many mode with one team made up of the nine classes and the other just playing as Saxton Hale who is stronger and more powerful than any individual character.
- Zombie infection: The red team must stay alive while the blue team as zombies are trying to kill them and turn them into zombies for their side.

And again, the modes I mentioned here don't count the many fan-made ones that were not picked up by Valve. *Team Fortress 2* succeeded thanks to both being a solid and unique shooter and building itself as an entire brand beyond just the gameplay (Figure 5.3). And while many shooters and live service games have copied this approach to character design and marketing, not one of them has had the staying and brand power of *Team Fortress 2*. As I said further up, Valve has stopped actively working on major updates for it, but the servers and all the functionalities are still playable at the time of writing this. As Valve is

Figure 5.3

There will never be another live service game like *Team Fortress 2* in terms of its success and how it grew over the years. It is the only game of its kind that never added in new characters, never changed the core gameplay over the years, and just added "more" of everything to turn it into a phenomenon.

a privately held company, there are no official sales reports I could find for the profit or revenue that *Team Fortress 2* has earned.

The monetization side of *Team Fortress 2* did grow and change over the course of its time. The game was originally a retail purchase but, when it went free to play, monetization shifted toward the different cosmetics. Through playing the game each week, players would earn random drops up to a specific amount weekly. These drops could be free items for any class, or "crates." Crates were tied to specific events or a generic one that would be changed from time to time. The crate itself was an example of a *loot box* – providing the player with a random reward from a fixed pool of possible ones. To open it, players needed to buy a key, the price of which could fluctuate depending on getting them from other players.

Valve implemented an entire trading system that allowed players to buy and sell any *Team Fortress 2* items, along with items from other games, through the Steam interface itself. On every transaction, no matter how big or small, Valve would receive a fee on every sale. This, on top of the 30% cut they take from developer sales on Steam, makes it impossible to determine just how much money Valve is earning year-by-year. They would also implement a pass system for accessing the Mann vs. Machine mode in order for players to earn the cosmetic rewards from playing it. Before the game went free to play, in 2010 the developers created the Mann Co. Store as a way of directly buying any item or cosmetic a player wanted with real money. Unlike the crate system, items bought in the store have a fixed price, but could go on sale for specific events.

*Team Fortress 2* succeeded thanks to being a fantastic game first, and then only grew bigger and more expansive over the years. It would not have been possible for the game to become what it did without going live service and changing its monetization model. Of the live service games released, it is the only one to this day that did not originally launch with any monetization from the get-go. Valve's success became a blueprint that has only gotten bigger and more elaborate from other studios over the 2010s. As of the time of writing this, there are no plans for *Team Fortress 3*, nor have there been any major content patches for *Team Fortress 2*.

## 5.2 The War of Military Shooters

In the 2000s and into the 2010s, both *Call of Duty* and *Battlefield* competed in the market to be the premier military shooter (Figure 5.4). As I mentioned in the last chapter, *Call of Duty* first came out in 2003 by Infinity Ward focusing on World War II conflicts and grounded shooting. In 2002, *Battlefield: 1942* was released by Digital Illusions CE that would then be acquired by Electronics Arts and rebranded to DICE.

In these original launches, *Call of Duty* focused more on its single player campaign, trying to build interesting missions and stories set during the war. *Battlefield: 1942* focused exclusively on multiplayer and its marketing point was about the scale of battles. Where most multiplayer shooters focused on small numbers of teams, *Battlefield: 1942* allowed 64 players to play at the same time on one map. This was

Figure 5.4

Looking at them today, both *Call of Duty* and *Battlefield* look and play nothing like their original versions, which is both a blessing and a curse of live service design. These franchises are massive today, but have also become monolithic with their audiences and userbases.

done by focusing on huge-scale combat, with players fighting as ground troops, in vehicles like tanks, and flying overhead in planes all contributing and trying to achieve their objectives. The only competitor at the time who had large-scale conflicts was *PlanetSide* (released in 2003 by Daybreak Game Company), which factions fighting across a huge map with conflicts all over the place.

*Battlefield* would not have a dedicated single player campaign until 2005's *Battlefield 2: Modern Combat*. While *Call of Duty* did have multiplayer modes, the major selling point at the time was the single player campaign. That changed completely with *Call of Duty 4: Modern Warfare* released in 2007. This was the first time the series moved to the modern era, but, more importantly, it came with a completely redesigned multiplayer experience.

Multiplayer games until this point featured no continual progression across matches. What the player did in one match would not impact anything in future matches, and, at most, the game would keep track of things like wins/losses, number of kills/deaths, etc. *Modern Warfare* changed that by giving every player an account level. Through play regardless of whether their team won or lost, players would earn experience. When they leveled up, they would unlock something new they could use on future matches:

- New weapons or mods for existing ones
- Killstreaks (special powers that activate if they score enough kills without dying)

- Perks (passive abilities that provide benefits)
- Cosmetics (profile pictures, gun skins, and more)

This provided long-term progression that anyone regardless of skill level could use and be rewarded through play. Even though being good at the game would reward someone with more experience and faster leveling, the system meant that, even if you had nothing but losses in matches, you still had the account progress moving up. This kind of progression would eventually be coined "meta progression," or I like to call it persistent elements in games.

It was this inclusion that would change multiplayer shooters, the *Call of Duty* franchise, and those who developed it for years to come. Over the 2010's *Call of Duty* would jump between different time periods, including going to the future in 2016's *Infinite Warfare*. Activision, who published the franchise, went with a unique development strategy to keep new *Call of Duty* games coming out. Instead of one developer working on the series, they would have multiple ones who would essentially take turns releasing a new game. While Infinity Ward still worked on the games, they were joined by Sledgehammer Games, Raven Software, and Treyarch who would develop their own entries throughout the 2010s or assisted in the development.

Like *Team Fortress, Call of Duty* would change with live service design and the growing use of monetization practices in the industry. The series would adopt loot boxes as a means of providing random cosmetic rewards. This would then be switched to a battle pass system, where players could earn different rewards over the course of a season (for more on these practices, please read *Game Design Deep Dive: Free to Play*).

With its design, the number and types of game modes would change from entry to entry. This means that the different modes are not consistent across the franchise. In the latest release of *Modern Warfare 3* in 2022, it shipped with the following base modes (may not represent the current list at this moment in time):

- Capture the flag
- Deathmatch – Where players fight against each other to see who can score the most kills first without any teams.
- Demolition: Teams take turns trying to plant bombs in specific parts of the map, while the other team defends
- Domination: Teams fight each other to control points on the map to score points and reach the score threshold first
- Ground war: Large-scale conflict with teams as high as 32 vs. 32
- Headquarters: A match of the king of the hill style
- Kill confirmed: Only collecting the enemy's dog tags counted as points in this mode
- Sabotage: Both teams have access to a bomb, and the team that plants theirs first wins
- Search and destroy: Like Demolition, but every player only has one life per round

- Team deathmatch – The same rules as deathmatch except now players are put onto teams.
- Team defender: Teams must protect the flag holder from the opposing team to score points

While those were the base modes, the series has since adopted two other game modes that were inspired by other games and franchises (Figure 5.5). The Zombies mode first appeared in 2008's *Call of Duty: World at War*. In it, players had to survive against waves of zombies that would attack their safe house. This kind of design is often referred to as a "horde mode" with the enemy waves escalating until either the players win, or they get overrun. It has since been expanded into its own unique campaign with story, voice acting, and more unique game elements.

Following the surge in popularity of Battle Royale games (more on that in the next section), *Call of Duty* had their version in the form of "Warzone." One hundred and fifty players can be dropped onto a large map and the last one standing wins. The unique aspects of warzone also include a chance for players who are defeated early on to get back into the match by winning a gulag battle.

From a design point of view, the series that first started with a more grounded approach with the original games would become more and more arcade like and over the top with the later entries. A major point of *Infinite Warfare* was adding more future tech and movement abilities than in previous games, and of course the zombies mode is not meant to be realistic or grounded at all. In recent ones,

Figure 5.5

The zombies and warzone modes represent how "*Call of Duty*" is no longer just one property, but its own universe of content; while the goal is for someone to do everything, just having someone enjoy one of the game options will keep them playing, and possibly spending, for more.

the live service style of rewarding daily play, limited events, and so on have been fully integrated into the *Call of Duty* experience. *Call of Duty* as a franchise has been one of the biggest moneymakers in the industry with an estimated profit of over 30 billion dollars lifetime.[2]

To switch over to *Battlefield*, they had a different path through the 2010s. They would experiment with single player-focused titles with the *Battlefield: Bad Company* series released in 2008 and 2010. *Bad Company 1* was a console exclusive while the sequel was available on PC. DICE also had a chance to work on the *Star Wars Battlefront* series which was originally created by Pandemic Studios in 2004 and they would release their take starting in 2015. The idea was to create a multiplayer experience based on the *Star Wars* license, where teams would control either the rebel or empire forces to complete different objectives. The series would expand this to include land, air, and space battles, as well as allowing players to control one of the main characters from the movies as a super unit for a limited time. The game earned a lot of controversy at the time for its live service and monetization practices that rewarded players who spent money with better advantages and access to stronger hero units. It received so much bad publicity that the game had to be reworked and those elements were removed or changed.

For the main series, like *Call of Duty*, each *Battlefield* would focus on different time periods and by extension had different weapons and vehicles (Figure 5.6).

Figure 5.6

*Battlefield* has been more self-contained compared to *Call of Duty* – treating each game up until this point as a completely standalone product with its own content focus. But they have been trying to mirror the live service successes of *COD* over the years, but it's unsure at this point what's next for the franchise.

5. The Live Service Shooter Era

As an example, *Battlefields 2-4* took place in contemporary times, *Battlefields 1* and *5* took place during World War I, and *Battlefield 2049* took place in the future, along with each game having multiple expansions and additional content. The series would integrate battle pass and season play into the later titles as part of their live service offerings. *Battlefield 2049* also changed the dynamics of the class system. Previous games allowed players to choose from different classes that affected their role, utility, and what weapons they could use. With 2049, the classes were then focused on specialists – unique individuals that made up each class with their own specific traits and abilities. Looking at this further, it is a way of trying to add hero shooter elements, and I will discuss more on them in the next section. According to VGChartz.com,[3] *Battlefield* as a franchise has sold an estimated 84.9 million copies.

These two series essentially wrote the script of AAA development from the end of the 2000s into most of the 2010s, which a lot of people view as a negative. When gamers and consumers make fun of how homogenized a lot of AAA games became during this period, they would reference one of these series in terms of how generic they looked. The push for multiplayer components in games became a mandate by many publishers.

During the 2010s, the military shooter market shrunk outside of the *Battlefields* and *Call of Duties*. But that didn't stop publishers from wanting to add multiplayer to any game, even if the designers didn't want it:

> No one is playing it, and I don't even feel like it's part of the overall package — it's another game rammed onto the disk like a cancerous growth, threatening to destroy the best things about the experience that the team at Yager put their heart and souls into creating.
>
> *Cory Davis, Lead Designer on* Spec Ops: The Line *(released in 2012 by Yager)*

During the 2010s, part of the reason why horror disappeared from AAA studios was developers chasing the military shooter/multiplayer trend, such as Capcom, and how they moved the series away from horror (for more about the history of *Resident Evil*, you can find that in *Game Design Deep Dive: Horror*)

Even though *Team Fortress 2* laid the groundwork for live service design and monetization in online games, *Call of Duty* went more on the unethical side of its design. There was a patent filed by Activision and went through in 2019[4] with regard to their matchmaking that they would purposely put players who spent money against those that didn't – making the latter feel like they need to spend money to compete.

However, these issues did not stop *Call of Duty* from becoming one of the biggest AAA franchises in the entire industry. In today's market, things have changed and, while *Call of Duty* continues to dominate its space, there are more unique multiplayer games and shooters that have carved out their own respective market segments.

## 5.3 Hero Shooters

The 2010s for the game industry was a period of three different trends – the growth of the mobile and casual game market, the rise of indie development, and the push by AAA studios to create live service and multiplayer experiences. At this point, I can't even begin to remember all the different live service multiplayer games that have come and went, let alone the ones specifically around shooters.

For shooters, there were three trends of design that would represent how most multiplayer shooters would go during the 2010s. The first is with the concept of the hero shooter (Figure 5.7). A combination of the class-based design of *Team Fortress 2*, with the focus of champions of a Multiplayer Online Battle Arenas (*MOBA*) like *League of Legends* (first released in 2009 by Riot Games). In most multiplayer shooters, players control nondescript characters; maybe they have a name and a face, but they are often just there for some light personalization. A hero shooter lets players control unique individuals with their own weapons, personality, and story. While there may be classes/roles, two characters of the same class may be completely different in what they offer to the team.

Developers were trying to capitalize on the viral nature and brand popularity of *Team Fortress 2*. By creating unique characters, people would resonate with them, enjoy learning about them, and hopefully, play the game and buy any content to go with them. Unfortunately, most of the ones developed during this time

Figure 5.7

While the concept of hero shooters technically could be traced back to *Team Fortress 2*, Valve did not turn the game into one. Each class in the game was a one-off; but with these games, part of the development process is the endless cycle of creating new characters, new abilities, and new promotional material to go with it all.

have either been shut down or the studio is no longer releasing content for them; they may still be played solely by their hardcore fanbase if the servers haven't been shut down. Some also have unofficial servers fans have set up to allow these games to be played but are not supported by the developer.

As of writing this book, there are four hero shooters still active at the time (*Apex Legends* is more of a battle royale game and will be discussed in the next section).

2015 saw the release of *Tom Clancy's Rainbow Six Siege*, which at launch did have issues in terms of bugs and people not liking the content. However, when the game fully adopted its live service design and received continued support, fans started to enjoy it and it is currently the oldest example of a hero shooter still with active support. What separated it from other shooters and hero shooters was combining the tactical shooting of previous *Rainbow Six* games with unique characters/heroes (Figure 5.8). Games are played 5v5 with one team being the attackers and one being the defenders. It's up to the attacking team to breach where the defenders are hunkering down and take them out. Of the hero shooters that are going to be mentioned here, it is easily the most complicated to play. The gunplay is on the grounded side and just running around will easily get someone shot. Both teams have access to specific abilities and options to either help their side or hurt the opposing one. The game also featured environmental deformation – shooting through a barricade, weak walls and floors, or using a breaching tool will destroy it and open more of the area for both sides. Combat is decisive, and no one can survive more than a few bullets.

Figure 5.8

The operators of *Siege* may not look as over the top compared to the other entries in this chapter, but they are still individualized characters whose different play-styles provide variety and depth to an already complicated game.

The two groups of operators are broken down into attackers and defenders, with each side having access to specific weapons and tools, and every operator has one unique gadget to distinguish them from everyone else. Monetization is based on buying cosmetics, new operators, and the battle pass, and there is still an eSports angle currently. According to VGChartz, *Rainbow Six: Siege* has sold an estimated 10 million copies, but this does not consider revenue earned through its monetization.

*Overwatch* by Blizzard was released in 2016 and was built from concepts Blizzard was going to use for another game that they ended up scrapping. Everything about a hero shooter is on display here – each character belongs to a specific class and comes with a primary attack, different skills, and an ultimate they can use after enough time has passed (Figure 5.9). The game attracted a fanbase thanks to Blizzard's name and the diverse cast of characters featuring people from different nationalities and species. The sequel released in 2022 did not fare as well, as Blizzard turned off access to the first game and required people to buy the sequel to keep playing and to continue spending money to acquire new costumes and champions. The gunplay here is on the arcade side, as every character has a different weapon and preferred range of fighting with an emphasis on constant movement. While *Overwatch* started with a major push to become an eSport, that has since fallen off and they have gotten rid of their original eSport league in 2023.

Figure 5.9

*Overwatch* and its sequel showcase the branding power of hero shooters. On this page, you can see completely different characters that look nothing alike, have their own stories that weave into the greater narrative, and are meant to be as marketable as possible. Just like with *Team Fortress 2*, there's no way you can confuse one character for someone else in the game.

Part of the problem that *Overwatch* had compared to other hero shooters was catering too much to the eSports angle and making balance changes and redesigns to try and keep the competitive side of the game going. As of writing this in 2024, they are still changing systems and basic rules around with *Overwatch 2*. For sales numbers, there were reports in 2022 that the first game has sold at least 50 million copies, but that number is no longer accurate today. And with *Overwatch 2* being free to play, there is no sales data to find.

*Paladins* first went into open beta in 2016 but was released in 2018 by Hi-Rez and their internal studio Evil Mojo. For this one, the genre combination that the developer stated was trying to combine *Team Fortress 2* with a hero shooter. Matches are fought 5v5 with players choosing from different paladins to play as (Figure 5.10). Each one has a different primary attack, secondary abilities, and an ultimate. In-between rounds and after someone is killed, they can spend any money earned in-game on passive bonuses to make their character stronger. A major form of progression unique to *Paladins* is that players can build loadouts of cards for each character that provide passive benefits. The player can only equip 15 points worth of cards to their character. Monetization is focused on buying new skins and new champions. *Paladins* is still going strong, and they have their own eSports league still running at the time of writing this. The gunplay is once again on the arcade side with its *Team Fortress 2* influences, and of

Figure 5.10

When *Paladins* first came out, there were arguments about them copying from *League of Legends* with their character designs. While the general aesthetics look similar, people did eventually move on when they played it and the gameplay was nothing alike. But this does serve as a cautionary tale when it comes to brand recognition and aesthetics.

course each character has their own abilities. Because the game is free to play, it's hard to find accurate numbers for the profit earned.

In 2020, *Valorant* developed by Riot Games was launched and became a hit by combining hero shooters with the grounded and challenging gunplay of *Counter-Strike*. Like *Counter-Strike*, teams take turns defending an area while the attackers are trying to plant a spike in a specific spot. After each battle, both sides can spend accumulated in-game money to buy new weapons. Agents fall into specific roles and come with different abilities they can use during a match. As with *Counter-Strike* and *Rainbow Six: Siege*, combat is decided quickly due to low health pools and matches are fought 5v5. What separates it from *Counter-Strike* are the different powers that each character has access to that can affect the level, their team, or the enemy, in specific ways. Monetization is focused on buying cosmetic items and access to new agents (Figure 5.11). While the game is the youngest of the ones featured in this section, the combination of hero shooter design with the high *skill curve* to play has made *Valorant* very popular and it is also an eSport. Riot has not disclosed any lifetime profits of *Valorant* as I was writing this.

In Section 8.4, I'm going to focus on the difficulty of balancing multiplayer shooters, but it's important to mention here why so many hero shooters have struggled in terms of their design. Much like live service and hero collector mobile games, these titles live or die based on the popularity and appeal of their characters. The more unique characters you add to a game, the harder it then

Figure 5.11

*Valorant* and *Rainbow Six: Siege* both share having grounded and more involved gunplay, but where *Valorant* goes with it is to pair it with its original characters who are more diverse and do more in a match compared to *Siege*.

5. The Live Service Shooter Era

becomes to balance. Gamers are exceptional at breaking down characters, skills, equipment, etc. to find the best of the very best to play a game with. This is part of the challenge of meta game design and trying to keep the meta from becoming fixed. If everyone knows that one sniper is the best, or one defender, then that's the only one people will use. And then matches will devolve into everyone using the best characters, and those that specifically use the counters to them.

To compound the difficulty of these games, if additional characters are locked to progression or pay walls, then newcomers will find it even harder to compete against other players who have access to "the right characters," and even more so if new characters are only accessible by spending real money to add them to your account. From an aesthetics standpoint, not one single hero shooter managed to outdo *Team Fortress 2* in terms of characterization and brand appeal. They often all devolve into the same basic tropes like:

- Cocky hero
- Solemn warrior
- Flirty or catty female character

Just to name some of the many. People to this day are still finding and checking out the meet the team videos from *Team Fortress 2* and enjoying them. Another issue in terms of balance is that, when you have unique characters, it can become frustrating when everyone is trying to play their favorite, when that favorite may not coincide with what the team needs, and this can be a nightmare if people are trying to play ranked games. From a UI perspective, it can be difficult immediately to figure out what is going on and who does what for a new player. That giant-looking monster may be weak compared to a three-foot-tall bunny rabbit whose ultimate power completely kills the opposing team. Onboarding on how the different characters and classes work has always been an issue for hero-focused games, because the rate of new heroes added in makes it impossible to keep updating tutorials and onboarding concurrently unless the team is large enough. Like with MOBAs, someone needs to play them regularly to be able to keep up with all the new characters or changes that are adopted.

Designing a hero shooter is all about figuring out what the core gameplay loop and gunplay of your title are going to look like, and then extrapolating how different characters can influence the gameplay in various ways. As I'll talk about at the end of this chapter, building a shooter like this year-round requires you to understand live service design.

When they work, like with *Team Fortress 2*, the combination of great character designs, branding, and gameplay can turn these games into moneymakers (Figure 5.12). However, reaching that level of fame and success is not something any studio can force, no matter how many of them tried and failed over the 2010s to achieve. Due to the interplay between different heroes, different roles/classes, and the basic mechanics, this kind of design is very hard to balance, and I'm not including gunplay. What you should take away from hero shooter design is that

Figure 5.12

I can't stress this enough for you reading this – do not doubt the power of marketing and branding that likeable, interesting, and well-designed characters can bring to any game. This has been part of the giant success mobile and gacha games have had for years now.

uniqueness will always trump generic in the eyes of the consumer. It would be a completely different world for the game industry if Valve decided to keep the military shooter aesthetic the same in *Team Fortress 2*. Anytime that you can put something unique in your game – a character, gun, map design, etc. – you want to market that to people so that they know that your game is different than the umpteenth game that played like *Call of Duty* that is no longer around.

## 5.4 The Battle for Battle Royales

The second major trend of the 2010s came with the creation of the battle royale style of multiplayer shooters. Inspired by the movie of the same name, battle royales focus on putting a huge group of players, typically 100 or more, on a single map and challenge them to survive until one is left (Figure 5.13). To force combat and keep the matches interesting, every few minutes, the play area will shrink and force the remaining players to move to the new area. Battle royales can be either played as small teams, or a free-for-all. The player must find equipment and weapons randomly placed in the world in each match to be strong enough to win. Apart from *Call of Duty*'s gulag system, battle royales only give a player a single life; once they are killed, they are taken out of the match.

The idea of playing against many people on a single map has been around in mod form for a long time. The first commercial product built on battle royale design would be *H1Z1* by Daybreak Games first released in 2015. The original

Figure 5.13

Battle royales have had the biggest shutdown of the different multiplayer shooter types of this chapter. Far too many of them tried to copy one of the four shown here, and even of this list, *Fortnite* and *Apex Legends* stand out the most.

plan was to have two different game modes, one being the battle royale, and the other being a king of the hill style. There are two styles of gunplay we've seen from battle royale shooters, a more arcade feel where characters are constantly moving and jumping, and the grounded gameplay with a focus on getting a drop on your opponent. While *H1Z1* was the first, it is the most dated now in terms of gameplay and presentation. Monetization is focused on getting new cosmetics, and the player is not able to buy any advantages for a match. In 2018, *H1Z1* was rebranded to *Z1 Battle Royale* and the king of the hill mode was removed. The game is now developed by a reformed team NantG. *Z1's* gunplay is a bit on the arcade side, but not as far compared to the later games mentioned in this section. With the rebrand and free to play status, I am unable to find accurate profit numbers for it.

*PUBG* once again started as a mod for *Arma 3* and was released as a standalone game in 2017. Like *Z1*, *PUBG's* monetization is about getting new cosmetic items for your character. The gunplay is more grounded here and firefights are often decisive by who can get the drop on the other first. While *PUBG* proved to be more popular than *Z1*, the game did have a steeper learning curve and technical issues at launch, which paved the way for the next game to blow up. *PUBG* is still being developed and around today, with its own updates and collabs (Figure 5.14). The mobile version that is published by Tencent has done very well. There are many different quotes regarding PUBG's profit, with some estimates saying it is now more than 10 billion over its entire lifespan to date.

Epic Games in July of 2017 released *Fortnite*, a multiplayer shooter where players would team up to defend areas from invading zombies by building various

Figure 5.14

*PUBG* has remained relevant and in the news thanks to the multitude of collabs it has had over the years. Not just with games, but restaurants, pop stars, you name it. And while it hasn't managed to catch up to *Fortnite,* it does keep it alive compared to the many other battle royales that are no longer around.

structures, traps and fight it out. While the mode was okay, it was not getting new fans with the surge in popularity of battle royale games at the time. To pivot, the developers released their own battle royale mode for the game in September of that year, and the mode exploded in popularity. *Fortnite: Battle Royale* became so popular that the original mode was set aside, and all development focused on the *Battle Royale* design (it is still playable within *Fortnite* today).

What made *Fortnite* succeed with its battle royale comes down to polish and support by Epic. Both *PUBG* and *Z1* were designed by indie teams with smaller budgets and manpower. *Fortnite* having the entire weight of Epic Games behind it allowed them to rapidly develop, iterate, and release content far faster than any other studio in the battle royale space. There were no other battle royale games at the time that had the quality of aesthetic, sheer number of cosmetic options, and the rapidly developed content that *Fortnite* offered (Figure 5.15). The continued support also meant radically changing the game by introducing new item types, new weapons, completely altering the map each season, and many collaboration deals. Today, you can play *Fortnite* as the original characters, or as anyone from different superhero properties, musicians, anime characters, and much more. Monetization focuses on buying new cosmetic items and the season passes/battle passes to get access to more content.

The gameplay was also different from other battle royales. This is the only battle royale to succeed with having construction as a major part of the gameplay. While players do search for items and weapons in each play, they are also gathering materials that they can use to build a variety of components. By using

Figure 5.15

The secret to *Fortnite*'s long-term success has been the constant flood of "stuff" to the game. Every season not only brings with it new collabs and characters, but also changes the map, adds in new weapons and items, and of the battle royale games of this chapter, has had the most number of updates and changes to it.

walls, floors, and stairs, it is possible to create massive structures and defenses anywhere on the map. Gunplay is 100% on the arcade side, with characters running, jumping, gliding, and more, around. It is possible to play the game either solo or team up with other players. In 2022, Epic released zero build mode which removes the construction in favor of just focusing on the combat. Of the battle royale games mentioned in this section, *Fortnite* has had the most success as a live service game. It has become a brand onto itself and has its own eSports league. While it's hard to find accurate revenue numbers for it currently, yearly earnings reports have stated the game earning billions each year since 2017.

*Fortnite*'s success created such a massive impact in the battle royale market that many studios could not directly compete with it. This is why most of the battle royale-styled games to come out are no longer in service. The only game that managed to be released after *Fortnite* and thrive in its own way was *Apex Legends* released in 2020 by Respawn Entertainment. Respawn are the makers of the *Titanfall* series that focused on high-speed, movement-focused shooting that I will talk more about in the next chapter. With the success of battle royale games, the studio decided to try and make their own with *Apex Legends*, and the game succeeded by standing out from all the other battle royales on the market, including *Fortnite* (Figure 5.16).

*Apex Legends* combined battle royale with the hero shooter design that I discussed in the last section. Unlike the other battle royales, *Apex Legends*' primary mode is three-person squads. The legends, or playable characters, are once again

Figure 5.16

Looking at these promotional images for *Apex Legends*, you should be able to spot something different about them compared to the other games here. There is a huge focus on the individual characters, this is because of *Apex*'s combination of battle royale and hero shooter play. I was tempted to mentioned in the last section, but the game does belong in the battle royale category. This unique take on the formula is what has allowed it to survive and grow alongside *Fortnite*.

defined by specific roles/classes. Each legend has one active ability, one passive, and one ultimate. As with the other battle royale games, teams will launch onto a map to see who will be the last one standing, and they will search supply boxes to get new weapons and equipment to aid them during a match. There is a greater emphasis in *Apex Legends* on teamwork thanks to the different abilities that can supplement the other players on your squad. Monetization is focused on cosmetics, their battle pass, and accessing new legends. There is also an eSports league for *Apex Legends* just like with the other popular battle royales. Again, it's hard to find accurate numbers for revenue with the game being free to play and built on monetization, but news sites online reported that the game reached two billion in sales in 2022.

Battle Royale became one of the many gold rush periods that occurs in the game industry. When *Fortnite* grew popular, studios tried to make their own or take an existing game and build a battle royale mode to it (which is what happened with *Call of Duty*'s warzone mode). The design is very appealing for a competitive atmosphere. Each match can have wildly different outcomes based on where people drop, what equipment they find, and where the safe zones go. This avoids some of the staleness and meta game issues seen in other competitive shooters. Besides shooters, there are battle royales for other genres, such as platforming with *Fall Guys* released in 2020 by Mediatonic. The Battle Royale genre can be very risky due to the fact that they are very sink or swim in terms of the market.

Getting 100 players connected and ready to play at any time is a tough ask for a multiplayer game. The second a battle royale starts losing its player base and it becomes harder to find people for matches, it becomes a self-fulfilling prophecy of people not staying around to play, which makes it even harder to maintain.

So many examples on the shooter side tried to copy *PUBG*, as no one wanted to directly compete with *Fortnite*. Many battle royale-styled games in the 2010s and early 2020s came out, had a moment where people checked them out, and then most of them went to other battle royales or back to one of the other ones mentioned in this section. The issue is that the core gameplay must be compelling enough to keep people playing and doing matches, and there must be continued and active development of new content, new challenges, and of course new cosmetics, to keep people engaged. There is huge money to be made if your game can succeed, but unless you can out-*Fortnite Fortnite*, or create something entirely original like *Apex Legends*, your game is not going to make much of an impact.

## 5.5 Coop Shooters

Coop, or player vs. the AI, shooters became popular as a way of playing a shooter with other people, without the competitive or high skill curve play that goes into a multiplayer shooter. By focusing on cooperative play, these shooters also avoid the challenges of balancing different characters, classes, etc., for each play. There may be a multiplayer or versus mode available at launch or after, but these games are primarily focused on player vs. the environment or PvE play (Figure 5.17).

Figure 5.17

Playing games with your friends without the worry of competition or rankings has been a pivotal part of the growth of coop games, and yet despite the popularity of some of the bigger names, it's harder than it looks to get this design right.

During the 2000s, early coop shooters focused on two-player coop with exceptions like *Halo*. The challenge of this period was that internet infrastructure was still being built around the world, and most homes at the time did not have easy access to cable modems. Even into the 2010s, there were shooters that only allowed for two players. Some examples of games at this time include *Army of Two* (released in 2008, 2010, and 2013 by EA Montreal and Visceral Games), the *Kane & Lynch* series (developed by IO Interactive and released in 2007 and 2010), and *Resident Evil 5* and *6* (released in 2009 and 2012).

The advantage of only having two players meant that puzzles and challenges were built to require and enforce cooperation. The team would be attacked by a force too big for just one person to take on. If there were puzzles, they would require the players to work together to solve them. *Portal 2* released in 2011 made waves with its coop campaign by taking the puzzle design of the main game and creating original puzzles that required two players to solve them.

The one that popularized this trend and would set the standard for four-player coop came out in 2008 with *Left 4 Dead* by Turtle Rock Studios and Valve. In it, up to four players control survivors following a zombie outbreak and they must work together to reach safe houses and eventually safety in a variety of campaigns. Teamwork is required thanks to the mix of hordes of normal zombies, and the special infected that each one has the means of stopping a single player (Figure 5.18). Boomers blind the affected player and summon a horde, hunters and smokers

Figure 5.18

The key to *Left 4 Dead's* coop gameplay was with the designs of the special infected. The boomer on the left had to be taken care of carefully or it would explode on one or more players. The charger on the right could knock down the entire team if they were positioned incorrectly or move in close and deliver damage with its punches.

5. The Live Service Shooter Era

incapacitate someone until they're killed, and the tank is so strong that it requires a combined attack to take it down. The game also featured a versus mode where another team of four would play as the special infected and had to team up to take out the survivors. *Left 4 Dead* got a sequel in 2009 that eventually had all the maps from the first game added to it, with the inclusion of new special infected. At this time, it is considered complete with no new content being developed for it. The gunplay is more on the arcade side even with the limitation of only holding a primary and secondary weapon. Players could find healing items and throwables that could even the odds against waves of zombies. The highly touted "AI director" which would decide where resources and infected would appear was a nice marketing point but couldn't stop advanced players once they knew how to work together.

Another successful take with players against the undead was *Killing Floor* by Tripwire Interactive in 2009, and the sequel in 2016. *Killing Floor* is a popular example of the horde-focused shooter that *Call of Duty* added their own form of with the zombies mode or the horde mode featured in *Gears of War*. A team of players must survive in different environments while waves of different enemies will attack them from all sides. The game scales the threat level based on the number of players at the start of a wave – the more people, the more enemies and the waves become longer.

Killing enemies will earn each player money that they can use to buy weapons that are categorized by what class they go with. Progression is tied to specific metrics for each class, with the usual one is killing a specific enemy with one of the weapons for that class. The system evolved in the sequel to have passive perks that the player could select at different levels that affected them while using said class.

Gunplay here is more about hunkering down in a location and trying to set up an area where you and your friends can defend yourself without being overrun. The enemy behavior is set to track the player/s to wherever they are on the map. Enemies will always spawn just out of the general area where players are, and part of the planning is finding an area with as few entrances as possible to force the enemies to come from one direction. Higher class and boss enemies require the whole team to cooperate and take them out before they start killing off the party. A match ends either when the team survives all the waves, or on one wave the entire team dies.

The game's monetization focused on opening loot boxes for cosmetics and buying *DLC* packs for new cosmetic items and the game is still being supported to this day.

The success of *Left 4 Dead* led to a chase by developers in the 2010s to be the new *Left 4 Dead* 4 vs. the AI experience. The one that succeeded the most in this respect would be the *Payday* series by Overkill Software (with releases in 2011, 2013, and 2023). The series is about the payday gang who are robbers who go around the world performing robberies and other crime sprees for fortune while dealing with police and other forces (Figure 5.19). The gunplay is slightly grounded, as the series does allow you to fully modify your guns to improve their stats, but, as it went on, more RPG-abstracted systems were added to give more progression and longer play times.

Figure 5.19

*Payday,* as a franchise, has benefited the most from live service than any other coop shooter to date. The game's updates, community engagement, and major events secured its position in the 2010s. As of 2024, the third game is going through a bit of an identity crisis among fans, and I don't know where it's going to be by the end of the year.

The series allowed players to approach maps going loud or attempting to do them in stealth. The dynamic is that to perform a heist with stealth requires the team to only equip the lightest weapons and armor. Being caught and triggering the loud portion like this guarantee a reset, as the team won't have the equipment needed to fight back.

Next to *Team Fortress 2*, it is one of the better examples of how live service design can keep a game growing in the market. Since the release of *Payday 2*, the game has had constant updates to add in new systems, new DLC, new characters, and much more. These updates and RPG elements represent a trend that will come up in the next chapter and is one of the major evolutions of shooter and action design. As of the end of 2023, Overkill is still supporting *Payday 2* and released *Payday 3* with content being developed for both. As an important point about live service, *Payday 3* has been almost universally downvoted by fans for coming out with fewer features and technical issues, and is a harsh lesson about the dangers of releasing a sequel to an already popular live service game.

There were many zombie-related games released in the past 20 years but finding a new *Left 4 Dead* game was a lot harder than people expected. In 2019, *World War Z* by Saber Interactive was launched quietly as far as game releases go. Based on the movie and book, the game challenged teams of four to complete missions around the world against overwhelming forces of zombies. Progression was

Figure 5.20

*World War Z* succeeded thanks to really being the game that was there at the perfect time – *Left 4 Dead 2* had no more support coming, and there wasn't another zombie-related coop game of this kind out. While it did take time for word to spread, the game appealed to fans of *Left 4 Dead*, but were looking for a harder take on it.

tied to playing as different classes that would unlock new perks and secondary gear. Every weapon type had an experience level, and the more someone used it they could upgrade that type for when it drops in a level. The game was on the harder side, as players can't run around when there are waves of zombies attacking them and teamwork was vitally important (Figure 5.20). Despite not having a lot of marketing at launch, word quickly spread of one of the best *Left 4 Dead*-like experiences and the game received content updates and additional support.

Part of the challenge of making a coop game is that, when you are required to work with other players, you want to make sure that the learning curve and general play are easy enough to understand. In difficult titles, having one weak link in a team can easily spell disaster for the entire group, and a game that embodied that fully was *GTFO* (released in 2019 by 10 Chambers). Players control a group of prisoners sent down into a destroyed mining facility in order to figure out what happened and why there are mutated creatures. The group has limited ammo and weaponry with few means of resupplying. To survive, they must work together to take out as many enemies in stealth as they can before alerting waves of them to show up. *GTFO* is by far the hardest coop game on the list, which also limited its appeal compared to the other games released. The difficulty came from how aggressive and numerous enemies were compared to what the players could do. Survival is about setting up how to properly defend against waves of enemies, and, if anyone is out of position or the team isn't prepared, they would be swarmed and taken out easily.

In 2020, *Deep Rock Galactic* came out after several years of being on early access by Ghost Ship Games. Focusing on coop and mining, teams of up to four players are sent to procedurally generated maps to drill for resources and complete objectives. There are four classes that each have their own weapons, secondary items, and ways of moving around, and all four can help the other players. Completing missions can unlock experience points and seasons are set up to reward unique cosmetics. This one is full on arcade-style shooting with lasers, grenade launchers, turrets, and more available. The game is still receiving content updates and has stood out from the other shooters as being more casual friendly and entirely focused on teamwork with no Player vs Player (PvP) content. The brilliance of the coop design is that the entire game is built solely on cooperation between the classes (Figure 5.21). While each class can move around the environment using a different tool, combining tools makes map exploration a lot easier and faster to do. Each class has a specific role and groups will want to have one of each to have the best chance of surviving.

Something that you need to keep in mind about cooperative shooters is they do not have the same moneymaking potential that competitive shooters have. What attracts people to competitive shooters is the thrill of high-level play against other players, with a focus on how each match can turn out differently. For coop games, it's more about progression and playing with friends

Figure 5.21

*Deep Rock Galactic* has succeeded by offering an original coop experience and one where every part of the core gameplay loop benefits from the team working together. Despite each class being unique, no one character can do everything by themselves.

Figure 5.22

Creating content for coop games requires the team to keep coming up with ways of making their gameplay grow and interesting without the inclusion of player vs. player content. Some games like *Deep Rock Galactic* make all their new season content free, while *Payday 2* kept game-changing updates free, but anything that added content became attached to purchases of DLC. You must have a plan in terms of how you will keep earning money if you intend on continuing to create content for your game.

or like-minded people. When fighting against an AI, you need to create unique elements and mechanics for how they behave. This also means having to create new and interesting levels to challenge the players. In a competitive shooter, map design is about forcing firefights and providing players with multiple routes of engagement. In a coop shooter, you need to build custom scenarios and make sure that your AI can engage the players. This is why major updates for cooperative shooters can take more time and resources compared to competitive (Figure 5.22). Monetization in these games is always about new gameplay-affecting content. While personalization with cosmetics and skins is certainly there, if there aren't new maps and scenarios being developed, or people are getting bored with the game, they are not going to stick around or support it further. Returning to *Deep Rock Galactic*, they frame their major gameplay updates around "seasons" – with each season changing the generation of the maps and having different event scenarios that can show up.

The potential for success is there, and the coop games that I talked about in this section did end up creating sizable fanbases[5]:

| Game Name | Copies Sold |
| --- | --- |
| Army of Two | 3.6 million |
| Deep Rock Galactic | 5.81 million |
| GTFO | 1–2 million (estimate) |
| Kane & Lynch series | 2.82 million |
| Killing Floor series | 10 million |
| Left 4 Dead series | 12 million |
| Payday 2[a] | 40 million (not counting DLC) |
| Resident Evil 5 and 6[b] | 17.8 million |
| World War Z | 3 million |

[a] From news sources online, couldn't verify directly from the studio.
[b] Taken from Capcom's PR site, updated 9/23.

The beauty of coop games over competitive ones is that, if a group of friends enjoys it, it can become a regularly played game for months or even years. This creates a very entrenched fanbase who will be happy to see what you have next. However, this still requires a long-term plan of content and growth to the game. The reason why *Payday 2* succeeded the most over the 2010s was the constant updates, new systems, and new monetization options released. These elements are separate from the initial development, and this takes us to discussing live service design, which I will touch on in Section 5.7.

## 5.6 Niche Shooters

For this section, I want to talk about a few multiplayer first-person experiences that are popular, but belong to their own specific niches, or the style hasn't caught on fully to become its own dominating genre. There are two multiplayer shooters I haven't talked about in this chapter yet – *Destiny 2* and *Warframe*. While both are examples of multiplayer shooting, they also represent the shift in shooter design that occurred in the 2010s and will be discussed in Chapter 6.

*Counter-Strike: Global Offensive* is niche not that it only has a few players, but that it has created an entire market onto itself along with its own eSports following. Following the popularity of the original mod and release, *Global Offensive* was released in 2012 and would become the definitive version of *Counter-Strike* until the sequel was released in 2023 (Figure 5.23). The gameplay of the first version has remained unchanged to this day, but a lot has been added in terms of rewards, updating the environment and map designs, and making it easier for eSports play. With the game completely free to play, even the 2023 sequel, monetization is handled differently compared to other live service shooters. Like *Team Fortress 2*, through playing the game, players will receive items each week, but in the form of cases. To open a case, the player must use a key which can only be purchased with real money, and players can buy and sell keys, cases, or the items

Figure 5.23

*Counter-Strike* is now the longest running eSport that is still being updated and maintained. And with the latest sequel released in 2023, it looks like it will continue to dominate its specific kind of FPS gameplay.

in them. Unlike *Team Fortress 2*, all items are entirely cosmetic and there are no gameplay-affecting items in any case.

*Natural Selection 2* came out in 2012 by Unknown Worlds Entertainment, presenting an asymmetrical experience. Two teams of players, one being humans and the other aliens, must fight each other on a large map to wipe out the opposing team. The gameplay here is unique with both sides playing completely differently from one another, and both teams had one player taking the role of commander, who views the match like a real-time strategy game and directs their team. Asymmetrical design means that both sides are not equal in terms of abilities. While humans have access to guns and high-tech equipment, the aliens evolve into different forms and can attack from any angle.

Asymmetrical multiplayer is very hard to pull off, as you must design a fulfilling experience for both teams. The most successful of these would be *Dead by Daylight,* first released in 2016 by Behavior Interactive. Here, four players are survivors searching for generators to power up a gate to escape the other player who is the killer that is stalking them. The killers are similar in design to hero units in the last section – each one has their own means of attacking, special skills, and passive benefits. As an interesting point about *Dead by Daylight*'s design, the survivors are all played in third person, allowing them a wider vision and better situational awareness compared to the killer that is played with a limited viewpoint in first person. Monetization is tied to buying DLC packs that include new survivors and killers, along with a season pass and cosmetic options.

Figure 5.24

Extraction shooters deliver the thrill of tense gunplay with the added weight that players have something to lose on every match. Both *Hunt Showdown* and *Escape from Tarkov* pictured here do give new players some leeway when starting out for keeping more, but eventually players will have to accept the fact that they could lose a favorite character or all their gear if they are killed during a match.

A trend that has been growing in popularity over the back half of 2010 are "extraction shooters" (Figure 5.24). Like battle royale, players are let loose on a giant map and forced to fight against each other. The difference is that instead of competing to be the last person standing, they are looking for resources and equipment that are randomly placed within the map. There are not only hostile players, but NPC enemies that can engage at any time. Once someone has found enough goods, they must reach an extraction point to bank any items and equipment they found during the play. Progression is built on the player using the equipment and items they found during a map to give them a better chance of surviving on subsequent plays. The high risk in these games is that, if the player is killed, they not only lose all the items they found while exploring, but also all the equipment and resources they brought in with them. These games can be played either solo or as a small group. The gunplay is grounded much like in the style of *PUBG*, with the added constraints that the player must be managing any items they've found and make plans to reach one of the extraction points.

Unlike the battle royale format, these games typically feature smaller pools of players on a map given the high risk of play. The attraction of these games is that the high risk rewards careful playing and good aiming as opposed to rapid movement and reflexes. There is a noticeable sense of progress as you find and recover better gear or level up, but you are always at the risk of losing your hard-earned prizes.

As of this time, there have been many extraction shooters released or attempted, but there are only a few now that have become their own market onto themselves. *Escape from Tarkov* was first released in beta in 2017 (it is still in open beta at the time of writing this) by Battlestate Games. Players are let loose in the fictional city of Tarkov and must go on raids to find items and supplies needed to survive and grow in strength. Besides buying new weapons, it is possible to modify them provided you have the accessories. Not only do players need to find equipment, but they also need food and water, and other resources to buy and sell on the game's virtual flea market. It is possible to put insurance on equipment so that, if someone is killed, there is a chance for that gear to be returned to them. *Tarkov* has grown in popularity thanks to the use of progression after each raid, and the game being focused on player skill and using modern weaponry. Maps can also have at max 14 players.

For something on the opposite end, there is *Hunt: Showdown* by Crytek released in 2019. Instead of being a military shooter, the game focuses on 19th-century weapons and supernatural elements. You play as hunters who are out to fight monsters and collect bounties in a bayou and must outwit the creatures and other players to come out on top. While *Tarkov* focuses heavily on progression and finding weapons and items while exploring, *Hunt* is all about the bounties. When players start on the map, they must find randomly placed clues to track the area's boss monsters. Upon killing one, they can pick up the bounty from the creature and become marked by all the other remaining players. To win, they must reach an extraction point with the bounty and survive there until the timer runs out.

The progression is focused on the player's character's/account's bloodline. Bloodlines provide players with randomly chosen characters that have specific skills and weapon loadouts. By winning matches and completing challenges, players can upgrade their bloodlines, which unlocks new weapons, new options, and game systems. When you select a new character for the bloodline, they come with different tiers that affect starting traits, weapons, and their appearance. Characters who survive matches can be leveled up to unlock access to traits that will give them a better chance of surviving. Once a player is past the intro levels, when they die on a map, their character and all the gear they had on them is lost for good. It is possible for a lower-level player to get lucky and kill someone higher up and take one of their better weapons for their own. No matter how many times someone loses, they will always be able to get a starter character from their bloodline selection. Monetization is about buying new hunter skins and legendary weapons.

Gunplay here is entirely grounded thanks to the older style of weapons. Where *Tarkov* leans heavily on military shooters with modern weapons, in *Hunt* every weapon is on the slower side to use and reload. While there are long-range weapons and rifles, a lot of fighting occurs in medium- to close-range quarters with weapons that most are single shot. Maps are designed for up to 12 players.

Figure 5.25

Here we have a tale of two different multiplayer games – *Rumbleverse* released in 2022 by Iron Galaxy and *Fall Guys* by Mediatonic released in 2020. Both games attempted very different takes on the battle royale formula; *Rumbleverse* trying to make a melee and grappler-focused game, and *Fall Guys* being about whacky physics and platforming. *Iron Galaxy* couldn't shake the similarities of other battle royale games and quickly lost interest, while the charm of *Fall Guys* and multiple collaborations helped the game grow and remain relevant.

Multiplayer shooters or any multiplayer game, which doesn't follow what everyone else is doing, is a risky strategy for a studio (Figure 5.25). If a game succeeds and can keep going, it will effectively corner the market on that design – leaving everyone else to try and catch up, and, in most cases, no one will be able to outdo it in that respective design as evident from its sales numbers[6]:

| Game Title | Copies Sold |
| --- | --- |
| Counter-Strike: Global Offensive | 40 million |
| Dead by Daylight | 10–20 million (estimate)[a] |
| Escape from Tarkov | Unknown |
| Hunt Showdown | 5–10 million (estimate) |
| Natural Selection 2 | 300k |

[a] All estimates provided by Steam Spy.

The risk is that getting people to try a new experience like this is very difficult. You must not only have a good enough game, but also be able to reach enough people to get them interested in it **before the launch**. One of the most important aspects of any multiplayer game is that there must be a respectably sized consumer base there on day one. What has been the kiss of death for many multiplayer shooters in the 2010s was not having enough consumers to support the game at its launch. This could be due to networking issues, marketing, or the game just not being enjoyable. As I said further up, once the consumer base starts leaving and it becomes harder to find a game, the entire game starts to go downhill. This is also why for any multiplayer game, shooter or not, it can have a snowball effect either positively or negatively based on what happens during its first month.

Cooperative game design, when done right, can create unique moments that can sell a game to people who are looking for something to do with their friends.

## 5.7 Making a Year-Round Shooter

For the games mentioned in this chapter and the next, they would represent shooters that would adopt live service elements. Again, for more about live service and free to play design in general, please read *Game Design Deep Dive: Free to Play.*

For shooters in particular, live service design requires specific considerations in terms of content and support. Like the other examples of live service games, cosmetics and personalization are always in demand, and there has been a lot of money thrown at unique skins for guns, knives, characters, etc. (Figure 5.26). But what keeps people invested in playing is the circular nature of developer-generated content and user-generated content.

Figure 5.26

The monetization of cosmetics in live service games is consistent and very lucrative. People who play competitive games love cosmetics as a way of showing off and standing out from everyone else. Counter-Strike: Global Offensive (CSGO) with its different weapon skins turned into big money for people who bought and sold them. On the right, the Mac update for *Team Fortress 2* brought with it exclusive cosmetics that I can't even begin to tell you how crazy it got in terms of people spending money to add them to their account.

Developer-generated content represents everything the designers add to the game through updates – new weapons, characters, maps, game systems, etc. User-generated content in this respect represents all the players on your servers that people can play against/with. Both are required for a game to keep working and keep earning money. If there aren't enough people playing your game to adequately find matches, then the ones who are still around will end up getting frustrated and leave as well. Without new content being developed, there won't be an incentive to keep playing for anyone who isn't a hardcore fan. And if the content at the start isn't keeping people entertained, they are not going to wait around for the developer to release more.

This is why the more players that are required for a match to work, the harder and riskier it becomes as a live service shooter. With balancing, you need to be aware of how every new weapon, skill, character, perk, etc. are going to factor into everything else in your game. This is like when I spoke about deck building design in *Game Design Deep Dive: Deck Builders*, something that is considered weak or not the best may find new life with new content that was added. And this can lead to a never-ending challenge of balancing your game, which will depend on the type of shooter you are making. I'll be discussing more about the balance in multiplayer shooters in Section 8.4, as both single player and multiplayer shooters have different approaches.

With new content, in shooters where there is not a leveling progression, you want to avoid introducing new weapons that are just flat out better than what's already in the game. This can create a power imbalance between the haves and the have-nots. For games with some kind of leveling progression that also acts as matchmaking, you can introduce better weapons that will not be used against players without a defense to them. For any hero shooter-styled game, you will need to decide whether your roster of characters will grow or remain the same as it did with *Team Fortress 2*. And once you start adding in new characters, this will become a major part of your development cycle and growth of your game.

Doing this right, much like other live service games, and you can have a game that keeps a studio going for years, but this requires a lot of work and challenge of designing a game with no real end in sight for its content.

## Notes

1  https://www.statista.com/statistics/189349/us-households-home-internet-connection-subscription/
2  https://www.statista.com/statistics/1244198/cod-lifetime-player-spending/
3  https://www.vgchartz.com/game/226219/battlefield/sales
4  https://patents.google.com/patent/US20160001181A1/en
5  Sources: VGChartz.com and Steam Spy for estimates.
6  Source: VGChartz.com

# The Evolution of Shooters

## 6.1 Role-Playing Shooters

The 2010s was a decade of a lot of changes for the game industry. One of the most profound changes was how action and abstracted design began to take elements from each other (Figure 6.1). In previous decades, the line between RPG and action design was fixed and so was the definition of RPGs. The industry soon started to see games that weren't quite RPGs, and they weren't pure action, and this would lead to new designs and subgenres.

In the 2000s, there were several RPGs that while they were designed fully with abstracted systems, they were still played in real time. The entire *Elder Scrolls* series is an example of this – while the player is moving and controlling themselves in a real-time space, everything that they do is decided by the abstraction of the design. An early example of this was *Vampire: The Masquerade – Bloodlines*, released in 2004 by Troika Games. Based on the pen-and-paper game of the same name, the game merged real-time combat with the tabletop rules and RPG abstraction. While you explored and fought in the game entirely in real time, your ability to do anything was dictated by your attributes.

In 2008, *Fallout 3* was released as the first main entry in the franchise not developed by the original designers or published by Interplay. When Interplay

DOI: 10.1201/9781003449959-6

Figure 6.1

It's finally time to talk about how shooter design evolved in the 2010s to feature RPG abstraction and progression. Attaching attributes and progression to gunplay in single and multiplayer games became huge. This goes beyond personalization to now allowing players to find and craft weapons that fit their own playstyles.

fell into financial trouble, Bethesda bought the rights to *Fallout* and made their own in a similar style to *the Elder Scrolls*. Played in first person, players explored the wasteland in real time looking for quests, equipment, and trying not to die. Unlike *the Elder Scrolls* that was built as a fantasy world, *Fallout 3* was a post-apocalyptic world with all manner of ranged weapons around.

The reason why *Fallout 3* and its later entries are considered more RPGs than FPSs is that the abstraction in the game dictates all. Even if you shoot an enemy in the face with a gun, it is possible for them to resist that damage; or if your stats in that gun aren't high enough, they may barely hurt them compared to a weapon that your character is built for. The game also uses "Vault-Tec Assisted Targeting System" or VATS so that someone who is not good at FPS gameplay can still attack enemies using the targeting system that will aim their gun for them.

In 2009, *Borderlands* by Gearbox Software was released, and they coined the term "role-playing shooter." Like RPGs before them, *Borderlands* has leveling and abstraction in it. Every weapon is procedurally generated, can be spawned with different perks and attributes, and their level will rise in concert with the player's character level. The difference, and what would go on to define a new age of FPS, is that the abstraction in the game is built on top of the player's skill and is not there to supplement or reduce it (Figure 6.2). If the player cannot aim or react fast enough, no amount of leveling up or powerful weapons will let them get past an enemy. To put this another way, games like *Fallout 3* and the rest of the series are RPGs first, FPSs second; *Borderlands* and other role-playing shooters

6. The Evolution of Shooters

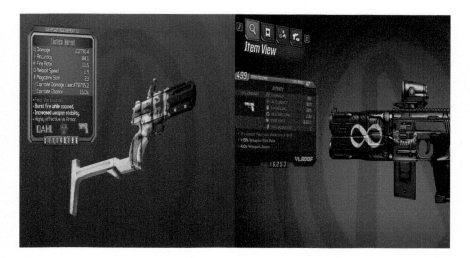

Figure 6.2

What *Borderlands* popularized was taking the idea of loot generation from the ARPG genre and applying it to its gunplay and weapon designs. Here are legendary weapons from *Borderlands 2* and *3*. Each one has a unique modifier that could make the gun better, worse, or just plain odd to use.

are shooters first, RPGs second. *Borderlands* would have multiple expansions and currently four main games were released over the 2010s.

By adding RPG elements on top of challenging shooter design, it was possible to not only create games with the high skill curve and intensity of any boomer or modern shooter, but also provide replayability and progression. The different shooters I mentioned in the last chapter that had unlockable gear and leveling up, all owe some aspect of their design to role-playing shooters. Another aspect of this design is providing players with abilities secondary to the gunplay. In *Borderlands*, each character had an exclusive power they could use besides having different gun preferences and passive trees. This was the next iteration of the design seen in games like *Bioshock* (released in 2007 by Irrational Games) where players could use guns, traps, and special abilities called "plasmids" to even the odds against their enemies.

Even if players couldn't upgrade their characters, tying weapon progression to leveling up and experience points became one of the cornerstones of multiplayer shooters that I talked about in the last chapter. For more about the abstracted elements and balancing, please read *Game Design Deep Dive: Role Playing Games*. Another term that would go on to define shooters with role-playing elements is "looter shooters." In the 2010s and beyond, there were a lot of shooters from major and indie studios that adopted RPG progression and wanted to be a live service looter shooter, and I'll be listing multiplayer-focused examples in Section 6.5, as many games offer both a single player and multiplayer modes.

Figure 6.3

Just as there were a lot of zombie-related games released, we saw more games that put the player in first person fighting them with gun and melee. In the *Dying Light* series, players not only could modify their weapons, but also upgrade their characters with new abilities to explore and fight.

First person, as I've talked about over this book, has been used mostly for shooters and shooting gameplay, but the 2010s also introduced several series and designs that focused on melee combat with guns as a secondary option (Figure 6.3). The *Dying Light* series (released in 2015 and 2022 by Techland) is an open-world action horror game where players explore a city that has been taken over by zombies. They are free to move, shoot, parkour, and fight their way around to complete quests and find resources. While there are guns, combat focuses more on melee with the ability to fight enemies with modified weapons. The series can be played both single player and multiplayer, with DLC that has added in new missions and equipment to find.

*Shadow Warrior* as a brand saw a revival in the 2010s, with each new game adopting systems and designs that were popular at the time. In 2016, *Shadow Warrior 2* was released by Flying Wild Hog and they implemented for the first, and currently last, time in the series an extensive weapon generation system. The weapons themselves belonged to specific classes like bow, shotgun, pistol, but all the stats and passive modifiers were randomly assigned to them along with scaling to the player's level. The gunplay itself was completely arcade-like, as players had to jump, dash, and constantly stay on the move while dealing with all manner of threats. It was also built for both single and multiplayer modes. Even though I enjoyed the concept, the loot generation was a bit extreme, and it was easy to become overwhelmed by the sheer number of items that were dropped. For the third game released in 2022, the style would change again, and I'll talk about it in the next section.

Figure 6.4

*The Division* series stood out from the likes of *Destiny* and *Warframe* by focusing more on cover-shooting and more grounded gunplay, compared to the more over-the-top nature of those two. Still, it did feature all the role-playing shooter elements with players trying to access higher-rated weapons and gear to do more in the late-game content.

Also in 2016, *Tom Clancy's The Division* was released by Massive Entertainment that combined looter shooters, RPG progression, and cover-based design into one game. Players controlled special agents who have been activated after a pandemic was unleashed that decimated the world. Guns were procedurally generated, and players could choose from different classes that affected what gadgets they could use in combat and to support their friends (Figure 6.4). The game also was the first to introduce the idea of extraction shooters with its player vs. player mode. The "dark zone" was an area where the best equipment could be found, but the only way to get it out was to extract it at specific points while other players could ambush and take your stuff. A sequel was released in 2019 that is still having content released for it at the time of writing this.

By 2019, the popularity of soulslike design was in full swing, and *Remnant: From the Ashes* was the first one to apply the model to a third-person shooter. Developed by Gunfire Games, the game was the first at the time to slow down shooting to try and create the pacing of a soulslike, but the gameplay of a shooter. Players could find and craft weapons and then upgrade them using materials found in the procedurally generated areas. Every boss fight had a unique reward that players could use to either craft a new gun or secondary ability that could be equipped. In terms of gunplay, this was a slower and more grounded game compared to other looter shooters. They released a sequel to more success in 2023 that also expanded the progression to feature upgrades to the different classes players could pick from. The game could be played as either single player or up to a max of three, and the game would scale accordingly.

It was also in the back half of 2010 that *roguelike* and *roguelite* design became popular thanks to the success of deck building roguelikes, and the entire design of roguelikes was covered in *Game Design Deep Dive: Roguelikes*. Not only were more games having roguelikes modes built for them, but also shooters were adopting these elements as well. *Risk of Rain 2* released in 2019 by Hopoo Games built off the side scrolling action roguelike design of the first and turned the sequel into a third-person shooter. Using different classes and a wide assortment of items, players had to survive waves of enemies in a variety of environments. Gunplay is completely arcade with each class having a primary form of attack, secondary attack, and special moves to use. The game could be played single or multi and would scale the threats per player.

One of my personal favorites was *Gunfire Reborn* released in 2021 after being on early access by Duoyi Games that combined the class-based design and gun-play of *Borderlands* with the structure of a roguelite. Every weapon was unique in terms of its functionality, damage type, and general appearance, and this could be further affected by having randomly chosen modifiers when they are gener-ated. Each class came with a passive tree that provided meta progression across runs. Gunplay was more on the arcade side, but not as over-the-top as other genre examples (Figure 6.5). To win, players had to figure out the build they wanted to

Figure 6.5

*Gunfire Reborn* is a great example of making a shooter that isn't focused on the same high-speed play as many of the ones mentioned in this book. The roguelike elements and RPG progression can allow someone who is not a high-level shooter player to dominate with the correct builds and weapons. And the characters pro-vide vastly different playstyles and strategies for players to find.

use based on the passive upgrades and weapons they would find over a run. The game became a breakout success for the studio, and they have been supporting it with new characters, new weapons, and new modes released as DLC. Like other examples mentioned, the game could be played solo or multiplayer, with enemy health and numbers scaling per player.

*Returnal* was released in 2021 and 2023 for PlayStation 5 and PC, respectively, by Housemarque and combined bullet hell and third-person shooting. The game was on the harder side as there was a greater focus on movement and dodging. Gunplay was on the arcade side along with the roguelite elements to provide players with new unlocks and options. *Returnal* is also special as having a large reach as a roguelite shooter thanks to the backing of Sony.

Here is a quick snapshot of the copies sold[1]:

| Game Name | Copies Sold |
| --- | --- |
| Bioshock series | 42 million |
| Borderlands series | 81 million |
| Dying Light series | 30 million |
| Fallout 3 | 2–5 million (estimate) |
| Gunfire Reborn | 2–5 million (estimate) |
| Remnant series | 4 million |
| Returnal | At least 1 million (estimate) |
| Risk of Rain 2 | 1 million |
| Shadow Warrior 2 | 1–2 million (estimate) |
| Tom Clancy's The Division series | 20 million |
| Vampire: The Masquerade – Bloodlines | 500,000–1 million (estimate) |

Adding abstraction and RPG systems to shooters and reflex-driven games opened these genres to provide players with another method of progression besides their skills. Someone who was already good at the game could use better weapons and abilities to push things even higher, and those that could supplement their play with getting better weapons. While popular, this kind of combination does present some challenges that would become more apparent in the multiplayer-focused ones. Some games designed their systems so that the RPG side would become more dominant than the reflex-driven gameplay. Even if the player was great at shooting, if the level of their weapon or their character was too low, their attacks would barely do any damage. Another trap developers fell into was not building their shooting gameplay around gunplay elements, leaving their weapons feeling flat and not keeping the FPS fans engaged.

Part of creating a good example of a genre combination is that the best of both need to be on display – just making a basic shooter with great RPG design or vice versa is not enough, and why this is advanced game development.

## 6.2 *Doom's* Return with Push-Forward Combat

Much of the first half of the 2010s was dominated by multiplayer shooters and the designs of *Call of Duty* and *Battlefield* when it came to the mainstream side of things (I'll talk about indies in the next section). In 2016, id Software returned with a new *Doom* after their 12-year gap previously with *Doom 3*. As it's referred to as *Doom 2016*, this was another soft reboot of the story of the original (Figure 6.6). This time, the original *Doom* marine or "Doom Guy" has now become a mythological figure in the universe as the Doom Slayer – a being so powerful that even demons from hell are afraid of him.

He awakens on a Mars base run by the UAC and Dr. Hayden who is trying to collect a power source from hell known as argent energy. When the portals once again open, it's up to the slayer to wage a one-man-army against hell. Where *Doom 3* tried to play this up as an action horror game, id learned its lesson about what the fans wanted and fully embraced the power fantasy and action this time around. For *Doom 2016*, id would go on to coin a new term to describe their methodology for creating it with "Push-Forward Combat." In a Game Developer's Conference (GDC) talk they gave in 2018,[2] id's designers talked about wanting to create a shooter that was entirely offense-driven. This would become the counter to the cover-based shooting and grounded gunplay of the shooters in the 2000s. Here, the idea was that the player should always be engaged in combat as a form of defense and offense – if they were standing still or hiding from enemies, then something was wrong.

Figure 6.6

*Doom 2016* was one of several games released over the 2010s that most people didn't really think much of before the release, but quickly blew up as a return to form and major success for the studio; much in the same way that *Resident Evil 7* (released in 2017) by Capcom was seen by fans.

Figure 6.7

Arena design has existed since the original *Doom* and is a way to create a specific encounter for the player to fight, with the severity and difficulty all determined by the designer. But every fixed arena always starts with the player being the one to initiate it, like activating the gore nest in this scene.

Gunplay is entirely arcade-styled, and the player has access to all available guns at any time. A lot was done to keep the player constantly active – from increasing the speed of climbing and moving around, to the complete removal of reloading weapons. The only limit guns had on them were their rate of fire and ammo. Every weapon in the game could be upgraded with an alt fire mode and these could be further boosted by completing challenges for every mode.

The level design also saw a merging of old and new school styles. Like modern shooters, a huge focus of the level design are arenas where the player must defeat all surrounding enemies to move forward (Figure 6.7). But where modern shooters would often not do much to the areas outside of them, id made each level massive with a variety of secrets and upgrades to be found. Besides finding collectibles, players could find bonus mini areas from older id games, passive buffs they could equip to alter their playstyle, and the options to upgrade their max health, ammo, and armor. In-between arenas players had to explore the level and make use of platforming to get around.

What would redefine combat and the crowning achievement of push-forward design was how health worked. To recap, boomer shooters used consumable healing which was placed throughout each level. The issue was that if someone took too much damage, there was no way for them to recover health before a major fight and they would have to restart the entire stage. Cover and modern shooters gave the player regenerating health via shielding or just staying out of combat. This worked, but it also upset the pacing and flow of the game with the player having to constantly stop what they were doing and heal. *Doom 2016* would borrow from action design the idea of implementing "finisher" moves which were dubbed in the game "glory kills."

Action games for years gave the player the option to finish off an enemy who is close to dying using a violent and over-the-top move; in some games, this could also provide healing as a reward. The glory kill system lets the player finish off any enemy who is flashing blue by getting close to them and hitting "interact." When an enemy is killed this way, they will drop health pickups for the player. Also, if the player is close to death, killing any enemy will also generate healing regardless of if they were finished with a glory kill. As an important note, when the player is doing a glory kill, their character is immune to damage and other enemies will stop engaging with them while the animation is playing.

This change altered the dynamic of combat and in line with id's design philosophy meant that the player must always be engaging with the enemy if they want to survive (Figure 6.8). The pacing of *Doom 2016* turned into peaks and valleys of the player fighting waves of enemies in brutal combat, to then dialing it down to explore the area for secrets and items to then bump it back up.

*Doom 2016* turned into a resounding success for id, and not only brought *Doom* back to the mainstream, but also proved that a single player-focused shooter could still sell well. The game did ship with a multiplayer component, but most of the fans preferred the single player campaign. Trying to find accurate

Figure 6.8

The importance of the glory kill and push-forward combat philosophy can't be understated for how much shooter design has evolved since *Doom 2016*. Being able to push the player to always engage with the enemies and putting resupply as the reward completely changed how someone approaches a shooter with this kind of system.

sales numbers for *Doom 2016* across all platforms proved to be difficult, and estimates from Steam Spy have it at between 5 and 10 million copies just sold on Steam, not counting the other platforms.

The success of *Doom 2016* may have been felt by the mainstream, but indie developers and studios were making shooters and mods for years. It wouldn't be until *Doom Eternal* that would trigger a new trend of shooter design and would also make it the most polarizing shooter in recent years.

## 6.3 The Indie Shooter Scene

Normally in the Deep Dive series, when I talk about the indie contribution to a genre, it's about indie studios either keeping a genre alive or being the new source for it. For shooters, the FPS genre never went out of popularity – there wasn't a point where studios were saying that shooters were no longer viable and that the market was shrinking. The likes of *Halo*, *Uncharted*, *Call of Duty*, *Battlefield*, and other shooters were all massive successes. What did change for the shooter genre was that studios invested heavily in modern shooting and multiplayer, with the boomer shooter style no longer being developed at major studios.

While fans weren't happy about this, it wasn't a case where the design disappeared forever, as PC gamers did not have a problem with finding new single player shooters to play (Figure 6.9). The modding capabilities of the PC allowed people to create their own mods for games. Many PC games over the years either

Figure 6.9

If you are someone new to PC gaming reading this, you cannot begin to comprehend how much modding and mod support has afforded games a new life thanks to fans. This is a scene from the final battle of *Eviternity* 1, a popular mod for *Doom 2* and is just one of the countless original mods for the game available today.

released the source code for their engine or put out software development kits, or SDKs, to encourage modding. Some programmers would create their own modding tools to then build a mod for a game they enjoyed.

The history and extent of modding are beyond the scope of this book, but it's important to understand some of the types of mods released for games. Many mods fall under the category of quality of life – where the mod doesn't add new content but alters or rebalances the base game in some way; maybe it makes it easier or harder, makes the UI clearer, or removes some frustration. Partial conversion mods add in new content that is integrated into the main game – new enemy models, changing the art style; the person is still playing the original game, but not the same as the base version.

A total conversion is building a new game within the engine or SDK. It can feature modified versions of the enemies and textures from the original, or completely original assets and gameplay that was never seen in the base game. For years at this point, fans have been making custom *Mario* levels and mods for *Super Mario World* using a fan-made game editor software (due to the gray area of this topic regarding Nintendo games, I will not be mentioning the name or where to find it).

For shooters, developers have been more than willing to allow people to create mods for their games. In 1997, the *Doom* engine's source code was released under the condition that it would only be used for noncommercial projects. However, Doom Builder and GZDoom[3] are considered as general public licensed software or GPL, meaning that you can now sell products made that use this software.

Doom Builder (or Ultimate Doom Builder) is a fan-made level editor created to make it easier to design levels in the style of *Doom 1* and *Doom 2*. GZDoom is a porting software that was made to let modern computers run the original *Dooms* and has since become included in the sale of any game on Steam that was built using Doom Builder to make it possible to play.

*Doom* is certainly not the last FPS to feature custom maps and mods made for it. Valve's Source engine and 3D Realms's Build engine have also been used over the years for mods of all sizes and creativity, or standalone games that licensed those engines. It is at this point in the book that trying to give you an accurate number of games or timeline for popular examples becomes impossible. Only a handful of places over the years would mention or cover mods for games, and those were only the ones that blew up so big that everyone took notice. Each game community has its own respectively sized fanbase of modders who have been creating mods for years. From the outside, it's easy to assume that mods are nothing more than just someone tinkering with the base game, maybe throwing in a few new characters and models and calling it a day; but for the communities of these mods, there are more fantastic examples than anyone could ever find the time to play every single one of them (Figure 6.10).

For over 20 years now, *Doom* fans have been having yearly best of awards called the "Cacowards[4]" that have featured all manner of mods for it. In 2023, one *Doom* mod that became popular online was "Myhouse.WAD" that started

Figure 6.10

This is a screenshot from *Ashes 2063*, a total conversion mod for Doom that completely reimagines the game as a post-apocalyptic FPS adventure. And again, this isn't even a 1/100th of a percent of the amazing and original mods for games put out that will never have a retail release.

out as a general *Doom* 2 level, but then turned into an existential horror piece where nothing was what it seemed. With *Quake*, there is an official programming language that was released by John Carmack in the 90s called "QuakeC," which modders have been using to create their own mods for the game for years.

One of the most famous pieces of software for meme and machinima purposes using the Source engine's assets was *Garry's Mod* released in 2006 by Facepunch Studios. An item in the game known as asandbox tool  lets players pose and manipulate assets from the source engine.

The Source engine for *Half Life 1* and *2* has also had numerous mods made for both games and standalone releases over the years. Besides how *Counter-Strike* and *Team Fortress* started as mods, there is an incalculable number of mods for both that became cult classics. Back in 2013, Team Psykskallar released the free survival horror game *Cry of Fear* that was built using a modified version of the Source engine called Goldsource. This was originally a total conversion mod that was turned into a game that focused on psychological horror and surviving in a city that is full of monsters and disturbing sights.

In 2022, Crowbar Collective, a group of *Half-Life 1* fans, released a multi-year project to remake the original game called *Black Mesa*. With Valve's blessing, the standalone release completely remakes *Half-Life 1* from top to bottom, featuring a new graphics engine, new enemy AI, redesigned levels, and its own SDK for modding purposes.

Most recently, the build engine version EDuke32 was featured in the shooter *Ion Fury* by Voidpoint in 2019 and 3D Realms has been publishing more indie projects since the end of the 2010s.

But in terms of indie shooters that have blown up, the one that has kick-started the boomer shooter revival would undoubtedly be *Dusk* (released in 2018 by David Szymanski) (Figure 6.11). In it, a man is brought back to life in a farmhouse to discover that some demonic force is corrupting the land, and it is up to the player with sickles and guns to stop them. The gunplay is completely on the arcade side, and an excellent use of sound sells the different gun effects. Where *Dusk* differentiates itself from the classic shooters is in the use of physics and level design. Almost any object can be picked up and thrown at enemies or used to create makeshift steps to reach secrets. One of the game's most famous easter eggs is that a bar of soap in each level can be thrown to instantly kill any enemy including bosses. The level design, like *Doom 2016*, mixes classic and modern design. Each area was designed to create a sense of place, but still features multiple secrets, routes, and arenas to fight in. Over the game's three episodes, the level design changes as the player leaves the farmlands and countryside for cities, mysterious factories, and other dimensions, each with their own aesthetics.

Since then, publisher New Blood Interactive has been publishing and promoting a variety of shooters; and in the time since *Dusk* came out, more boomer

Figure 6.11

*Dusk*, in terms of its release and impact, is like *Doom 2016* and was the game that gave a new life to indie shooters and helped propel developer/publisher New Blood Interactive into one of the major names for indie games.

shooters and GZDoom-developed games have been released on Steam and major platforms. For games that are conversion mods that use any of the assets from the *Dooms*, those are not sold commercially. What's interesting is with the revival of boomer shooters, there are now so many coming out or have been released, and it has become harder for them to stand out. Just like any other genre, just repeating what has been done before is not enough to market yourself anymore. The shooters that are succeeding today have had to differentiate themselves from the pack in some way. Just saying "this is *Doom*, but in a jungle," is not going to sell a game (Figure 6.12).

Some favorites that I have played that have done something different (with more that will show up in the next section) include *Hedon BloodRite* (released in 2019 by Zan_HedonDev), which features huge levels with a focus on exploration on top of shooting. *Vomitoreum* (released in 2021 by Scumhead) combined metroidvania design and exploration with shooting. *Prodeus* (released in 2022 by Bounding Box Software Inc.) merged old and new school designs into their own unique experience. *Nightmare Reaper* (released in 2022 by Blazing Bit Games) was designed as a roguelite with procedurally generated weapons and levels. *Cultic* (released in 2022 by Jasozz Games) focused on a variety of weapons with the ability to upgrade them, and there are more currently in early access at the time of writing this book. For these smaller games, finding accurate sales

Figure 6.12

Here are images from episodes 2 and 3 of *Dusk* to show how the game grew over the course of it, and the variety. There is a noticeable difference in terms of level and environmental design that can be seen in the game, and this is something that is important to convey as a designer.

numbers is harder as major outlets did not cover them. I will be posting the estimates available from Steam Spy (note: this only tracks sales directly on Steam and does not count physical releases, or sales on any other platform):

| Game Name | Copies Sold |
| --- | --- |
| Cultic | 100–200k |
| Dusk | 200–500k |
| Hedon: Bloodrite | 100–200k |
| Nightmare Reaper | 200–500k |
| Prodeus | 200–500k |
| Vomitoreum | 20–50k |

In the last chapter, I mentioned newer types of shooters like extraction and battle royale, and there were many indie studios who tried to build one of their own. However, just like with boomer shooters, just repeating what *Fortnite* did, or *H1Z1*, with a different aesthetic did not work. Creating a good shooter in any style is hard enough; creating one that will resonate with the market is even harder. And to that point, it is time to talk about one of the biggest changes to shooters in recent years.

## 6.4 Bringing Action Design to Shooters

Shooters for most of the genre's life span relied on the same basic practices and design philosophies. The major changes I have talked about so far with multiplayer and RPG progression pushed things further, but they still followed the same gameplay loops. During the 2010s, we would see the idea of combining action game design with first- and third-person shooters (Figure 6.13).

When I talk about action design in this capacity, it refers to a focus on movement and advanced enemy patterns and behavior. For games that have additional movement or motion-based abilities beyond "walk, run, and jump" as the only verbs, a popular term used to describe them as I discussed earlier is movement tech. The only example seen in single player shooters for the longest time was crouch jumping. Returning to the *Tribes* series, this would be one of the earliest examples of a shooter where additional movement tech was a factor in the combat.

That last part "factor in the combat" is an important distinction that may sound like I am splitting hairs but is important to understand the differences in design. There are third- and first-person shooters which gave the player additional powers and abilities outside of shooting to move around levels – double jump, jet pack, slow descending fall, or attacks like a melee or super move. But the point is that those abilities must not only be integrated into combat, but the enemies must be able to react accordingly to them.

There are examples of games that gave the player additional ways of moving around tie them to fixed points in the level – the player can teleport, but only at magic glowing points in the level, or a wall that the player can grapple to, but it

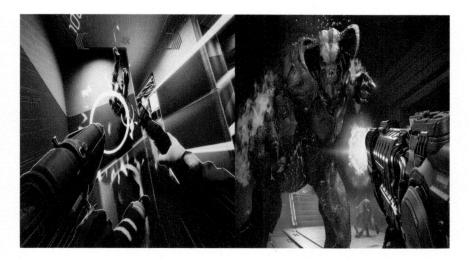

Figure 6.13

For this style of shooting, the player is now the absolute aggressor – with abilities and weapons that reward them for never standing still, never hiding, and just rip and tearing across the map.

is never used in combat or put into an arena. With different abilities in combat, the enemies never change their behavior or have any impact based on what the player is doing.

In the 2010s, there were several examples of shooters that leaned into action design and became cult classics.

A popular trend that developers tried to capitalize on was combining shooting with score-based challenges. The idea was that the player wasn't just being tested on surviving, but how well and stylish they were during combat. This is an evolution of the idea of rewarding style frequently seen in action games in the 2000s. *Bulletstorm*, released in 2011 by People Can Fly, was one of the best examples of this by tying score to progression. In it, players must not only survive against enemies in a destroyed world, but they are rewarded for how inventive their kills were. By combining different guns and their alt fires, along with a grapple and kick, it was possible to kill enemies in ever more ludicrous ways via the "skillshot" system. The gunplay was arcade-style, but the player still had to hide behind cover to recover health.

The *Titanfall* series by Respawn Entertainment (released in 2014 and 2016) combined gunplay with the ability to wall run, jetpack around, and get into titans and fight the other players in them. The first game only had multiplayer, but the sequel did have a single player campaign. *Call of Duty: Infinite Warfare* mentioned earlier also gave players movement tech for first person in both single and multiplayer modes.

An example that people did not think about at the time was *Sunset Overdrive* by Insomniac Games (released in 2014). The game was played entirely in third person and, even though it was an open-world title, all combat was built on third-person shooting – with players grinding rails, wall running and jumping, and just constant movement and avoiding masses of enemies.

A game that came out of nowhere to become a sensation was *Superhot* released in 2016 by Superhot Team. This game built its entire gunplay and game-play around one unique gimmick: the game only moves when the player does (Figure 6.14). When the player fires a gun, the bullet does not begin traveling to its target until the player starts moving, but that also makes all the enemies and their projectiles start moving. It was possible to block bullets with a sword, throw your empty gun to stun enemies, and the game's situations got more and more over-the-top over the course of playing. This is also another popular marketing point from indie developers – by focusing and highlighting one unique element of their game, it was possible for them to go viral on social media and reach an even larger audience.

But the example that has become the one most associated with this kind of practice in the mainstream is *Doom Eternal* (released in 2020) by id Software. The game's story is a retelling of *Doom 2*, with hell unleashed on earth and the Doom Slayer must now save the planet by killing every demon he sees. Instead of just repeating the same push-forward combat in *Doom 2016*, id completely changed how movement, weapons, and enemies worked. In 2016, the Slayer was fast in aligned with keeping the player engaged with the enemies. In *Eternal*, arenas now

Figure 6.14

*Superhot* became a sensation thanks to its unique element which is very hard to see in still images. This was not the first or last indie game to make a shooter build around something different that would make it stand out from the rest of the pack.

feature a variety of different interaction points – jump pads, walls to climb, bars to swing from, and hazards to avoid. Most notably, players are now able to dash forward, sideways, and backward. Dashing forward allows the player to reach platforms and ledges they would not be able to with a normal jump. By dashing sideways or backward, they now have a defensive move beyond just running away from enemies. Being able to dash lets them quickly get in and out of combat and is a far safer way of avoiding incoming damage.

Enemies are far more aggressive and diverse in their attack options, which is also a part of how weapons were redesigned. In every arcade shooter ever made "damage" is the primary attribute of the player's weapons. As an example, a pistol could do 20 points of damage and a rocket launcher could do 200 points of damage. The actual weapon itself has no bearing on the damage itself, only on the amount that it is doing. There are exceptions to this rule – games where the player can use different kinds of ammo in their weapons, and the role-playing shooter trend mentioned in Section 6.1. In *Doom Eternal*, damage now has a property to it – grenades do explosive damage, plasma gun does energy damage, and so on (Figure 6.15). Ammo has been split into several types to go with the corresponding weapons. By using specific weapons and their damage properties, it was possible to quickly kill enemies or reduce their effectiveness. The single barrel shotgun's alt fire shoots out a sticky grenade. If the player lands any grenade on a mechanical part on specific enemies, it will destroy it and reduce their ability to attack; the same goes for the assault rifle's precision mode.

Figure 6.15

*Doom Eternal* was the first mainstream FPS to design its enemies and encounters like an action game – the player is not just mindlessly shooting an enemy or aiming for the head, but must be constantly aware of who they're fighting, what weapons work the best, and how to quickly deal with the major threats of each wave.

Now, the player must pay attention to their enemies they are fighting to quickly figure out what weapons to use and the best and most efficient way of fighting them. Due to the increased focus on the weapon types, the glory kill system was further altered to allow players to now replenish health, ammo, and armor using it. Finishing off enemies who are stunned still grant health. The chainsaw in the first game has now been expanded to work on all minor enemies and refills up to one charge over time: with larger enemies requiring discoverable fuel. A chainsaw death will now drop all ammo types to allow the player to quickly restock. Lastly, a shoulder mounted flamethrower called the flamebelcher can light enemies on fire and they will drop armor shards gradually and more when they are killed. In this respect, it is now possible to fully restock all the player's reserves through combat. Generic zombies infinitely spawn during arena encounters as their purpose is to be an easily killable source of supplies. While the different behaviors of the enemies pushed people out of their comfort zone, it was the inclusion of the marauder that has caused an endless debate about *Doom Eternal* (Figure 6.16). Marauders are introduced as a boss fight before being integrated into normal encounters and they are the only enemy in the base game that has unique rules for fighting it. They are immune to all energy weapons, including the BFG, and they cannot be fought at long or close range. Instead, the player must keep them at medium length to bait out an attack that can be countered and leave them stunned.

What makes the marauder such a polarizing enemy is that they don't fit within the rules of a traditional shooter – where enemy behaviors are secondary to the

Figure 6.16

The Marauder's design is an alien concept for FPS games, but a highly reactive enemy who must be approached differently from everything else is a common practice of the action genre. To this day, people are still arguing whether the marauder fits within *Doom Eternal's* design.

6. The Evolution of Shooters

player's actions. The player is always the instigator, the one who controls how aggressive they are and what they're doing in combat. Here, the marauder dictates the pacing, and everything the player is doing is tied to them. This is a common aspect of action game design when the designers create elite enemies that have their own rules of engagement, but this was unheard of at the time for a shooter.

Admittedly, I do think *Doom Eternal* from a UI/UX perspective is a bit much. In terms of player actions that must be always considered:

- Running
- Jumping
- Shooting
- Double jumping
- Dashing
- Switching to different weapons
- "Quick swapping" between weapons
- Using alt fires
- Switching alt fires
- Grenades
- Switching grenades
- Flame belcher
- Glory kill
- Blood punch
- Crucible attack
- Hammer strike (DLC 2 exclusive)
- The best way to kill the current enemy

Outside of the weapon-specific ways of hurting enemies, combat is free-form in that the player can decide how they want to approach each arena, but the number of buttons required to play *Doom Eternal* far exceeds that of other shooters, especially with memorizing the loadout and quick swapping between your weapons. Expert level play is something to behold, with players who can perform three or more different weapon attacks in the span of a second or two done via quick swapping that I will talk more about in the next chapter. In the DLC chapters, this is further heightened by introducing new enemies that have unique rules and extending the length of arenas for additional challenges. There are also "master level" remixes of specific levels that change every encounter in them to be harder than they were in the regular version. *Doom Eternal* at its highest level of challenge is by far the most skill-intensive single player shooter with a high skill floor and ceiling to go with it. If the player learns all the subtleties of all their different options, it is fantastic to play. If they can't, the design will explicitly punish them by making encounters harder and take longer to go through.

Following *Doom Eternal*, there have been more shooters released, and some still in development, which are elevating shooter design beyond just being about either modern or arcade-styled shooting. For single player shooters, there are several examples that have been adding more to their first-person gameplay. Multiplayer shooters have also had different evolutions in their design, which will be discussed in the next section. For more Doom, it has been confirmed that id is working on a new game in the series subtitled "The Dark Ages" that will be released in 2025.

*Ghostrunner* released in 2020 by One More Level is more of a first-person action game with ranged attacks as the secondary option. The entire design is built on high-speed play and movement to avoid taking damage, where every character including the player can only take a single hit with some exceptions (Figure 6.17). A sequel was released in 2023 that added in more tools and an open-world section.

*Severed Steel* released in 2021 by Greylock Studio builds off the slow-mo powers of *F.E.A.R.* but adds in movement tech and destructible environments. The player is trapped in a facility with an army after them, and they must use all their powers and guns to get out. The trick of this game is that the player can only take one hit, but when they are doing any kind of movement ability, they are invincible. Due to the high-speed of movement, the player can slow down time by command for proper aiming and killing enemies restores their slow down meter. And for a more direct continuation of *F.E.A.R*'s design, there was *Trepang 2*, released in 2023 by Trepang Studios.

Earlier, in Section 6.1, I talked about how more games added in RPG and roguelike elements, but there are also other designs that have also created their

Figure 6.17

*Ghostrunner 1* and *2* were designed around very deliberate combat. Because everything dies in a single hit normally, the player must be more aware of what's going on around them and fight carefully, despite the high-speed of moving around the arenas.

6. The Evolution of Shooters

own niches with shooter design. Using rhythm to timing game mechanics has been another well-established concept for many genres, and shooters have had a few over the years to do just that. *BPM: Bullets Per Minute* released in 2020 by AWE Interactive was a first-person shooter roguelike where all combat is tied to a rhythm indicator that dictates how much damage your weapons do. For a metal take on this practice, there was *Metal: Hellsinger* released in 2022 by the Outsiders for one that focuses on score chasing and less on the roguelike design.

Another aspect that has been seen is combining trick-based or arcade sports design with shooting. In 2022, *Rollerdrome* by Roll7 came out that was about rollerblading and fighting enemies while performing tricks. By doing tricks, the player would increase their score, which is a factor for unlocking new content, and it would refill their weapons. Due to the double focus on tricks and shooting, neither system is as involved or as technical compared to games that are just about one or the other, but it did present a unique mix of designs.

In 2023, RyseUp Studios released *RoboQuest* after being on early access that pushed the roguelite shooter genre to include the movement tech and movement focus design (Figure 6.18). Like *Gunfire Reborn* mentioned earlier in this chapter, weapons were procedurally generated, and the player had to balance the weapons they found with the passive items and their chosen class. What *RoboQuest* did differently was have a greater focus on movement and environmental obstacles.

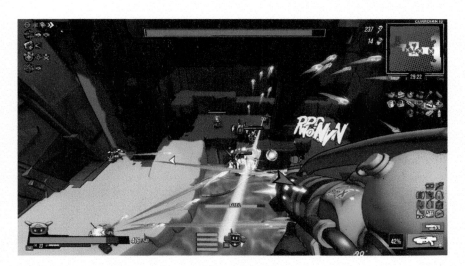

Figure 6.18

*Roboquest* is my favorite of the roguelite FPS games as it is the most movement-intensive take on this kind of design. In this screenshot, standing on the ground at any point during this arena is just asking for these robots to destroy me. While it's not as fast as *Doom Eternal*, this one challenges the player to be constantly adjusting their plan and movement at a moment's notice.

By finding and unlocking gadgets, players could grapple around areas and get a jetpack that lets them fly, completely transforming how someone approaches the combat in the game.

The gunplay features more generic-styled weapons compared to *Gunfire*, but this is compensated for by the fact that modifiers and special abilities on guns are not tied to specific types. It is possible to get a pistol that could also shoot a rocket, a shotgun that fires like a machine gun, and other combinations. Of the roguelike/roguelite combinations, it is the most movement-focused which does add to the skill needed to play it. With the mentioned unlocks and movement tech, the game became more focused on verticality and movement the more the player unlocked gadgets. While they are technically not required to beat the game, their inclusion and use completely change how someone approaches the game to the point that it feels like a different game once they are unlocked. And as another recommendation of the roguelite meets FPS, *Deadlink* was released in 2023 by Gruby Entertainment that goes for a heavier feel to its character and gunplay.

Also in 2023, *Turbo Overkill* by Trigger Happy Interactive finished up in early access to deliver easily the most extreme FPS of the year, featuring multiple weapons, movement abilities, the option to customize your character, and incredibly difficult arenas. This is a game where the player is not only the most powerful character on the field but is also the most fragile given all the different enemies and their attacks coming at them.

Last but not least, *Ultrakill* by Hakita is still in early access while writing this book. The game looks to be the next successor of push-forward combat. While it doesn't feature as many tech-related elements and combat systems as *Doom Eternal*, it features a far more interesting assortment of weapons, different level designs, and it takes the combination of action and shooter design even further (Figure 6.19). Instead of using a glory kill system, any damage to an enemy in close range of the player will heal them based on the attack. Meaning that to recover health at any time, the player must actively get close to the enemy or boss and risk more damage to heal. This is also tied to the style meter that the rate at which the player recovers health and their ability to heal further is based on how high their grade is at a given moment. Each weapon has multiple alt fires that can be switched to during play that change the utility of the weapon and how it can be used with the player's other guns. Defense is tied to a dash that grants invincibility and being able to punch/parry incoming attacks to send them back at the enemy along with general movement and jumping.

The gunplay is built heavily around combining the attacks and capabilities of your weapons to "combo" off them. As an example, the shotgun can be charged to shoot out a grenade that hits enemies, but this grenade can also be shot by the player – triggering a larger and more damaging blast.

Figure 6.19

The current frontrunner in my mind for best action meets FPS game is *Ultrakill*. In many ways, it's more of an action game first, with weapon combinations and movement tech, and hardcore FPS second. This is also a game where trying to get good screenshots of is very difficult due to how fast everything is.

Push-forward combat to me is one of the best evolutions of shooter design and fits perfectly with how I like to play games. At its best, it turns every fight into a puzzle that you solve through action and a lot of combat. However, there are legitimate criticisms of this design by fans of traditional shooters. The shooter genre is one where the simplicity of the mechanics lends itself well for players to get in the flow of constant movement, shooting, and having a good time. Push-forward design greatly complicates this – the player is no longer able to just go through the flow, and they must be constantly thinking, adjusting, and changing their strategy and weapons on the fly. For the people who love this, it provides a sense of intrinsic reward by mastering the game and being able to cut loose and show off. But it is a lot to take in and does remove the simplicity of just engaging with the shooter mechanics. Push-forward combat is also an anthesis to modern or grounded shooting that typically favors people who learn the maps for the best places to attack and can follow a plan. In a game like *Ultrakill* or *Doom Eternal*, you cannot just come up with a plan that is repeatable in every circumstance. The enemies are too erratic and dangerous with their attacks that a passive strategy will not work.

For you reading this, just like with any design trend discussed in this series, when deciding what you want to focus your game on, you'll need to decide what kind of game you want to make and how it relates to the market. The reason why push-forward combat and its philosophy became popular was that no one was doing it at that style at the time of *Doom 2016* or evolved it in such a way with *Doom Eternal*. If you're thinking of just copying *Doom* or *Ultrakill* and doing nothing else with it, then you risk people looking at your game as just a carbon copy of those. As I'll discuss in the next chapter, there is an infinite well of inspiration to draw from when designing weapons, enemies, and scenarios for your game. Lastly, here are some sales figures that I could find for the games mentioned.[5]

| Game Name | Copies Sold |
| --- | --- |
| BPM: Bullets Per Minute | 500k to 1 million |
| Bulletstorm | 1.5 million |
| Doom Eternal | 5–10 million |
| Ghostrunner series | 2.1–2.2 million |
| Metal Hellsinger | 1–2 million |
| Roboquest | 200–500k |
| Rollerdrome | 100–200k |
| Severed Steel | 200–500k |
| Turbo Overkill | 100–200k |
| Ultrakill | 2–5 million (The game was still in early access while checking this statistic.) |

As I mentioned with push-forward design, these games represent the shift away from just arcade shooting into a mix of shooter and action gameplay. The challenge from a design standpoint like everything else with genre combinations, you need every system to be fully working. If you're making a game about 3D platforming and shooting, then movement tech and the gunplay need to be solid and intertwine. What you don't want is for the game to feel like you're switching between genres – this is the platformer section, this is the shooting segment, this is when you sneak, etc. And again, this is why these kinds of games can be very demanding to an unaccustomed player who now must be actively doing multiple mechanics at the same time.

Approachability is a huge point, and I'll talk more about it in the next chapter, but when you combine genre qualifiers and systems, you must be careful with how high of a skill curve you are going for. In *Metal Hellsinger*, the gunplay and general FPS design is noticeably easier than that of *Ultrakill* or *Doom*, but this is balanced by the added consideration that the player must time their shots to the beat. If the game was just as hard as *Doom Eternal* in terms of gunplay with the rhythm matching, it would be popular for hardcore players, but a lot of people would not be able to keep up.

As a final point, whenever you do genre combinations, shooter design or not, you are not creating a game for fans of both genres – you are creating a game for someone who is looking for the combination of genres X and Y, and that is always going to be a smaller market (Figure 6.20).

Figure 6.20

Games like *Metal Hellsinger* and *B.P.M.* are original takes on FPS design, but uniqueness doesn't mean "mass market appeal." Someone who wants to play these games has to be a fan of both shooting and rhythm gameplay – and that market is smaller than the separate genres.

## 6.5 Redesigning Multiplayer Shooters

The 2010s was a period where across the industry, multiplayer games were viewed as the next big market. Thanks to the popularity of MMOGs in the 2000s, military and modern shooting, and mobile and live service games as discussed, many studios went all in. As I discussed in Chapter 5, there were plenty of shooters that would try to capitalize on these elements.

For this section, I want to focus on multiplayer shooters that did something different from the crowd and became their own niche market because of it.

2013 saw the release of two indie games that would dominate and became studio definers – *Path of Exile* by Grinding Gear Games for Action Role-Playing Games (ARPGs) (this was discussed in *Game Design Deep Dive: Role Playing Games*), and *Warframe* by Digital Extreme for third-person shooters. The original concept for *Warframe* that was in beta in 2012 focused more on a competitive multiplayer shooter – with players fighting against each other in a variety of environments. While the gunplay and movement were solid, people were not responding to the competitive design, progression, and monetization. That original version was heading to become a failure for the studio. They decided to pivot and rebuild the game as more focused on PvE content and would publish the game themselves (Figure 6.21).

In the redesign, players explore the galaxy as a Tenno – cybernetic ninjas who have awakened after being asleep for a long time. The campaign and different

Figure 6.21

*Warframe* is a unique game among live service and shooting design. It's a shooter but has a heavy focus on movement and melee; it's completely free to play, but also features the most extensive store and monetization of any other live service game. But without that monetization and the support from their fans, the game would have never grown and changed to where it is today.

story expansions follow the player learning more about the galaxy and what has happened to the Tennos and other species that are still around.

The gameplay and gunplay are built on high-speed combat nothing like modern/grounded shooting. The player is free to slide, jump, and dash around areas looking for resources and objectives. The main equipment that players have access to are different range weapons, different melee weapons, and different warframes. The warframes themselves represent various classes in the game – each one comes with different stat ratings and powers that are unique to them that they can use during combat. An important note is that the warframes themselves do not restrict or prioritize weapon usage.

Weapons come in all different shapes and sizes – from guns, bows, rifles, shotguns, on top of all the different melee weapons that have different combos to use. Weapons can be upgraded by using them along with adding different modifiers to them.

One of the defining aspects of *Warframe* is its monetization. The game's store is legendary at this point for the sheer amount of purchasable content available. However, it is possible to unlock and get access to weapons, warframes, and anything that is progression-related, through play. By completing missions and special events, players can find resources and blueprints to craft items and gear aboard their personal spaceship. With enough time, someone can craft the weapons and frames they want to use and not spend a single cent in the game (Figure 6.22).

Figure 6.22

*Warframe* is a live service game where you could spend literally $0.00 and get a fleshed out experience, or you could spend a whole lot more in their store lifetime if you want to acquire everything.

The game will routinely put out special packs to buy that come with warframes and discounted premium currency.

What has kept *Warframe* going has been the constant updates, extensive progression systems, and new stories and modes on top of the game's solid combat. Over the years, new modes and features were added including open-world areas, a customizable mech, capital ship fights for guilds, more ways to improve weapons and gear, updated warframe models called "primes," and a lot more. Like *Team Fortress 2* and *Payday 2* mentioned earlier in the book, playing *Warframe* today is a completely different experience than it was at launch. As of drafting this book, *Warframe* is at its 35th major update with "Whispers in the Walls." In terms of revenue, finding exact numbers has been difficult, with estimates online from different sites saying it has earned at least 200 million lifetime.

The next example comes from Bungie. Following their split from the *Halo* franchise they would team up with Activision to create *Destiny*. Released in 2014, the game combined the role-playing shooter aspects of *Borderlands* with Bungie's skill at designing shooters and gunplay. In it, players become guardians who are trying to keep the last remains of humanity alive and fight back against forces trying to take over. In terms of the broader plot, this has been expanded thanks to the numerous expansions over the years. In 2017, *Destiny 2* was released to the major platforms, and in 2018, Bungie bought the publishing rights from Activision and are now in full control over the game.

The basic play is that players can create a character from one of different classes, these classes determine what powers and abilities they have access to, but

Figure 6.23

The other side of this live service looter shooter coin is *Destiny 2*. *Destiny 2* feels more MMOG-inspired in terms of its progression and general play compared to *Warframe*. Instead of having unique characters, *Destiny 2* goes for unique weapons.

no class restricts weapon usage. Through play, they will be able to acquire different pieces of armor and weapons that they can use to customize their character (Figure 6.23). The overall power level of a character is based on the strength of the gear they are using, and their current level in any season of the game. The gunplay is on the arcade side, with a focus on using the different powers and defensive and support moves. While the game can be played solo for general content, most of the higher-level content is designed around having a full group – either three for the vanguard missions, or six for the raids. High-level play and the monetization are driven by acquiring the highest rarity tier of weapons known as "exotics." Weapons come in different types which affect ammo usage and rarity that affects any modifiers attached to it. Exotic weapons are designed as one-offs – each one is completely unique and comes with utility that only it has. In a way, this is like the design practice we see out of gacha games with their highest rarity characters, but *Destiny* ties their exotics to their content (Figure 6.24).

With each new expansion, the game is updated with a new chunk of story content and missions to do. By completing these missions, players can acquire new exotics to be used in the high-level raid missions and PvP play. The monetization is centered on the seasonal battle pass and buying access to expansions to unlock their content. Bungie has gotten in trouble with fans by removing access to older expansions to keep the file size of the game manageable, but this comes at the expense of being able to keep up with the story. Trying to find accurate sales numbers for *Destiny 2* and the series is all but impossible, as this information has not been released by Bungie, and any retail sales charts would not track any in-game purchases along with the

**LUMINA**
HAND CANNON

*There must be meaning in my roar.*

WEAPON PERKS

WEAPON MODS

INTRINSIC TRAITS

**NOBLE ROUNDS**
Kills with this weapon leave behind Remnants. Absorbing a
Remnant converts your next hipfired shot into an ally-
seeking Noble Round and partially refills the magazine.

POWER
**1620**

Enemies Defeated 0

Impact 84
Range 63
Stability 80
Handling 76
Reload Speed
Aim Assistance
Zoom
Airborne Effectiveness

Rounds Per Minute 140
Magazine 12
Recoil Direction 100

APPEARANCE

Ⓐ Show Lore 🔲 Hide Menu 🔳 Dismiss

Figure 6.24

Exotics in *Destiny 2* are one part of the moneymakers for buying their continued
expansions. While I don't know if the fanbase sees them the same way I do, but this
focus on unique, one-off, content, is very reminiscent of the kind of design I see in
gacha and mobile games that save their coolest content for their rarest.

expansions. The only numbers I could find put the game having sold in the millions
at this point. And due to the game removing access to expansions, I'm not going to
mention what is available currently as that can change in the future.

As part of the trend of trying to make a new multiplayer coop game, Fatshark
grew in popularity with their series based on the "Warhammer" property owned
by Games Workshop who licenses the **IP** to developers to make different games
on it. For Fatshark, they created the *Warhammer: Vermintide* series starting in
2015. Taking place in the Warhammer universe, the first game involved a group of
unlikely heroes who are trying to save the town Ubersreik from an invasion by the
Skaven – a race of rat-like creatures. Of the games mentioned so far in this book,
*Vermintide* focuses more on melee combat in first person with guns as a secondary weapon. Each character has different melee weapons, and each weapon varies
in terms of damage, attack speed, and reach. The ranged weapons are limited by
finding ammo in the levels but can be used to deal with specific targets.

The gameplay itself is like the *Left 4 Dead* series, as up to four players go on
missions in fixed levels with randomly appearing groups of enemies to fight. The
skaven come in different types, including special ones that are reminiscent of the
special infected from *Left 4 Dead* and will require team work to deal with quickly.
The mission structure here is more varied as players are not required to complete
an entire campaign in one sitting but can make progress level-by-level.

Gear for each character was randomly generated as rewards for completing
missions, and these were required to have any chance at winning on the higher

Figure 6.25

All the *Tide* games focus more on melee than shooting, despite what this screen-shot will lead you to believe. Guns are often reserved for higher threats or a way to thin out mobs of enemies before engaging in close range.

difficulties. This loop was expanded on with the sequel released in 2018 that expanded on the progression by introducing different variants for each character that would change how they would behave. The most recent game from the series is *Warhammer 40K: Darktide* released in 2022 which moves the franchise to the 40K universe of Warhammer which is sci-fi as opposed to fantasy (Figure 6.25).

From a design point of view, a point of contention among fans and critics is how much gear matters to progression. The series has always had a gear rating system that dictates the quality of items dropped, and this can greatly affect how well someone can help their team on the higher difficulties. However, focusing on melee as opposed to range does give the series a unique feel to it that we don't often see from multiplayer games. Estimate from Steam Spy put *Vermintide 1* at 1–2 million copies, *Vermintide 2* at 2–5 million, and *Darktide* at 2–5 million.

2021 had *Back 4 Blood* by Turtle Rock Studios that was marketed as a new *Left 4 Dead* experience by the original creators. This time, the developers went all in on abstracted design with the ability to upgrade weapons over the course of a campaign, and players could create decks of perks that they could use. The perks came in the form of cards that could be unlocked at random from vendors at the hub/lobby of the game. Cards would be categorized by their utility and whether they could be used in the campaign mode or the vs. which played like *Left 4 Dead* with survivors vs. infected (Figure 6.26).

Unlike the other multiplayer shooters discussed, the campaign structure greatly factored into the difficulty and pacing of a match. Originally, players only earned the supply points needed to unlock new cards by finishing every

Figure 6.26

The problem that *Back 4 Blood* faced was that it tried to push the monetization and live service design by making progress slow. The card on the right is something that is too good on the higher difficulties in a game where enemies can disable one of the players, and many people felt that the game was keeping them from being able to enjoy it until they were able to get all the necessary cards for their build.

level in a campaign, and they would be penalized if the team lost before the end. Each campaign was made up of a series of levels where resources, guns, and the as-for-mentioned perks would persist. Levels would feature randomized elements such as different infected cards that would change the rules of the map, and different weapons and gear to equip. Over the course of a campaign, it was possible to find different guns of various rarities and weapon mods that could be equipped to change their properties.

The problem with the design for gamers was that success on a campaign was heavily determined by the perks each player brought in, more so than anything else. The strength of the perks greatly varied with many cards that were deemed too situational, and some cards so powerful that they became the cornerstone of every deck. This, combined with the difficulty of getting supply points to unlock more cards, led to many people giving up on the game. Despite that, hardcore fans who did learn the game and get access to all the cards found one of the more challenging and coop-heavy shooters released. In 2023, the developers announced that no more content would be developed for the game, and they rebalanced all the card drops and progression. According to Steam Spy, the game sold an estimated 1–2 million copies on Steam, but it was also released on the other platforms as well.

While the likes of extraction shooters, battle royale, and the major names mentioned in this chapter continue to dominate, that doesn't mean multiplayer design is only locked to those games. Whether you want to go big and design massive scale like *Planetside* or make something more intimate and focused like *GTFO* is entirely up to you. What you do need to understand about multiplayer design today is that the established designs and popular games are entrenched. There will not be a studio that is going to outplay *Call of Duty* in terms of gameplay and features with a single game; likewise, no other studio is going to have access to the resources and money afforded to the different studios that work on it. What you want to strive for is to create your own market with a unique multiplayer experience that people won't be able to get anywhere else. *Deep Rock Galactic* succeeds by offering a multiplayer experience that no other game is doing at this design.

Case in point, when I was finishing this book in 2024, the game *Lethal Company* by solo developer Zeekerss was released at the end of 2023 – being a combination of extraction shooter, coop, and survival horror (Figure 6.27). In that span of time, the game has an estimated sales count of 10–20 million copies according to Steam Spy. The game certainly doesn't provide the graphical fidelity of the likes of *Call of Duty*, but it does give its audience a multiplayer experience that no one has done specifically before.

Figure 6.27

To sell a multiplayer game in the market today, you need to offer people an experience they haven't already seen before and being able to provide more content and grow what's in the game. Every multiplayer game being released today that wants to succeed must have a live service plan for where the game is going to go, as people will not stay with a game that has no future content.

6. The Evolution of Shooters

Standing out with fantastic design, whether it's single player or multiplayer, is how you want to sell your game today. As I'm going to talk about in the next chapter, there is a lot that goes into just making one weapon feel fantastic, let alone an entire shooter.

## Notes

1 Data provided by VGChartz and estimates by Steam Spy.
2 https://www.youtube.com/watch?v=2KQNpQD8Ayo
3 https://zdoom.org/downloads
4 https://www.doomworld.com/cacowards/
5 Sources are VGChartz.com and Steam Spy for the smaller games and estimates.

# The Foundations of a Great Shooter

## 7.1 The Decimals and Design behind Weapon Balance

When we look at reflex-driven games, before you can start building anything tangible in your game, you need to start thinking of your core gameplay and the options that you will provide to the players. In a platformer, this is all about the kinds of jumps and movement tech; in a shooter, it's all about the weapons. I'll be returning to gunplay in Section 8.2 as the feel of your weapons is the next step.

The relationship of your weapons to jumping in a platformer is perfectly apt – changes to what weapons are in your game or how they will behave will impact everything around them (Figure 7.1). The first thing you need to decide on are the overall types of weapons to be included. This will also be a factor for multiplayer games and the differences between single and multiplayer will be discussed in Section 8.4. Before we start talking about balance, here are the attributes that are a part of any ranged weapon in a shooter (and note: many of these attributes will also correspond to enemy design in the next section):

DOI: 10.1201/9781003449959-7

Figure 7.1

Every good shooter must begin with what do you want the player to do in it, and then create the weapons and gunplay meant to facilitate that. This is why for games like *Doom Eternal* and *Ultrakill*, their gameplay can only work within this specific design, because everything was built from their foundational aspects.

- Hitscan or projectile
  - If projectile
    - Projectile shape
    - Projectile size
    - Projectile speed
    - Projectile physics
    - Blast radius (for explosions only)
- Bullet spread
- Damage
  - Damage type
- Range
- Rate of fire
- Reload speed
- Ammo
  - Ammo type
  - Storage capacity
  - Loaded amount
- Stability/recoil
- Tracking
- Alt fire
- Weapon class/type

- Rarity
- Utility
- Modifiers

As a reminder from earlier, weapons can be designed as hitscans or projectile-based, and both have their places in any shooter. A hitscan weapon can be either for novices or for advanced players based on the other attributes of the weapon. A fast-firing hitscan with low recoil can easily be aimed and used to hit any fast-moving target. Conversely, a hitscan weapon that has a slow rate of fire and slow reload could be a high-skill weapon designed for maximum damage. The only shooters where I've seen them not have any hitscan weapons are ones where the player has access to a hard lock-on. And again, these would be games where movement and avoiding damage is more of a focus than attacking. Part of the design of a hitscan weapon is that the actual reticule is the smallest on screen. The reason is that, as a hitscan, the game is calling a function instantaneously when the player presses the fire button. If the hitscan is literally the player's screen, then they can just hit anything without needing to aim. That said, having an ultimate power or ability that gives the player a mass hitscan attack could be a way to mix things up.

The factors for your projectile all have an impact on the balance behind it. A very large projectile is easy to hit with vs. a small one; but a speedy small projectile can be easier to hit with compared to a very slow large one. The most common projectile shape is a circle, but there are cases where developers have created different shapes to make their weapons stand out. A lightning blast that arcs out from a gun, a giant fist; in the game *Armed and Dangerous* (released in 2003 by Planet Moon Studios), one of the weapons simply fired a shark that would travel underground to track and eat enemies. One exception to mention with projectiles is if the attack is meant to cause an area of effect blast, like a rocket launcher. If your weapon features splash damage or a secondary effect after the projectile connects, that will also need to be balanced.

Projectile physics matters in games where part of the challenge of using the weapon is that there are simulated physics for how projectiles behave (Figure 7.2). Details like the weight of the bullet pulling it down in the air, wind affecting the trajectory and other factors. This is often used in games that are trying to be more grounded or realistic with its weapons. The *Sniper Elite* series by Rebellion was built around balancing real-world physics on how bullets travel for players to hit their targets. Many arcade games can have some physics elements, such as grenades that will bounce and have drag once they are fired. This is optional and whether you want to have these factors will depend on the game you are making.

Bullet spread is a point for semi/fully automatic guns, and shotgun-styled weapons. This is about how the bullets travel out of the gun. Even though the player's reticle is pointed in one area, it doesn't mean all the bullets are going to hit exactly in that range. The size of the reticle on screen will give the player an idea where bullets will go when the gun is firing. This is also why hitscans

Figure 7.2

"Bullet Physics" can be vastly different depending on the game in question. In *Roboquest*, the entire game is arcade-style, but projectiles behave differently depending on whether we're talking about a shotgun with shells, grenades, rockets, and so on. In the *Sniper Elite* series, physics are about how wind can drag a bullet down over time and making that one shot connect. Just remember, the more realistic you are aiming for (no pun intended), the harder it can be for new players to grasp it.

feature the smallest reticle, as the point is that the "bullet" is instantaneous and exact. Guns with a widespread arc are meant to be used in close range, and how shotguns are balanced with their damage. An individual bullet from a shotgun doesn't do nearly as much damage as an individual bullet from another gun, but that shotgun could be putting out 20 or more bullets in a single pull of the trigger. As someone keeps firing, automatic weapons will have the size of the reticule get wider to indicate the difficulty of keeping the gun aimed at a specific point while it is going full auto and is often a balancing element between going semi vs. full.

Damage is the amount of damage an individual pull of the trigger should provide, but to get the DPS of a weapon (damage per second) you must factor in the rate of fire as well. Many weapons in shooters have been balanced as having low damage combined with a high rate of fire, or high damage with a low rate. Some games have used randomized damage – instead of a weapon doing 10 points of damage or 20, it could do 10–15 points per attack. For most shooters however, damage values are kept the same. Just like with RPG design, if you want numbers to matter more to the player, then you can use low number design as opposed to saying that a pistol does 40 points of damage, and a rocket launcher does 5,000 (Figure 7.3). Again, this will be balanced depending on the rest of your game and the enemies that you are going to design.

Figure 7.3

You may not believe it from the screenshots of *Ultrakill*, but the game uses low numbers for health and damage. The pistol seen here does a whopping 1 point of damage per shot, and the mighty railcannon that is one of the strongest single-shot weapons in the game...does 8 (number values subject to change with updates).

Range means different things depending on the game and weapon in question. In some shooters, guns just have infinite range – that bullet or projectile will keep traveling until it collides with something. In other ones, the projectile will only exist for a specific number of seconds before disappearing. Part of the balancing of range will be the level design. If you're building areas out of a lot of enclosed areas, an infinite range can be fine as there are always going to be walls or obstacles that will cause the bullets to stop traveling. From a programming standpoint, you do want to make sure that any generated projectiles are deleted to avoid memory leaks and performance problems if your game will have thousands of projectiles during a play. Some shooters have their range be more explicit in how it is used, with weapons having a minimum and maximum range for peak damage. While any gun can be used at any range, if the player is not within that sweet spot, the weapon will do less damage.

For weapons that are specifically not gun-based, you'll need to be more careful about how range works. Many shooters and first-person games have featured melee weapons as either a last-ditch weapon, or something for high-skill play. Even though the player is in close range, you still need to give it some range for it to be functional. For a weapon that works as a launcher to knock enemies away or attacks as an arc, you'll need to decide just how far it can go. As a specific quality of life feature, if your melee or close-ranged weapons are built as special attacks that can't be used rapidly, having an on-screen indicator when the player is in range for them can help during the heat of combat.

7. The Foundations of a Great Shooter

Rate of fire is an important attribute in any shooter – it defines the DPS of a weapon, how effective it is when attacking fast-moving characters, and affects the feel of it. Some of the most powerful moments in a shooter is when the player gets their hands on a high-DPS weapon and are free to cut loose. A popular set piece featured in many shooters is when the player gets behind a gatling gun emplacement and must hold out against waves of enemies while firing at full auto at them. The rate of fire also has an impact on the aesthetics of your game – having every weapon be slow to fire can be used to build up tension or work in a horror setting, while fast firing can be used if you want a lot of action. As a point about rate of fire, this is one attribute where the difference between it feeling good or bad can come down to tenths of a second. The rate of fire will also be a factor with the movement speed of your enemies or other players. Slow rate of fire weapons are not as effective in close range – such as trying to hit someone with a sniper rifle when they are a few feet in front. In team multiplayer games specifically, weapons are always on the faster side in order to keep the fast pace of a match going.

To that point, just because fast rate of fire is used a lot in multiplayer doesn't mean that it's always the best. As I said further up, having a slow rate of fire weapon balanced with having high damage can be of use for players who prefer to hit an enemy once and be done with it. In games where weapons can have modifiers or additional on-hit effects, high rate of fire weapons are preferred as the more bullets that are hitting the enemy, the more changes for those effects to work (Figure 7.4).

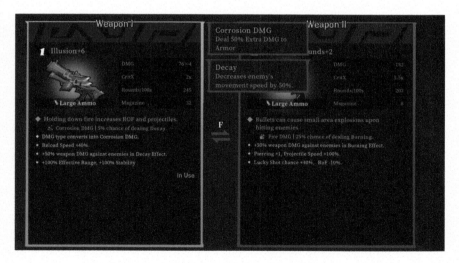

**Figure 7.4**

Elemental and to-hit effects are a mainstay of high-level play in any roguelike/lite shooter. The trick about them is that it will often take multiple passive bonuses/perks for them to blow up, but when they do, like in *Gunfire Reborn* here, players can decimate even the mightiest of bosses with a "low" DPS weapon.

Reload speed is something that its inclusion is no longer a gimmie for shooters. Games like *Doom Eternal* and *Ultrakill* showed that you don't need to have reloading weapons as a form of balance. The role of reloading and reloading speed is to limit how much the player can use their weapon at any given time. Some weapons are balanced by having a lot loaded into the gun, but with a slow reload to compensate. In games that are built on additional RPG systems and design, reload speed is often tied to a perk or modifier that could increase its speed. Like with everything I'm discussing in this section, reload speed is just another factor that the rest of your game must be balanced whether you have it or not. Multiplayer and competitive shooters still make use of reloading and can be a major part of how encounters play out – run out of bullets at the wrong time and the opposing player could rush and finish them off before they have a chance to reload.

The variables when it comes to ammo are another one where there are no hard rules for what you should do. There are several approaches to ammo types that have been used in different shooters. The first is that every gun has its own unique ammo, case closed. This way, stronger weapons are balanced by having their ammo type harder to find compared to the other guns. Another option is that guns are categorized by different classes or types, and ammo is tied to each class. This is often used in games where the different classes have a form of balancing to them: normal guns are standard weapons, heavy guns are stronger, and special guns are the ones that don't fit standard characterizations. In this approach, the player can always swap between the different weapon classes if they run out of one ammo type. Another option is that every gun simply exists as its own ammo. Instead of the player having to pick up ammo, the ammo is infinite, and the guns are balanced by details like the amount that is loaded and reload speed.

For games that are meant to be more involved with ammo and shooting, there is also the case to have different variations of ammo that can be used by guns, such as having normal bullets, silver bullets, exploding bullets, etc. The gun itself doesn't change in its use, but the bullets affect the properties of attacking on top of the stats of the weapon itself (Figure 7.5).

Storage capacity once again depends on the game itself. If you're designing a game where ammo is infinite, then you could also say that the weapons have infinite storage as well. Other games may still have a fixed capacity for each gun that will require a reload. You may have noticed that I'm using the word "storage" as opposed to a magazine or a clip. The reason is that many games will feature unconventional weapons where those designations wouldn't apply, like a living weapon or a sci-fi laser blaster. The same can be said about how much is loaded into the gun at one time. In games that have different loaded amounts, the fewer bullets that can be used at one time will also relate to the damage of that weapon. What makes sniper-based weapons high risk/reward is that they are usually single shot – the player must reload each time after they fire. Some games can have modifiers on guns that increase the storage on a gun, even if it doesn't make sense realistically, such as allowing a double-barreled shotgun to hold four rounds.

Figure 7.5

Multiple ammo types is often used in shooters that feature more grounded or slower gunplay, as the means of rewarding someone for properly scoping out their target and using the right bullet for the job. In *Blood West* pictured here (released in 2023 by Hyperstrange), the different ammo types do make a big difference when fighting larger or spectral enemy types.

The storage capacity of ammo will also affect how someone gets more ammo for their weapons. The boomer shooter way was just having bullet supplies throughout the map. Modern shooters allowed players to swap between guns, or picking up a copy of a weapon already in the player's hands will just take the ammo and add it to the player's supply. For powerful weapons that are meant to have limitations, one option is to set limits to them that require the player to switch to a new gun instead of just using it constantly. In *Ultrakill*, the nailgun is the only weapon in the game that can overheat which prevents the player from using that weapon mode until it cools off. And the rail cannon is a single-shot high-damaging weapon that always takes 16 seconds before it can be fired again. Just remember, the limit of how often someone can use a gun must factor into the pacing and gunplay of your game. In *Ultrakill*, which is a fast-paced shooter, 16 seconds is a very long time. In another game where things are slower and the player is not getting into frequent fights, 16 seconds could mean nothing in terms of limiting the player.

Stability and recoil are about how easy it is to control the weapon while firing. When a gun is fired, the kickback of it can prevent the user from shooting at the same exact angle if they are trying to fire rapidly. For semi- and full-auto weapons, the recoil is so intense that the person must try and fight it to keep the bullets going to the correct target. This is another factor that will be based on how realistic or grounded you want your weapons to be. In games where realism is out the window, there may be no recoil to deal with while the character is jumping, dashing, or sliding around the room. In multiplayer-focused games, recoil and the impact of stability are used as other factors for the player to have to deal with when trying to attack another player. It's also used as a form of balancing between different strengths of weapons. A single-shot pistol will have drastically lower recoil compared to a shotgun or assault rifle. However, a magnum or higher-caliber gun that is single shot, may have huge kickback to balance how unwieldly it would be to use it rapidly.

Tracking refers to any weapons that have the ability for their projectiles to home in on the opponent once the gun is fired. Some of the most dangerous enemies in shooters can have tracking on their shots as well. This is also a part of games that have soft and hard lock-on systems and is another way for the player not to worry about aiming when they are focusing on movement. The amount of tracking on a projectile can vary quite wildly between games and weapons. Low tracking could mean that the projectile will simply list to the direction the character is in relation to the projectile. Medium tracking will have it turn and change its heading based on where it is to the player. In this situation, wide-open areas would allow a projectile to keep coming at the character even if they dodge it. High tracking is only used in rare situations, and this is where the projectile essentially becomes a heat-seeking missile and can follow the player around walls. In this situation, the player must either destroy it or trick it into colliding with something to stop it. Tracking is not a required factor for any shooter, and your game must be designed and balanced around it if you choose to put it in.

Alt fire is for games where each weapon can have one or more additional ways of firing it. There are no rules or standard elements for if you want to feature alt fires in your game. They can be a way of letting a player customize how they want to use that weapon, or they could provide completely different use cases for it (Figure 7.6). Alt fires can also be a way for weapons to share ammo or utility if the player doesn't have the ammo for one – like a grenade launcher attachment to a rifle to let players use explosive damage if they don't have any rockets for a rocket launcher. Returning to *Doom Eternal*, every gun in the game with exception to the BFG-level weapons had two different alt fires. The shotgun could either turn into a single-shot firing grenade launcher or fire its shells like a machine gun for a rapid source of high close-ranged damage.

If you include them, you also need to factor in how swapping alt fires will work in your game. Some games may only let the player swap fires at a save point or rest area if they're trying to make the decision more strategic. In *Doom*, the player could swap alt fires in the middle of combat, but there was a slight delay between swapping them and being able to fire again. In *Ultrakill*, keeping with the high-speed play, alt fire swapping is instant. Just remember from a UI perspective, the more things the player must be thinking about at one time, the harder it can be to play the game.

For the remaining variables, I've marked them differently as these are used more in games that have RPG abstraction or roguelike/roguelite design. They are

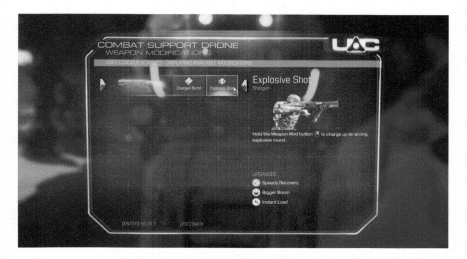

Figure 7.6

Alt firing can be used to give weapons new utility and further expand the diversity of your gunplay. In *Doom 2016* and then to *Doom Eternal,* the different firing modes become a major part of someone's strategy and high-level play of swapping between them depending on the circumstance.

not required to be in your shooter, and the decision to include them will radically change the structure of your game and its gunplay.

Weapon class/type is when the player is not using a fixed number of unique weapons such as in *Doom*. Instead, weapons can drop that belong to different classes and rarities. The "class" is just a way of distinguishing each weapon from one another. A simple example would be having different pistols, shotguns, rifles, etc. In *Gunfire Reborn*, each weapon class is a unique one-off, so that each weapon behaves completely differently from the others.

Rarity is carried over from RPGs and ARPG design. Different rarity tiers affect the quality of the weapon, with the highest tier often built as one-off weapons. Higher-quality weapons can have higher base stats or come with additional modifiers and abilities I'll discuss further down. A huge draw of *Destiny* 2 discussed in the last chapter was the exotic tier that the player can only equip one on their character at a time and they will have unique modifiers to go with them.

Utility is a more advanced concept, and this is for if the weapon has any additional means of affecting enemies or the world around it. This is also where weapon design can dip into immsim territory. In *Prey* 2017 by Arkane Studio, the "Gloo Cannon" fired out a material that could either freeze enemies if they were hit by enough of it or be used to connect to surfaces to create makeshift platforms and climbing points. Another popular feature is to design utility specifically around puzzle solving, such as *Half-Life 2*'s gravity gun that could not only

Figure 7.7

The gravity gun seems novel today, but it was quite unheard of at the time to introduce a device in shooters that had other applications besides shooting. With it, players could use it for puzzle solving, or for combat using the many random objects littered throughout the world.

launch objects at enemies but was also used to solve puzzles (Figure 7.7). Like with alt fires, if you're going to include this feature in your game, then it needs to be fully integrated, and the player needs to be explained about what their guns can do. Utility effects on weapons must also be balanced around their own variables and considerations separate from the gun itself. As an example, if the alt fire of a weapon is designed to specifically do damage to one type of enemy, then the attack rate of it must be considered when designing encounters with that enemy type and allowing the player to adequately fight that enemy type.

The situation you want to avoid as a designer is creating an enemy or encounter that requires X weapon or Y alt fire, but the player is unable to use the specified attack. Maybe there aren't any ammo supplies, or the weapon has a long cooldown period. There is always a difference between saying that weapon X is better against an enemy vs. weapon X is the only way to actually fight them.

Modifiers are additional variables and effects that can be attached to the base properties of any weapon. This is full-on ARPG design and has been a major feature in many shooter roguelikes/roguelites. Modifiers can also be rated by rarity that affect how potent they are. On the low end of the spectrum, a modifier could give a gun slightly more damage or a few more rounds. On the high end it could completely change how the gun is used, add new properties for attacks, or give the player a unique bonus for having the gun out. Modifiers can be either locked to different gun types or any modifier can appear on any weapon depending on the design you are going for. That last point is important if your gun classes are designed to be one-offs or have generalized functionality between them. In *Gunfire Reborn*, weapon modifiers are weapon class-specific, because every class functionality is different. Whereas in *Roboquest*, the guns are meant to be more generalized and, with few exceptions, every modifier could show up on any weapon. When combined with weapon rarity, rarer weapons can have the possibly to come with more modifiers compared to a lower-quality version.

Discussing modifier design, there really is no limit to how far you can go with a modifier system. *Gunfire Reborn* has modifiers that provide bonuses if the same one is on the player's second weapon, many games let players reroll modifiers to try and get a better combination, and *Roboquest* had active modifiers that give weapons a secondary attack. The best kinds of modifiers are those that have a pronounced and easy to see impact on the weapon. While it is easier to balance small changes like "1.0% more damage," if you want players to engage with your rarity system, then you want to go big with them, and quality is better than quantity when it comes to modifiers.

Another example of modifiers is the use of "weapon mods" – being able to change out parts like the stock, barrel, trigger, and so on, to change the property of the weapon. This is a feature in grounded and military-styled shooters and has become a major part of the progression seen in the *Call of Duty* series. Instead of weapons coming with a random selection of mods, the player acquires new mods through play and progress that they can then swap on and off the weapons where they are applicable. Part of the balance of weapon mods is that the player literally can't attach every mod to their gun – you can't have a 27-barrel pistol as an example. In return, weapon mods of the same type will be designed to stand out from each other in terms of utility. A popular example is whether or not to have a silencer on a gun, with the trade-off being that the gun does less damage but won't alert enemies when it is fired.

With all the attributes mentioned in this section, it now falls on you to build the weapons you want with your shooter. If you're hoping for an exact breakdown to the decimal point of how to build a perfect pistol, shotgun, sniper rifle, or the prefect list of weapons for a shooter, that is impossible. Just like how every jump in a platformer is different, so is every weapon and weapon type. A hitscan pistol in one game could be the weakest weapon; in another, it could be designed as the most powerful gun in the game if it's meant to be a powerful magnum or have additional functionality. In *Ultrakill*, the game goes as far as to have combos with specific weapons and their alt fires, creating even more combo potential and damage for the player to use (Figure 7.8).

The absolute first thing you need to figure out before designing your weapons is what kind of shooter do you want to make? If you're going for something grounded or hyper realistic, then half the work is done for you, as you can use real-world weapons (or non-copyright alternatives) to build your weapons around. As a legal point, you cannot put a real-world gun manufacturer, ammo supplier, or weapons maker in your game without seeking approval to license their brand. And just because you have realistic-looking weapons,

Figure 7.8

Combo blasts like this one with the rail cannon and shotgun are hard to pull off during combat, but are a few of the advance tactics for playing on the higher difficulties and going for the highest rank possible.

it doesn't mean that those weapons must work like in the real world, as many boomer and arcade shooters can testify to.

Building something unique like the portal gun, GLOO cannon, or the weapons from *Doom Eternal* and *Ultrakill* is going to take more work. You not only have to create something that no one has ever seen before, but it must fit within the world and level design of your game and allow the player to fight the enemies. Remember, the pacing and speed of your shooter will also impact how your weapons will feel and what it means to use them. If you're building a slower-paced game where every bullet counts, having a slow rate of fire and reload speed can work; in a fast-paced shooter, even waiting 1 second can feel like an eternity. The only way you will know for sure if a weapon works in your game is to build it and test it out; just looking at a spreadsheet of attributes is not going to do it. This is part of the feel that goes into reflex-driven games and where there is such a gulf between bad, good, and amazing shooters. Returning to the platformer comparison, just like how good it can feel to make a character jump, if using your weapons don't feel good in the player's hands, then you will lose their interest in your game.

One point is universal among every shooter type: quality is always better than quantity. *Borderlands* put an idea into designer's heads that giving the player "all" the guns will make their shooter better. This is the same fallacy that ARPG designers have struggled with and thinking that procedurally generating an infinite number of weapons will lead to a better game. Good weapon design is about making each weapon, or each weapon class, feel unique. There should be a credible reason for each weapon to exist in your game. Does weapon A do something different than weapon B? And within the same class of weapons, does each variation bring something different to the table?

Let's go over the weapons from *Doom 2*, to demonstrate this point.

- Fists: low-damaging melee attack (higher with the berserk item) used as a last resort.
- Chainsaw: medium-damaging melee weapon can stun low- to mid-class enemies and has infinite ammo.
- Pistol: low-damaging hitscan weapon with no range limitation and high accuracy. Uses bullets.
- Shotgun: hitscan weapon that does more damage at closer range but has a longer range than the super shotgun. Uses shells.
- Super shotgun: hitscan weapon that does high damage at close range, but quickly loses damage the further the enemy is. Uses shells.
- Chain gun: hitscan weapon that shoots rapidly and can stagger low- to mid-class enemies; lower accuracy at longer range compared to the pistol. Uses bullets.
- Plasma gun: projectile-based weapon that does medium damage but fires rapidly. Uses cells.
- Rocket launcher: projectile-based weapon that does high damage and creates splash damage at the point of impact. Uses rockets.
- BFG: projectile-based weapon that travels slowly and does high damage to the target and any enemies nearby. Uses cells.

This list of weapons has stood the test of time thanks to the number of mods that have been built from *Doom's* weapons. There are *Doom* mods that introduce new weapons or change the attributes of the ones mentioned above. Looking over the list, you can see that the different ammo types are spread across different weapons, with the rocket launcher the only one that has no carryover. Once again, every weapon on this list does "damage"; there is no difference between the kind of damage the pistol does compared to the rocket launcher. What is different is the ammo type, and that the Super Shotgun and BFG use more shells and cells, respectively, when firing. How much and what kind of ammo the player finds on each level will dictate what weapons they are going to be able to use. This point will come up again when I talk about level design in Section 7.3 and how weapon and ammo placement will affect your levels.

Regarding classes of weapons vs. unique ones, this point will heavily affect the level design of your game. When the player must swap between weapons based on what is available in the level, you must make sure that enough weapons are able to be found off enemies or in the field itself for them to be able to fight back. With older boomer shooters, levels were designed to provide the player with enough weapons in the level itself that they can succeed even if they die and lose the weapons they entered the level with. There was also the

Figure 7.9

One of the hardest aspects to balance in a shooter is how far do you escalate the combat over the course of playing? With the DLCs for *Doom Eternal*, they both featured far harder and more complicated arenas to test players who finished the base game with new enemy varieties. Some players liked the increased the difficulty, and there were some put off by how far the difficulty was ratcheted up.

option in older shooters that the game would wipe the player's weapon inventory at the start of a new level – requiring them to build back their arsenal each time.

Going the unique route means that the player will always have their complete stock of weapons level-to-level, and now the challenge becomes providing good enough level and enemy design to keep challenging the player to use them (Figure 7.9). In the next section on enemy design, I will be talking about what the enemies mean to the world and the player's weapons, and why it is a lot harder than it sounds to get all this right.

Weapon design is where you can create your own unique mark on the shooter gameplay, and where you can just as easily fail. In Section 8.2, I will be discussing how this gets tied to the gunplay and UX of your title. I've played countless shooters from indie teams over the years and the one defining point that either makes or breaks the experience is how does it feel to shoot your gun for the first time. If that first shot doesn't feel good to the player, then everything else after it is not going to work. If you're reading this as someone who has built games featuring abstracted design like RPGs and going into reflex-driven for the first time, my starting advice for you is to go and play the original *Doom*. If your game cannot even meet the gunplay of the original *Doom* that is over 30 years old, then you do not have a shooter that's going to work in the market today.

Figure 7.10

Good enemy design hinges on building them as different threat levels that can then be used throughout your game. In both *Doom Eternal* and *Ultrakill*, part of the escalation is taking a strong enemy that is introduced in a 1v1 fight (or 1v2 with the Cerberus enemy), and then using them in regular arenas.

## 7.2 Enemy and Encounter Design

Reflex-driven games are all about testing the player's mastery of the systems and mechanics, and to do that they need interesting and challenging enemies and level design. Enemy behavior and design have changed over the years as designers focused on different aspects and skill levels for their games.

Before we talk about encounters, you need to start thinking about the design of your enemies. Like weapons, each enemy type should have a purpose for its existence in your game (Figure 7.10). And just like weapons, there are no hard rules for what must be considered an enemy type. Series like *Serious Sam* keep the enemies very simple in terms of behavior but use overwhelming numbers to drive challenge. *Doom Eternal* on the other hand can make even a handful of enemies very dangerous thanks to the different rules and behavior they exhibit.

When I talk about reflex-driven enemy design, I like to use a tier system to categorize them:

- Tier 1 – Common grunts: Basic enemies who are only dangerous in high numbers.
- Tier 2 – General threats: Stronger enemies that the player needs to pay attention to.
- Tier 3 – Supporters: Enemies who empower the other ones or are dangerous if the player is not watching them.

- Tier 4 – Elites: Very powerful enemies who can destroy the player if they're not taken out fast; can also be considered on par with mini-bosses.
- Tier 5 – Bosses: One-off enemies who play by their own rules and will challenge the player.

Multiple enemies can exist within each tier, and the mix of tiers and enemies will determine the difficulty and complexity of your encounters. Fighting one elite in a wide area can be easy; fighting one elite, a group of supporters, and grunts in a small room could be a bit hard.

Just like the weapons in the game, the attributes of your enemies are also built on a similar list with a few differences:

- Health: The amount of damage needed to stop them.
- Damage: How much damage does an individual attack do to the player?
- Defense/resistances: Do certain types of damage (if applicable) do more or less to them?
- Weak spots: Are there parts of the enemy that will take increased damage?
- Attack speed: How fast is the actual attack of the enemy?
- Aggressiveness: Once active, how often will the enemy attack the player?
- Behavior: What will the enemy do while attacking?
    - Different behaviors based on enemy health and distance?
- Type of attack: Melee, projectile, or hitscan.
    - If it's a projectile: How does it travel, does it track the player and if so how strongly?
- Utility/special abilities: Will the enemy do something other than attacking?

It's important to note that every attribute mentioned above can be tweaked either while playtesting or be modified based on the difficulty level the player has chosen if you decide to have them. While health and damage are easily understood, how much of both you have on your enemies can affect the pacing and overall difficulty of your game in relation to the weapons you've designed. If the player only has a pistol that does 5 points of damage, and every enemy at the start has 80 health points, it's going to take a long time for each enemy to stop them. Likewise, if enemies can do 40 points of damage per hit to the player who only has 100 points of health at the start, that can be viewed as unfair. In reflex-driven games, it is often better to make higher difficulties more interesting to fight rather than just increasing the attributes of enemies. In *Doom Eternal*, the enemy base attributes are not adjusted going up the difficulty levels, instead their aggressiveness and behaviors are altered to be more threatening to the player (Figure 7.11).

With defenses and weak spots, this will be dependent on the kind of shooter you're making. It's common in games today that hitting an enemy on the head, or any glowing part, would do more damage to them. If you are going to feature different damage types and defenses around them, they need to be conveyed to

7. The Foundations of a Great Shooter

Figure 7.11

Action game design for years now have used their difficulty settings to create different experiences for the player. This could be having a higher chance of seeing elite enemies in action RPGs, to completely remixing levels and enemy placements in hack and slash games. The reason why this is better than just attribute raising is that it makes your game feel different difficulty by difficulty and gives players a reason to push higher if they want to.

the player, such as a different color on the impact, different color numbers, or the enemy reacting differently. If your game features enemy deformation, this can be used to allow the player to destroy parts of the enemy that are holding weapons/ is a weapon to weaken them. In games that procedurally generate enemies, one tactic is to build an enemy as a collection of individualized parts – so a generated "enemy" can have each limb be different that could affect its behavior/weaponry. However, if you are building a game around a campaign and fixed arena designs, this kind of generation may upset the balance of your game.

The attack speed is literally the rate of fire at which the enemy can attack the player. If the damage type is a projectile, the speed of the projectile in the air is also factored here. Another attribute that can radically impact the difficulty of your game -- the faster the enemy can attack, or their attacks can travel, the harder it will be for the player to react in time. In games that provide the player with the means to counter attacks, such as parrying them, attack speed will also relate to the difficulty to perform that maneuver. This is often the X factor that designers tweak when raising the difficulty of the game up instead of making enemies take longer to kill. The danger is that attack speed can change the threat level of any attack too far if it's not kept in check. In *Turbo Overkill*, on the highest difficulty, the projectile speed, along with damage, for enemy attacks is increased. To the point that small bullets that did 6.66 times the damage (on the first patch after 1.0) could travel across entire rooms before the player could even process that they're coming at them. For enemies with melee or close-ranged attacks, the attack speed is important when it comes to avoiding attacks at that range. If it's too fast, the enemy can almost instantly damage the player the second they get in range and the player won't be able to respond; if it's too slow, then the player is never in any danger of getting hit.

Aggressiveness relates to how often will an enemy go after the player and is a part of designing encounters and groups of enemies. If every enemy attacks at the same time, it may not be possible for the player to survive, much less dodge those incoming attacks. Part of the design of your game will be figuring out how many enemies should be actively engaging the player at one time. This was a major design consideration for both *Doom 2016* and *Doom Eternal*, and the developers came up with a system that would rank enemies by threat level and determine the order and severity of incoming attacks accordingly. The idea is that one enemy or some of the enemies will be considered "aggressive", they will chase the player and do their best to attack. The rest of the enemies may take potshots at the player if they are within range, but will hang back and not actively pursue them; with this constantly changing based on the player's position and which enemies are still alive. In many other shooters and action games, enemies that are off screen or not directly engaged with the player may hang back and not attack as aggressively compared to the ones the player is actively fighting. The more aggressive enemies are, the more the player will need to be able to react and deal with them accordingly. If an enemy has a very powerful attack, or does something that massively changes the encounter, they should not be set to perform that rapidly or before the player has a chance to try and response. For enemies that are supporters or have unique abilities, you need to be aware of how often they should be using their powers. In *Doom Eternal*, the arch-vile is slower to use its ability to summon enemies, but this is compensated for by the fact that it will summon multiple stronger enemies that can quickly escalate out of control no matter how good the player is if they managed to use it.

Another point about the aggressiveness of the enemy and something to consider with your design is whether the player's character has invincibility after being hit. In many action games, if the player takes a hit, they are granted a few milliseconds of invulnerability to let them try and get away due to how often the player is mobbed by enemies. Many shooters do not have this option, but it needs to be weighed by how aggressive enemies will attack the player. If the player walks into a room and is immediately attacked in five directions and takes full damage from each one before they can respond, there's not much someone can do to avoid that. Part of what makes push-forward combat good in this respect is that if the player can easily take damage, they can also easily recover as well.

The behavior of the enemies consists of what the enemy can do during combat – including attacking, defending, movement, and how they engage with the player. Enemies who have range attacks will often try to stay back or keep away from the player to get a shot off; while melee enemies will want to charge the player and get as close as possible. You will also need to decide if the enemy has any means of dodging or avoiding the player's attacks. This could be implicit by having the enemy move and be active, or explicitly if they will automatically try to dodge certain kinds of attacks. This is another way of providing a "defense" for an enemy that the player must keep note of. There is also the option to give them a literal defense move – blocking, putting up a shield, teleporting, etc. to avoid damage. Beware of giving the enemy a defense move that is constantly triggering such as teleporting or an invulnerability shield, as these can slow down the pace of a fight dramatically. Having certain weapons or skills that can counter defensive moves is also an option.

An advanced element of designing behaviors is coming up with different attack patterns or changing how the enemy behaves based on specific conditions. The marauders and shamblers in *Doom Eternal* and *Quake* respectively are examples of this – the enemy will change what they do based on the player's position to them. Having an enemy or a boss change their behavior when they lose a certain percentage of health is another option that has been done heavily in action games and soulslikes. Part of the evolution of shooter design mentioned in the last chapter has been borrowing cues from action design with how enemies behave. For example, on the high end, there is the V2 fight from *Ultrakill*. V2 is essentially a clone of the player, with the same movement abilities and weapons that the player has access to (Figure 7.12). Beating it relies on the player figuring out how to kill themselves and deal with the same attacks they've been using up until this point.

Figure 7.12

This is V2, before the madness of the fight begins. Due to its speed and movement, trying to get a good action shot to show just how hard it is to fight it proved to be too difficult for me.

One other consideration regarding behavior is with the use of friendly fire. A mainstay of the *Doom* series and boomer shooters was that enemies could hurt each other with their shots. It was possible through careful movement to bait an enemy to hit another one which would cause them to focus on each other rather than the player. Many expert *Doom* mods encourage this tactic by filling rooms with so many enemies that it wouldn't be possible given the ammo restraints for the player to kill them all. This is not a required element in your game but could give it more flavor.

Before we talk about special abilities for enemies, you must think about the kind of attacks you want to give your enemies. The strength of the attack itself should be proportional to the tier it's on. Just like the player's weapons, you'll need to decide the kind of attack enemies can do, and enemies can certainly have multiple attacks.

Let's talk about the three base categories of damage – melee, projectile, and hitscan. Melee attacks mean that the enemy must get close to the player to use them. These attacks are often designed to be higher damage than the lower-ranged attacks to make these a greater threat and punish unaware players who let them reach them. Tracking also relates to melee attacks and needs to be balanced with the player's own defensive measures. Games like *Doom Eternal* and *Ultrakill* will often give melee enemies tracking with their attack combos, as the player has a defensive dash they can use to get out of the way. If the player's only way of avoiding damage is to run, but enemies attack and track so fast in melee that the player literally can't get out of the way, this will be viewed as an imbalanced design.

Projectiles are often the common attack as the player can actively dodge them either with a defensive move or by simply getting out of the way. Projectiles can come in all varieties and shapes and sizes. In *Returnal*, the projectile design was meant to emulate the same style of over-the-top patterns seen in bullet hell games, and that could only have worked by the fact that the player had a defensive move available. The speed and intensity of projectiles can also factor into the tiers of enemies. In *Ultrakill*, many enemies have fast-moving projectiles that do small to medium damage, but there's also the "black hole" attack – a slow-moving tracking ball that if the player runs into it, their health is automatically reduced to 1 and can't heal out of it for a few seconds.

Hitscan attacks on enemies is trickier than they are for the player. Since the player is always going to be outgunned in these games, unless they can use cover or some kind of defensive move to go in and out of combat, there is no way to directly engage with the enemies without taking damage from hitscan attacks. What makes *Blood* so frustrating to play is that the player is always overwhelmed with enemies who have hitscans. Unless they use indirect weapons like bombs or explosive attacks to quickly kill them, their health will be reduced fast. While *Doom* also had hitscan basic enemies, their shots did not do a lot of damage, and the enemy behavior is more erratic and not as constant with attacking.

Having hitscan enemy attacks will test your ability as a level designer to provide the player with fair challenges (Figure 7.13). An encounter in a large room with no cover against multiple hitscan enemies can be an imbalance experience.

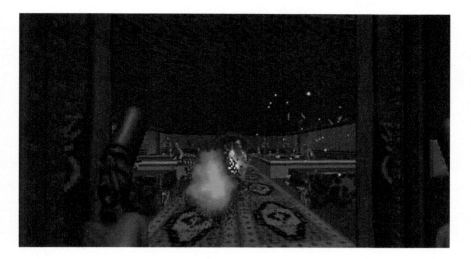

Figure 7.13

*Blood* was infamous for its high difficulty, and a lot of that comes from the waves of hitscan enemies in rooms with little to no cover. As part of the talk about level design in the next section, this room here can only safely be done by using the previous room to move away from the open door as the sole means of avoiding the hitscan.

If you're going to design elite enemies with hitscans, there must be a way for the player to mitigate or avoid those attacks. Returning to *Quake* with the shamblers, in the remaster that was released in 2023, one of the hardest rooms comes near the end of the game's added expansion – the player is in a circular area against two shamblers at the same time. With how they are spaced, there's no way to get into cover that will stop both from targeting the player. This creates the challenge of having to dodge behind cover, when need be, deal with the melee enemies in the arena, and try to stay close enough to the shamblers to get them to use their melee attack rather than their hitscan.

Since there's no way to dodge a hitscan besides using cover, or a defensive move if you build it into your game, you can also have additional rules for how those attacks work to give the player a chance to stop them from being used. The Arch-viles in *Doom 2* always take a few seconds once they start targeting the player before the attack goes off. This is indicated by a fire effect that is shown on screen, and if the player can get out of the sight of the Arch-vile in time, the attack will be canceled. *Ultrakill* features sniper-class enemies as well but provide the player with different options for how to deal with them. Knocking them in the air prevents them from attacking, electrical attacks short circuit their aim, and they can be heavy punched out of their firing stance. And if those don't work, skilled players can time their dodge to avoid the shot. However, as the game goes on, arenas get larger and it becomes harder to focus on snipers while avoiding everything else coming the player's way.

When designing enemies as specific threats against the player, you want to pair this with the weapons that you came up with, and why this chapter started with weapon design first. If all the player's weapons are single-shot, slow-firing attacks, creating enemies that attack quickly in groups will be a challenge. What you don't want is to design enemies and encounters that don't fit within the roles and strength of the player's current weapon lineup. If a level only has close-ranged weapons in it like shotguns or sub machine guns (SMGs), building an entire section where enemy snipers are attacking from far range with no cover can feel like the designer is cheating the player. The more variety of weapons the player can use, the more interesting encounters you can build the game around. This is why games with unique weapons have an edge with their encounters, as the designer can build them fully around all the techniques and options they have given the player.

When creating enemies that have unique ways of dealing with them or they play by different rules compared to the other enemies, you need to be more attentive to how they are positioned in an encounter. An enemy who makes all the other enemies in the area stronger is obviously a huge threat that should be taken out fast, but if you hide that enemy behind walls of other enemies, it becomes a lot harder. The trick about supporter-type enemies is that it doesn't take a lot of them to greatly increase the difficulty of an encounter. In *Ultrakill*, there is an enemy known as a "virtue" who stay in one area and attack by summoning a beam of light directly over the player. If the player doesn't kill one after a few seconds, they will glow red and start actively tracking the player better with their beams. One kind of placement that is used a lot is to put one virtue on one end of the arena, and another on the complete opposite side with enemies in the middle. Many of *Doom Eternal's* advanced arenas will place down a "totem" that while it is active, every enemy is immortal, attacks faster, and does more damage. When they appear, the player's only recourse is to stop fighting the enemy and track down the totem before they are overwhelmed.

As you're thinking about enemy abilities and their roles in your game, look at what you gave the player and the tactics they have available, and see if you can design enemy abilities meant to counter them to some extent. Let's say as an example that your game features a powerful rocket launcher that can destroy most enemies with ease without any further thought from the player. Instead of making the weapon weaker, you could put in an enemy that creates a shield that reflects all projectile-based weapons – including rockets – back at the player. When this enemy is in an encounter, the player must either use other kinds of attacks or try and kill them first to take them out of the equation. This is how supporter-class enemies can be the most dangerous threats if they can stop the player from using their best tactics or force them out of their comfort zone. An encounter with nothing but supporter enemies would be easy, as the support-ers don't do enough on their own to be a threat but surround them with other enemies, and suddenly that encounter can get very difficult and hectic fast.

Speaking of encounters, it's time to talk a little more about them. An encoun-ter or arena is when the player is put into an area and they are not allowed to leave until either enough time has passed that the exit opens, or they have killed

Figure 7.14

Arenas can be large or small, easy or difficult, but they are a required part of building a shooter, as this is where the player is going to be tested the most by the enemy designs and enemy placement in your game.

every enemy. Some games may require the player to hit multiple switches, which can prove difficult when they are surrounded by enemies (Figure 7.14). These are the big moments in your level and are meant to be a test not only of your enemy designs, but the level as well. For modern shooters, arenas are often placed where there is a checkpoint before and after one so that the player is not wasting time repeating areas they've already done.

When setting up the encounter, there are several event triggers that designers have used. The first and most popular is simply walking into the room, the door locks, and enemies begin appearing. If you want the player to be in a specific position before the fight starts, you could set up an important item that acts as bait – the player needs a key or hit a switch in the room, they do it, and then all heck breaks loose. Another popular tactic is to fill the hardest arenas full of weapons, ammo, healing; anything to completely resupply the player before they unleash the enemies.

Encounters can be designed either as one huge battle where every enemy spawns at once, or as a set of waves. A wave trigger can either be killing a specific enemy, activating something in the arena, or wiping out the existing wave. One style that I haven't seen before until *Ultrakill,* but I'm sure has been used by other games by now, is the idea of a cascading wave – the player enters a big room, and instead of spawning enemies all around them, they trigger individual groups at select trigger points in the area. Instead of having one giant wave, the player triggers micro-waves until the entire room is cleared. You can also design encounters to be on a timer – every X seconds, another wave spawns in or part of the environment changes. This rewards players who are fast enough to clear out enemies but will punish someone for taking too long by having waves on top of waves attack them.

Since part of encounter design includes your level design, I will be talking more about the environment itself in the next section. For the enemies, the frequency, types, and number of waves will all factor into the difficulty of your encounters. If you're going to introduce a brand-new enemy, it is typically considered fair to the player to have them be the only enemy in an encounter or wave to let the player learn how the enemy behavior before integrating it into the regular routine. The best designers will not only create unique and interesting levels, but will design every arena as a one-off, and this is why level design is such an important aspect of your enemies.

For a rough idea of building the style of your encounters, you should treat each encounter as a level within the level: what are you trying to test the player on, how does it differ from the other encounters, do you want to do something special (Figure 7.15)? Encounter design encompasses a lot of different ways of building combat encounters. Some designers treat an encounter as a big test of the player's abilities – throwing huge numbers of diverse enemies at the player. For most of the expert-aimed *Doom* mods, expect to fight many more times of enemies in a level compared to anything from the original games.

Another way to view encounters is to treat them as combat puzzles – the player must deal with a specific threat or threats; how do they use the environment and their tools to win or even the odds? This is where having enemies that are designed around specific abilities or rules of engagement can lead to unique fights that test the player beyond just using more guns. A good example in the advanced side would be the later chapters in *Ultrakill*, and how they mix new and old enemies in new levels to create challenges that feel different than anything else that came before it.

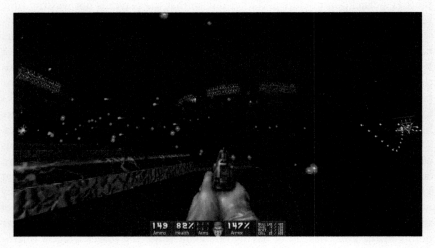

Figure 7.15

In this screenshot from Eviternity 2, the player is put into a series of unique arenas in a later level. Here, the player must dodge projectiles coming from all around them until a specific time has passed.

7. The Foundations of a Great Shooter

For examples of both the gauntlet and the puzzle style, you can examine the expansions for *Doom Eternal* titled The Ancient Gods Parts 1 and 2. Part 1 features some of the hardest arenas in the entire game outside of the master level challenges. Arenas are filled with more enemies, have more waves, and the environmental hazards have been cranked up to make things harder. In Part 2, the difficulty gets dialed down in favor of making more varied areas and arenas. The pacing of your encounters is a major aspect that will affect the overall difficulty of your game. The more waves, and harder waves, in a single encounter will add to the challenge. One of the worst feelings in these games is when the player is on the final wave and gets killed forcing them to restart the entire encounter.

To sum things up, encounter and enemy design will determine the overall difficulty of your game. It is very easy to make encounters too easy or too hard depending on the mechanics in your game, the weapon design, and the level design (Figure 7.16). Just like with platformers, many designers will have hidden battles or bonus stages that push the design and difficulty far higher than the base content. Part of the attraction of reflex-driven design is the very act of pushing the player's skill level higher and higher, and to do that there must be adequate challenge and a reason to explore the game's systems in full. The master levels I mentioned in *Doom Eternal* are all about pushing each encounter as far as it can go and testing the player's mastery of all the mechanics in the game. *Ultrakill*

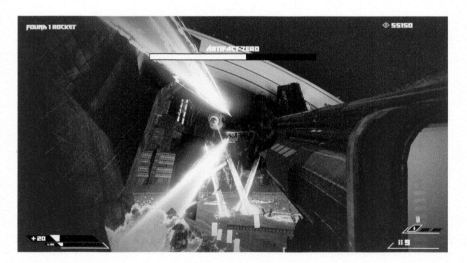

Figure 7.16

This section is very hard (no pun intended) to get good screenshots for that convey what I'm talking about, as a still image of bullets, enemies, etc., doesn't really show why something is too easy or too hard. In this scene from *Turbo Overkill*, this is the act 1 boss on the higher difficulty and it was a huge pain to fight, not because of the boss and its patterns, but the infinitely spawning enemies with their increased attack and projectile speed.

features several experts-only stages that can only be accessed by beating the other levels in an act with the highest ranking. If you're trying to build a shooter that is approachable for everyone, it's better to segment content that is meant for experts from people who aren't ready or aren't interested in it.

What makes reflex-driven design so challenging and diverse is that there are many ways of using the same enemies, the same hazards, and mixing them up to provide different degrees of challenges. Putting the player in a small room with 40 cyber demons in *Doom* would be hard, but it wouldn't be interesting to fight. Having them set up as turrets that are attacking the player as they try to reach switches or items could be a unique section. As a lesson from platformers, just constantly escalating the difficulty curve of your levels will eventually cause people to stop playing who can't keep up. Just as a good level needs pacing and time to wind down, so should your encounters in a level. If there's one encounter that would be rated a 10/10 in difficulty, you don't want to follow that up with another 10/10 or 11/10. The final encounter on a stage should be the most interesting and unique one to end on a high note. The more ways you can challenge the player to make use of their full arsenal, the more your shooting and gameplay will stand out.

For boss encounters, if you are building your game around them, this entails creating a unique enemy, with unique behavior, all taking place in a unique environment that fits the boss fight. For reflex-driven games, bosses can come in two forms – an actual fight or a puzzle. An actual fight is quite simply the player having to fight a boss with all the tools and tactics they have available (Figure 7.17).

Figure 7.17

The reason why *Ultrakill* is brought up so much in this section and chapter is that it features a lot of design elements that aren't normally seen in shooters, and this on full display with the boss fights. The bosses in this game are not the kind we typically see from an FPS, but from an action game, and this is from their attacks, patterns, and the use or design of the arena that you will fight them in.

A puzzle fight is when the player must defeat an enemy using unconventional methods that aren't always about just shooting them.

Boss design is about creating an enemy whose behavior and tactics outrank any common enemy in your game. Due to their challenge, many games will either checkpoint the player before any boss so that they don't have to repeat the stage, or the boss fight is the entire stage and once defeated, the player moves on. Boss design in shooters has always been a weak part of the fps genre, as many games just feature a larger enemy who shoots a little more and has far more health. *Ultrakill*, with its embrace of action design and push-forward combat, does feature some of the most dynamic and interesting bosses in an FPS to date. However, boss design, like your enemies, must always be balanced based on the weapons and abilities you provide the player. To make boss fights easier, an option seen in shooters and action games has been to have checkpoints between the major phases of a fight to cut down on the amount of time lost and repeating content once the player gets through it.

Good enemy design is something that has existed since the very beginning of the genre, but its importance has only grown as designers have gotten more creative with the tools and gunplay of their games. Just as it must be exciting to shoot a gun in your game, it needs to be exciting to shoot it *at something*. And just like your gunplay, there is an unlimited number of ways to design enemies, and the very best shooters will fully capitalize on that to create a unique roster of foes for the player to go up against.

## 7.3 The Different Philosophies of Level Design

The third piece of the equation for making an attractive shooter is the level design. To clarify, level design is creating the layouts, enemy placements, and set pieces that the player will go through in each stage or area. Environmental design represents the aesthetics of the level – where does it take place and what does it look like.

Level design has changed a lot over the years for shooters, and you'll need to decide early on what kind of level design, or designs, you want to feature in your game. There are also differences between designing for single and multiplayer and I'll talk more about those differences in Section 8.4.

As I've said over the previous sections, the weapon and enemy designs in your game will dictate the foundation of your levels. If your game is focusing on being more horror-minded and have tense encounters with enemies in close range, then you want to use a lot of enclosed areas where the player will have blind spots. For games focused on cover shooting and trying to circle around the enemy, then wide-open maps with cover will be needed. If the mood and pacing of your game changes from level to level, so should the level design change. A good example of this would be the evolution of levels in *Dusk* (Figure 7.18). As discussed, each act features different environments and styles of levels, so that no two levels feel the same way to play. For this book focusing on the overall shooter genre, I'm not going to be detailing the structure of every style, as there are books out there that focus exclusively on them.

Figure 7.18

Level design today means more than just creating hard arenas or maze-like environments, but having a sense of place that feels unique and distinctive from everything else in your game. This is something you can see from *Dusk* – the player is doing the same thing every level – shooting enemies, but where they're doing it is completely different.

Let's start at the high level (no pun intended) and there are two ways to test the player – exploration and puzzles, or gauntlets of fighting. For shooters that are about exploring the world and are more story-driven, they may have sections and levels exclusively around solving a puzzle or getting through an area that is not about fighting. *Half-Life* 1 and 2 featured areas like that; there may not even be a point in the area where the player needs to use their weapon.

When I say the word "puzzles," this is not the same as talking about puzzle design in an adventure game, although some designers can put in areas built on puzzle logic to do something different. The most common wall the player runs into when exploring is that there is a door they need to open to keep going, but they need to find the key. Said key could be anywhere in the level and will often be the trigger event to spawn or release enemies to fight the player. *Half-Life 2* was one of the few shooters to feature actual puzzles using the physics of the world for the player to figure out how to get past a section.

Another popular use of puzzle design is creating a level that is about finding the way around. The corridors could be maze-like, the player must teleport through different areas, and other examples. In these levels, combat is secondary to the act of finding the way to the exit. Some designers use puzzles as the gate for harder or original content, such as having bonus stages hidden in some levels.

A holdover of boomer shooter design as discussed was maze-like levels where there wasn't a focus on creating an actual place, but just hallways and rooms for the player to fight in. There is no attempt at creating a realistic environment or one that would make sense within the world. On the spectrum between focusing on environmental and level design, this would be 100% on the level design side. While this can work if the focus is on combat and only combat, the moment you try to add puzzles and exploration, it can become a confusing nightmare for the player to figure out where to go.

Some of you reading this may be thinking "what about designing a fictional world, how does level design work then?" Unless you are trying to recreate a real-world area or realistic setting in your game, the goal isn't to go for 100% realism, but that the level and environment make sense within the setting and world of the game (Figure 7.19). If the player is exploring a butcher shop, there should be freezing rooms for the meat, display cases for product and so on. I'm going to assume that everyone reading this has never been aboard an alien spaceship and have had to find their way off an alien world. Would a ship have 15 identical office spaces, 600 closets that all look alike, and the bridge door only opens by finding 10 multicolor keys that have been placed in corners all over the ship?

Many games, shooters notwithstanding, will "hang a lantern" on these points or try to ground them within the setting. With the bridge door, maybe the captain went crazy and paranoid and purposely made the door hard to open to keep people away. Creating a sense of place through the architecture of your level is very hard to do, and why level designers have studied blueprints, architecture,

Figure 7.19

Replaying the original *Halos* and the series does jump between human, covenant, and outdoor sections quite a bit. But it does suffer when it comes to indoor environments and repeating room designs and architecture to the point where some of the minor rooms just look like they're being copied and pasted from one area to the next.

and floor plans of building to get an idea of how rooms are set up and spaced and using that to guide people around.

For modern games today, part of designing an attractive level is having the world, the story, and the level design all be in sync. The environmental design becomes the basis for the levels, and the level design makes sense within the environment. For an example of this, I want to talk about *Left 4 Dead*. Each level in the campaign is meant to show the progress of the survivors going from the start of the campaign to the escape at the end. In each level, the level design draws from trying to present a realistic-looking area as a challenge within the logic of the world itself. In the No Mercy campaign, the survivors are trying to reach the helipad on top of Mercy Hospital. In the fourth level of the campaign, it is built entirely within the hospital itself and the path is like this:

1. The players arrive at the front desk reception and start climbing up floors, with enemy groups already placed along with the special infected.
2. They reach the ICU and must call the elevator to go to the roof and trigger a horde of enemies.
3. The elevator takes them to a construction area where there are open walls all around them.
4. The level ends with them reaching a planning room for the construction with the path leading to the helipad for the final level.

Part of good level and environmental design is using the environment itself as a guide for the player. Simple tricks like having a light over the door the player needs to go through, signs in an office building pointing to various services, and many others provide the player with information they need without having to directly tell them to "go here" (Figure 7.20). Many action-adventure games will literally stop the game every time the player pulls a level or hits a button to show them what changed. Depending on the game, this can either be too apparent, or necessary depending on the size and structure of your level. As part of the UX of games today, if your levels are maze-like or confusing, you do want to provide the player with something that can direct them or provide them with a general direction as to where to go. The most explicit example would be a quest or objective pointer that shows the player the exact direction to the next required task.

When you are thinking about your level, you want to approach the level from the question of: what should this level be about? As I talked about in platforming design, every level has a mission statement or focus to it. That focus should drive the environmental design, the shape of the level, and what you want the player to face in it. It's always better to create a focused level around one central theme, rather than try to fit two or more into one. Level length is a nebulous point that is going to depend on the gameplay and style you are aiming for. Many arcade and boomer shooters have levels that could be finished within minutes, or seconds if the player speed runs through them. For grounded shooters or those that are

Figure 7.20

When environmental design lines up with your level, it can make it far easier for someone to navigate. Here's a subtle example from *Left 4 Dead* – the light is being shown on the tunnel that is the correct way, while the dead end is left dark to indicate that the player should not go down that route.

trying to be more cinematic, a single level could take 10–30 minutes. If you can keep creating unique challenges and situations within the scope of your central theme, then you can get away with having large levels, with one exception.

If you are building your game around skill mastery and ranking the player on how well they play, long levels can become a detriment. The reason is that the more level there is to master, the harder and more painful it becomes to do everything perfectly, not just one individual section. Returning to *Doom Eternal*, the master levels can easily take an hour or more to play due to their extreme difficulty. What keeps them out of the reach for more people is the time commitment to dedicate to one level of the game, compounded by the fact that you cannot save and return to the level; it must all be completed in one go. Conversely, getting the highest rank in *Ultrakill* requires master play through a level, but the levels themselves average 3–5 minutes at length through the early content and five to eight for the later levels. As a point about good level design, the more extreme the challenge you are putting on the player, the shorter the level should be to compensate. While there will be an audience of people who want that incredibly difficult 2-hour-long level in your game, they will always be in the minority compared to the rest of your consumer base.

An important balancing consideration you need to take note of when designing a boomer shooter or arcade shooter is the placement of supplies. As mentioned already, every level should have enough health items, weapons, and ammo, to deal with all the enemies in it, and you can have a bonus challenge to play each stage starting with the default weapon, or dying removes the player's inventory. If you are building a grounded shooter or one where the weapons are generic among the player and the enemies, you still need to make sure that the player is finding enough ammo to be able to engage. And remember, there should always be more supplies than necessary to beat a level, because most players are not going to be landing every shot and avoiding every incoming source of damage. Push-forward combat is an exception when it comes to requiring supplies in the level, and I will return to it in section 8.6.

It's time to talk about how encounters and enemy placement factor into your level design. The placement of your enemies will dictate the flow of your level. As a point about the difference between old and modern shooting, arcade and older shooters will have enemies set up wandering around the level along with those that appear during encounters. For modern shooters, as I mentioned earlier, they will segment their level design around specific points – this section is a cutscene, this section is all about platforming, etc. In this case, while there may be one or two enemies outside of encounters, the real fighting will always occur in an arena.

Where the player is going to fight enemies is one of the hardest aspects of level design, due to having to create something that allows both the players and the enemies to adequately fight one another. An example of what not to do goes back to the 90s era of shooting and the infamous level "sniper town" or Sniper's Last Stand in *Medal of Honor*. The entire level is framed around the player exploring a town with snipers hidden all over the place. Enemy snipers in shooters will always do a lot of damage, and the goal is to hit them before they can get a bead on the player. But in a city where the enemies blend in, the entire level is a long slog with the player inching around trying to spot the snipers.

There are several other don'ts, or weaker forms of level design in shootings to keep note of. The first is an empty area. *Serious Sam*'s arenas were mostly large empty areas with no cover and enemies would spawn all around them (Figure 7.21). The problem is that this turns every arena into pretty much the same arena; yes, different enemies will require the player to respond differently, but there is just no level design present or anything within the space that the player can use. This kind of shooting can get repetitive, especially if the gunplay is boring as well. If you have enemies with tracking projectiles, empty rooms also make it almost impossible to dodge their projectiles without getting lucky and having them hit one of the other enemies.

The next weaker example is a plain corridor – a long room with enemies at one end and the player at the other and nothing else in the corridor. While corridors are a necessity to connect rooms and you can fight a few enemies in them, building encounters around them greatly reduces the player's ability to maneuver and what you can do with them. An extension of this, and why arenas typically lock the player in them, is exploiting doors. When there is a door that connects a corridor to a room, the player can open the door, fire a few shots, go back into the corridor where the enemies aren't at, and repeat until the major threats are gone. While this may be boring, never underestimate a player's willingness to optimize their

Figure 7.21

A major weakness of the *Serious Sam* games is in their arena designs or lack thereof. Part of this is due to the limited AI of the enemies who are mostly those that charge the player. Here, the challenge is about figuring out how to survive against overwhelming numbers, but the arenas and their level design aren't really remembered by the player.

play in such a way that they end up ruining the experience for them. Tight spaces can lead to challenging arenas, as even just one dangerous enemy can be enough to test a player when they don't have the luxury of creating space between them. If you're going to have encounters in corridors, make sure that the player has room to maneuver, something else going on in the corridor, or keep them quick.

If an empty area is bad, then filling a spot with "stuff" should be good, right (Figure 7.22)? The point of level and encounter design is that the shape and structure of the level must push the player to fight. An infamous example of cover shooters was entering a large room with two chest-high walls on either side of the area. The second the arena starts, the player gets behind one wall, the enemies get behind the other, and neither group will move until the other is defeated. In this situation, the arena by its design doesn't give the player any reason to move, to think of the best place to go, it's all been decided for them.

Good level and arena design is about giving the player an entire space to play around in. They shouldn't just stand in one corner and not move out of there. If your game is built around movement tech, the player should be using them to get out of trouble, get into a spot to fight the enemies, anything that isn't just standing on one spot. And on that point, the more ways the player can actively move around, that must be factored into your arena design in the form of having platforms, walls to jump off, or anything else that lets them control the space around them. You can

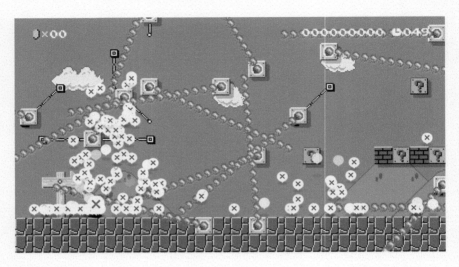

Figure 7.22

The *Super Mario Maker* series by Nintendo has given everyone the license to make levels however they want, and that includes a huge variety of troll levels, frustrating levels, and levels that someone just filled with everything and then posted them online. While these can work in a free or rage game, if you are trying to build levels for a commercial release, you should not follow their examples.

also use the enemy design to persuade them to keep moving – if the player hides in a corner, the enemy could throw a grenade in to flush them out. When the level design, enemies, and weapons are all working together, the player will be engaging with the enemies using their weapons and the level design itself to aid them.

*Shadow Warrior 3* built their arenas on this very notion of using the environment to even the odds. Every arena had death traps and hazards, not for the player, but for the enemies. Corralling enemies around a trap allowed skillful players to quickly deal with huge groups or stronger enemies far quicker than just using their weapons.

As you are thinking about your arenas and encounters, the shape of the area has a monumental impact on the difficulty and pacing you want to convey. As I said, having one fewer or more enemy in a room can completely change the strategy for that arena fight. In *Doom Eternal*, on one of the master levels, a hallway that originally was just there to provide a brief respite from combat fills with sticky goo that prevents jumping and dashing, and then has the player fight two higher-class enemies one right after another. The encounter itself is over in seconds, as either the player quickly kills them, or they will quickly kill the player. This encounter is short and meant to catch an unassuming player off guard but is overall not that hard. Shortly later, the player is put into a wide-open area with pinky demons, cacodemons, and multiple waves of other enemies that is a far harder fight despite the room to maneuver.

7. The Foundations of a Great Shooter

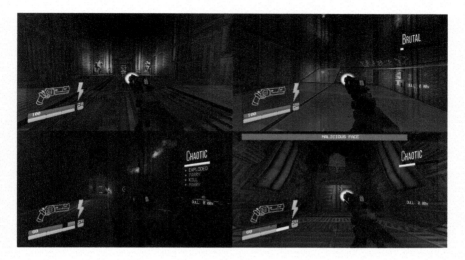

Figure 7.23

Here are some screenshots from the first level of *Ultrakill* showing different parts of the level. The level's goal as a tutorial to the base concepts works and it can feel weird going back to it after the player has unlocked more weapons and understands more of the tech and play it with just the starting weapon.

Balancing an area, master levels notwithstanding, requires you to fully understand what your enemies and the player can do in any given room. One hitscan enemy in an open area can be a nightmare to fight; put that same enemy in a room with a lot of cover and the fight becomes a cakewalk. This is why you need to approach your level design and your arenas as part of the same whole (Figure 7.23). In games that feature a lot of advanced tech and movement, the difficulty of an encounter can fluctuate between players who know how to use the expert tricks vs. those that don't. To demonstrate, I'm going to run through the encounters of the first level of *Ultrakill*:

1. The player is in a small square room and fights two waves of filth enemies.
2. Two groups of filth in a hallway.
3. One group of filth in a room with destructible floors.
4. Large room with many destructible floors in it and a large group of filth.
5. First official arena with groups of filth and strays.
6. Hallway with strays and filth used to teach parrying.
7. Large room with strays and filth that focuses on moving around and jumping.
8. Narrow bridge with a death trap below with husks on the bridge and filth on the side of the walls meant to either practice parrying or quickly leap over and kill them.
9. A fight with the malicious face enemy.

At this point, players have access to two weapons: the starting pistol and punching. Only three enemy types are introduced in this level, one melee, one range, and one stronger enemy, and it also does double duty to give the player a tutorial on the basic mechanics. Using levels and arenas as tutorials is another factor to consider. The "boss" at the end of the first level is just another enemy type that gets folded into basic encounters in later levels; the same goes for the final fight of the opening act of the game. For someone brand new to *Ultrakill*, these fights can be hard, but returning to the areas later for the highest rank with more weapons, and any player should be able to clear the prequel act easily.

When building the overall shape of your arenas, you want to encourage the player to move around or go to specific points in it for different reasons. The *Shadow Warrior 3* example mentioned further up is an example of this, and any games that reward the player for fighting stylishly using the environment or different abilities. What you want to avoid with your level design and arenas is that there is exactly "one" place that the player should stay for the entire arena. This can be due to the enemy behavior – if every enemy is melee and there is a platform up high, the player could just stand up there and fight them one at a time. Another example is that the enemies are so dangerous that the only safe measure to fight them is to hide behind a corner and peak out and shoot them once and retreat.

Here's a point about level design, while the original *Dooms* are iconic as shooters, they also feature some of the weaker level designs; not because the game was bad or the designers didn't know any better, but by the limitations of the gameplay and what the player could do. It wouldn't be until the modding scene when other creators would go much further and build encounters designed to capitalize on *Doom*'s mechanics and enemy design far more than the base games. What makes a level become iconic in a shooter is providing a unique and memorable challenge that "forces" the player to engage with the mechanics. I put force in quotation because it's easy to think of that word as being a negative, but again, if the player is given the option to play the game the safest and most boring way possible, a lot of people are going to choose that. Great games, not just shooters, are all about exploring what is possible within the mechanics and scope of the design. The worst thing you can strive for with your game is just making something boring that won't hold the player's attention. If every level is the same, people will not stay around for that one level many hours in where you did innovate.

And repetitive design also means designing levels that are too long or repeat content. If the first encounter in a level is three machine gun enemies and two shotgunners, and then the next encounter is the same, or it's two machine gun enemies and three shotgunners, that's also going to bore players. Remember, how enemies are set up in an area is just as important as which enemies are there. Long-ranged enemies set up where the player can run up and kill them fast is a different story compared to putting them on high-up ledges that require the player to get to them first. The rate that you introduce new enemies or higher-class enemies into your levels will affect the difficulty curve of your

Figure 7.24

Don't treat numbers for the sake of numbers as the sole metric for the quality of an arena, and by extension, the entire level. You can have fantastic set pieces with hundreds of enemies at once in a huge area, or a few enemies in a small and detailed room. And you can see this entire spectrum on display with the many mods built for *Doom 1* and *2*.

game. For someone building an expert-level mod for *Doom*, they may have cyber demons and arch-viles on their first map. Remember this point – the number of enemies in a level in no way has an impact on the quality or difficulty of the level (Figure 7.24). Figuring out different ways to place enemies or designing unique arenas is a great way to get more value out of your enemies and the player's weapons, and this also goes with multiplayer maps that will be discussed in the next chapter.

Part of the form of progression that I will talk about in the next chapter is how you must design your levels around the tools and options currently available to the player. That also means not purposely designing encounters that go against the rules of your game or how your weapons behave. The sniper town example I mentioned earlier would fit here, and any time you create an encounter that explicitly contradicts your gameplay. As an example, if you design an enemy that is incredibly tough and frustrating to fight unless you use the ice gun to slow them down, don't create an arena where you remove the ice gun and have them fight nothing but those enemies without giving the player some other means of dealing with them. As new weapons are unlocked or made available to the player, the complexity of your encounters should grow to match.

Complexity and challenge are good to a point, but you always want to avoid constant escalation where the difficulty curve always goes up from arena-to-arena and level-by-level. Even in mods and games that are meant to be on the difficult

Figure 7.25

Being able to reuse enemies in new and interesting ways is the hallmark of a good level designer. Whether you are building an easy level, nightmarishly difficult, a weird level, or anything else. This is an image from the first level of *Sigil 2*, a *Doom* mod created by John Romero and released for the 20 anniversary of *Doom* and every level is on the difficult side if you play on the higher settings.

side, there must be a flow to your levels and game. If one arena in a level is considered the hardest, you don't want the very next one to be equally or even harder; likewise, if a level ends with a difficult fight, the very next level shouldn't start with an equally hard fight. A contact of mine, Pattrick Holleman who writes the "Reverse Design" series talked about this in the form of the Nishikado motion named after Tomohiro Nishikado who created *Space Invaders*. Level should get progressively harder and more interesting, but the start of a new level should be easier than the end of the previous one.

A point I brought up with designing platformers is that any enemy or obstacle in your game can be designed around various difficulties and complexity of fighting them. In the best shooters, these games don't just keep adding new enemy types every level, but instead will design original encounters that put said enemies in new configurations to test the player (Figure 7.25). You are going to be limited by the design of your game in terms of how you can keep changing things around each level, but even basic enemies can be given a new light based on how they are put into the environment.

Here's a hypothetical example of an easy, medium, expert, and master arena using nothing but imps from the original *Doom*:

- Easy: The player is in a room with one imp, with enough room to dodge any projectiles and no cover.

- Medium: The player is in a large room with six imps set up on pillars with boxes available for cover.
- Expert: The player enters a room with narrow ledges in a rectangle shape suspended over a lava pit. Four imps spawn on different corners that the player must kill while staying on the ledges.
- Master: A long tunnel-like section with stairs set up at an angle connecting to various square tiles. There are sliding walls that will knock the player into the lava below. Imps are set up in groups of three along the walls at an angle where they can fire on the player, but the player can't hit them. They must reach the end of the room to hit a switch that will open up the walls enabling them to hit the imps. However, several stairs and all the square tiles will go into the lava, requiring the player to run fast enough to "jump" over gaps to make it out of the room.

One aspect I haven't touched on yet is the inclusion of secrets. Many boomer shooters and arcade shooters will have hidden sections in their level. These could be accessed by making a tricky jump, finding a fake wall, or doing some random task. Secrets can hide everything from bonus resources, access to stronger weapons earlier, new stages, new arenas, or anything else that comes to your mind. They are not required to be in your game but is another way of adding more content and rewards for players to uncover.

Another part of level design and your overall game that hasn't been discussed yet is having power ups within the level itself. This is different from giving the player unique abilities they can use at any time, but having one-time pickups that give the player something special for a specific duration. Here is a quick list of power ups from the original *Dooms,* not counting only health or armor pickups:

- Auto map: Reveals the entire map and any secrets for the one level.
- Berserk: Heals the player to 100 health and increases the strength of punches for a set period of time.
- Invincibility: Makes the player immune to all sources of damage for a limited time.
- Invisibility: Reduces the enemy's ability to spot the player when they are doing anything other than shooting.
- Mega sphere: Fills up health and armor to 200 points while providing the benefits of damage reduction from a mega armor.
- Night vision goggles: Lights up the player's vision allowing them to see everything easier.
- Radiation suit: Enables the player to go into acid and lava pools without taking any damage.
- Soul sphere: Gives the player 100 points of health and it can heal them for over their maximum health to a total of 200 points.

Power ups can greatly change the dynamic of an encounter and overall difficulty of a stage. Their inclusion in your game and within your levels is entirely up to you.

Meshing story and level design for most shooters is not the primary draw of a shooter, but the ones who can not only build an impressive game but tie a story that makes sense to those levels, is a sign of an expert designer and can add value to your game. Even within the *Doom* modding scene and building new content for it, the creators who go above and beyond with their environmental and level designs are the ones that stand out each year. Just like with any genre today, the bar has been raised in terms of quality and what people want out of their games.

## 7.4 Putting It All Together

Originally, this chapter and the next one were combined, but as I thought about shooter design and what weapon, enemy, and level design mean to a shooter, it was important to separate them. The shooter genre, much like with platformers or any other reflex-driven design, is created as a sum of its parts. Your goal isn't to just get one element right, but all three, and that is the hardest aspect of creating a shooter.

It's also why there is difficulty in talking about what makes a great shooter. Everything once again begins and ends with your gunplay – if the player isn't excited to fight in your game, then your game is going to fail. After that, you need to create enemies that are going to test the player and your weapon design level by level, and then you need to create interesting levels that fit everything in.

I've been comparing the shooter genre to platformers a lot in this chapter, and there's good reason for it. Both genres from the outside look easy to build; one could assume that just watching footage of a platformer or a shooter is enough to then go and design one (Figure 7.26). However, if you can't grasp why using the super shotgun in *Doom 2* is great, or how *Doom 2016* and *Doom Eternal* are fundamentally different games despite being about shooting, then you are not going to be able to create something new.

With the renaissance of boomer shooters following the success of *Dusk*, just like every other genre and gold rush period, there were countless shooters released or developed trying to become the next *Dusk*, and something I've seen time and time again from every genre that has a breakout hit. A point I bring up with every genre is that you only have minutes from your start screen to get the player invested in your game. If all someone sees when they start playing is nothing but someone copying *Doom* or *Halo*, or any other shooter, they're going to uninstall and never look at your game again.

The best shooters are built to push the player to learn their mechanics and quirks. As a point, *Doom Eternal*'s level design is not memorable in the sense that the player is going to remember where they are or what they're doing, but the arenas are built to fully capitalize on the mechanics the developers built and the enemies, and why the game was highly praised. Ideally, you want the player to be engaged with not only fighting enemies, but also the world and story of the game.

Figure 7.26

Creating a good platformer, good shooter, or any genre takes understanding all the aspects of the design. Heights of the genre like *Mario* or *Ultrakill* aren't designed in a vacuum or just throwing random ideas against a wall, but having a clear vision for the kind of game the designers want to make and fully exploring that idea.

While this is certainly a goal for story-driven games, RPGs, etc., shooters and reflex-driven design are always approached from a mechanic and gameplay side first. If it's not enjoyable for the player to run, shoot, jump, etc., then no amount of creating interesting levels and enemies is going to fix that. And to that point, this is why level and encounter design can be treated as two separate aspects of your game, and why making them both work is the hallmark of a fantastic designer.

Enemy design is often where designers "get it" or they don't. Part of the evolution of shooters with the integration of action game design is the notion that an enemy's behavior isn't just "stand still and shoot" or "charge the player." For you reading this, you can see how much of a difference this makes when comparing *Doom Eternal* or *Ultrakill* to any other shooter in terms of enemy design. There's a reason why I said that these games had action game elements in them. However, enemy design can only work with the abilities and options you provide the player; there is no way that any boomer or modern shooter would work if someone just threw in enemies from *Ultrakill* in them. Even if you are making a boomer shooter, there is still plenty of areas where you can innovate or create unique enemy designs.

And with level design, this is something that has seen the most changes with the evolution and different periods of shooter design. Thanks to the modding scene, there are so many different types of level designs and innovations that it would take years to look at them all at this point. Level design must be in sync with your weapons, enemies, and any other unique abilities or movement you give the player.

The differences between a bad, good, and amazing level are very wide for shooters. The challenge once again is that everything is connected to create the gameplay of your title. Great level design is always about establishing a "place" that your game is taking place in. What separates the good and amazing levels from each other is that amazing levels take that extra step to integrate the story and the world into the environmental and level designs. You're not just running and gunning through nondescript hallways with no sense as to where you are, but you're exploring an environment where around every corner is something new and dangerous to throw you off, and this continues level-by-level. Level and enemy design go together because of this – what enemies and where in the level can completely change the flow and pacing of a level. There must be a beginning, middle, and end to your level that makes sense, and build up to these sections throughout it. This is something that is hard to put into words, but you know it when you see it and why great level design can be a painstakingly process to get done.

As I said earlier, level design of the three points in this chapter is often the weakest of the three – if your gunplay and enemy designs are phenomenal, most people won't care if your levels are generic, or they are just running through the same looking areas each stage. However, being able to take those fantastic elements and build levels that fit them, and the story and environmental design of your game, is a sign of a master designer. As of drafting this book, *Ultrakill* is in my opinion the strongest example of how fantastic level design combined with the world and story can elevate everything about your game.

With the three points, and I can't stress this enough, you need to start with the gunplay and overall feel of your game, as everything you build, and balance will grow from them. Just like failing to finalize your core gameplay loop early, changing your weapons and what abilities you give the player will require a redesign of your level and enemy design to accommodate.

There are a lot of people, designers and consumers alike, who treat action-heavy games as being "simple" or "mindless": that you don't need to put the same amount of work into making a good one like you would an RPG or another genre. It's also why a lot of designers who switch from another genre to an action one end up failing despite years of experience making games compared to an action fan whose first game is about reflex-driven design. Making a game that's enjoyable simply to walk from point A to point B is a lot harder than it sounds, and if you can't do that, amazing graphics and a thought-provoking story will not save your game.

# Advanced Shooter Design

## 8.1 First- vs. Third-Person Perspective

Throughout this book, I've discussed first- and third-person shooting interchangeably, but it's important as a designer to understand the differences between the two in relation to how you build your game from a design and technical perspective (Figure 8.1).

Of the two, first person is the easier one in terms of development. This is because there are more free engines and modding software for FPSs than there are third. When it comes to the actual development, first person has no camera issues because the camera is literally the player's screen. Simply removing the need to build a 3D camera for your game will make things a lot easier for you.

The main disadvantage of first person is that while it works well for shooting, it is weaker when it comes to any other gameplay loop revolving around action. Because the player can't see their actual character model, it makes anything related to needing to see the character harder. This includes jumping, any kind of close-ranged combat, fine movement, stealth, and of course dodging. With this said, I am not including VR games played in first person that allow the player to see their hands or their actual body being used to dodge attacks.

DOI: 10.1201/9781003449959-8

Figure 8.1

First- and third-person perspectives for shooting are similar, and there are games that offer both perspectives as an option, but you still want to figure out what is the preferred method of playing, and the strengths and weaknesses of both that are discussed in this section.

Developers have found ways of getting around this limitation to some extent – showing an indicator for where the character is going to be landing, modeling legs and feet that the player can look down and see where their character is and having an on-screen indicator for stealth-related gameplay or dodging to name a few. While they have worked, they are not as effective as just having the character model on screen.

A unique issue present in first person is that, without having a character or something to focus their eyesight on, motion sickness and the symptoms of sea sickness have been known to affect some consumers when they play any kind of FPS. This also exacerbates any photosensitivity triggers like flashing lights or colors. This will come back up when discussing accessibility, but you want to be mindful of how someone is going to play your game, and putting in elements that purposely can cause issues in consumers can hurt the appeal of your game.

Third-person shooting means that the character model is always on the screen – usually in the bottom-left or bottom-right corner of the screen, giving the player as much view ahead of the character as possible. Due to being able to see the character model, anything that requires the player to measure depth and perspective is easier compared to first person. Many third-person shooters will have more platforming or movement-based challenges compared to first person.

However, third person does come with some noticeable drawbacks and limitations. The first is that it is a lot harder to develop a great third-person game than a first-person game, and the reason why comes down to one thing: the camera.

8. Advanced Shooter Design

Developing a functional and effective camera is beyond the scope of this book, but it is required in any game built around 3D movement that isn't first person. The camera has been the bane of many developers over the years and if it doesn't work right, your entire game can become borderline unplayable. Even in the best circumstances, the camera can still present issues if the character gets too close to a wall or too close to a large enemy. This can cause the player's character model to disappear, making it incredibly hard to gauge enemy attacks or even see where they are currently located.

Depending on whether projectiles are generated at the point of the reticule or from the character's weapon model, this can affect how easy it is to hit close-ranged targets. There is an issue when the reticule is used as the spawn point for projectiles or the hitscan that if the enemy is too close to the character model, the attack will miss even though the reticle is on the enemy model.

The question you are wondering now is does it make a difference to build a game in third or first person, and the answer is yes. First person allows for a greater sense of fidelity with weapons and gunplay. Because the player is only seeing enemies on the screen, it allows them to better read the situation and quickly line up targets. Third person is better if you want to challenge the player with movement tech and dodging as a focus (Figure 8.2). You can create more complex and varied level designs that involve movement in third person, as the player is able to see

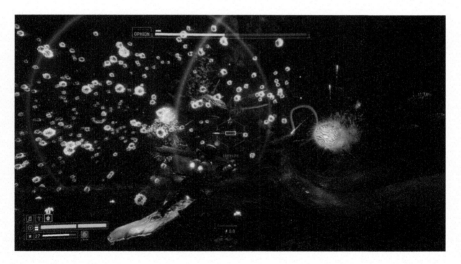

Figure 8.2

In a game like *Returnal*, while you could play it in first person, the amount of dodging and situational awareness required to win would be far harder to do with a first-person perspective. And for FPS that do focus on a lot of dodging and bullet patterns, you do want some kind of indicator for off-screen attacks if you want the player to be able to respond from 360 degrees around them.

the greater environment around their character and plan accordingly with better situational awareness. With that said, there is a subgenre of first-person games specifically built around speed running through environments in first person.

The decision to build your game in either first or third person should be decided as early as possible, as it can be difficult to switch between the two if you are not familiar with creating a 3D camera. Some designers have put in both first- and third-person modes in their games for people to have a preferred way of playing. One final point about third person from a UX point of view is that there should be an option to switch which side of the screen the character model is on while aiming. Typically, the character model should always be on the opposite side of where enemies are to allow for aiming without the character getting in the way.

## 8.2 The UI/UX of Gunplay

Creating the UI/UX of your game, whether you are making it first or third person, is very important to learn as a designer. One advantage of working in a reflex-driven genre is that most of the basics in terms of information and controls have been standardized by developers. There are some specific cases and GUI elements that designers have used that I will be going over in this section as well.

With every shooter in existence, the player needs to be able to always notice the following information (Figures 8.3):

- Where are they aiming?
- Their current health
- Their current armor (if applicable)
- Current weapon
- Current ammo

These points should be self-explanatory, but I want to touch on the current weapon. It is customary to have the weapon's model on screen in either the left or right hand of the character. Good aesthetics and art design should make your weapons visibly distinctive from one another; not only does this make your weapons stand out, but it reduces the chance that someone is going to be confused as to what weapon they're using. A common trap I see designers fall into when designing futuristic or otherworldly weapons, is that they are built from the same general shape with few details different. The more ways that each weapon looks different – shape, coloring, details, and size, the better it will be for your game. If you provide the player with the option to dual wield – use two weapons at the same time, a good quality of life feature to include is to set the fire buttons in relation to where the guns are on screen – left weapon for left mouse button; right weapon for right mouse button.

Part of the UX of your weapons and gunplay also involves the sound effects and animations. Going back to the original *Doom*, what made it stand out and gave its

Figure 8.3

I want to emphasize GUI design from three different shooters starting with *Doom Eternal*. Ignoring the boss information at the top, let's look at the reticule in the middle. The reticule shape itself will change based on what alt fire the player is using for the weapon. Surrounding it are icons showing the charges of the player's different abilities. This was updated after launch, and previously that information was only available along the bottom-right, and blood punch on the bottom-left. The reason why this is good is that it allows the player to focus on fighting and always know what abilities are available. However, it does not include anything about grenades or grenade type which is a mistake in my opinion. You can see health, armor, dash, and blood punch on the bottom-left. When the player is close to death, the screen will flash red and a warning noise will play, along with audio cues for when some powers recharge. This is a solid GUI that doesn't distract the player from the main focus in the middle.

timelessness was the impact and feel of the guns. You're not just firing a weapon and hearing someone say "bang" in a monotone voice, every gun looks different, sounds different, and feels different to use in the game. Another trap I have seen designers fall into when building any shooter is having their weapon aesthetics fall flat. Not only is the weapon a factor, but also the impact on the enemies and environment. If someone is using explosives and hits an enemy with a rocket, and the only thing the enemy does is faint, that's going to hurt the feel of your weapons.

This point is obvious but needs to be said regarding your guns. The animations tied to your weapon should be 1:1 in terms of how they are being used. What I mean is that the reload animation should be exactly how long it take the gun to reload, likewise, the rate of fire of the weapon should be consistent with the firing animation. Remember, reflex-driven games are all about how the game handles in the player's hands. Feel trumps realism in this respect, such as having a character reloading a gun super-fast thanks to an upgrade or powerup.

Figure 8.4

Let's turn to *Ultrakill* (note with the game still in development, this GUI can change). Like the last one, we can ignore the boss health bar at the top. This one features more information that takes up the screen, namely the combo and score indicator on the right-hand side. Not picture here is the ranking breakdown that is shown on the top-left, as that is only for expert play and is optional. The most important part of the score section is the ranking, and why that first letter is so big. The second part is the multiplier at the bottom, because scoring big in a level requires the player to keep swapping between weapons. The reticule shows on the right-hand side the number of dashes remaining and the left side shows the player's health once they've been hit and if they have any hard damage, with this information repeated on the bottom-left. The lightning bolt indicates the charge of the rail cannon, and there is an audio cue when it's also fully recharged. The only information that is locked to the bottom of the screen is what fist type the player has equipped. However, an update now allows the player to bind each fist type to a separate key to make it easier to use during the heat of combat. All and all, another solid GUI for a game where you shouldn't be looking directly at it during a fight.

With the overall GUI for your shooter, because these games are focused on the player's ability to aim and process what's going on, the main screen should be kept as clean as possible (Figure 8.4). Most people prefer to keep GUI elements like health, ammo, etc., either along the bottom of the screen or the top. But there is one problem with this – any games that feature special powers, abilities, unique items, etc. Part of the growth that I've discussed in this book and that I will be returning to in this chapter is giving the player more abilities beyond just shooting and jumping. The player's eyes will always be focusing on the reticule on screen – for the obvious reason as that is where they are aiming their weapon. The more additional details the player needs to be keeping track of can make it hard to focus. What you do not want when someone is playing your shooter is having to keep adjusting where they are focusing their attention in the middle of combat. Many RPGs and abstracted titles like to frame their information to different corners of the screen to compartmentalize the types of information the player is looking for, and that is something you want to avoid doing in shooters, especially fast-paced ones. The reason is that the more places the player needs to look at, the less time they are spending being able to focus on moving and shooting.

There are several innovations that designers have done to balance keeping their screens clean while providing the player with information. In third-person shooters where the player needs to be focusing on their character model as well as their reticule, essential information will be placed near where the character model is located, such as on the bottom-middle, bottom-left or bottom-right of the screen. This way, when the player is focusing on their character, they don't need to shift their eyes too far away to see their health and ammo. Speaking of, from a UX perspective, allowing the player to swap the corner of the screen where the character model goes when aiming makes it easier to aim and shoot depending on the layout of the level.

The reticule itself has also seen improvements in this respect from designers. Instead of just being used to show where the player is aiming, designers will put additional details around the reticule corresponding to any secondary or special abilities – how many dashes the player has, special attacks, what alt fire is on, grenades and so on. This way, the player never has to take their eyes off the reticule in the middle of combat to know what abilities they can currently use. If one of your abilities is predicated on being within a certain range of the enemy or interactable, then the reticule or something on screen should indicate when the player is within range to use it.

*Diegetic* GUI elements allow designers to combine the aesthetics of their weapons and models with providing essential information. Instead of having a readout on the bottom of the screen for ammo, there could be a display on the gun that shows current ammo. While this is far harder to do than just having floating GUI elements, it can add a touch of style to your game and improve the aesthetics as well. With *Metroid Prime* (released in 2002 by Retro Studios), the developers turned the protagonist: Samus Aran's, suit into the GUI for the game. The information was displayed as if it was being fed to her visor by the sensors in her suit.

One recent development that I have not seen before was in *Roboquest*. Instead of putting the reticule directly in the middle of the screen, they put it a quarter up from the bottom of the screen. This provides better visibility when dealing with enemies who are vertical on the screen as opposed to being on the same ground as the player (Figure 8.5).

Just as you don't want the player's eyes to be focusing on different parts of the screen, the player's hands shouldn't need to move or adjust their positions on the gamepad or keyboard.

Figure 8.5

For *Roboquest*, while the player is not as actively moving compared to *Doom Eternal* and *Ultrakill*, there is more to pay attention to as evident by having more GUI elements. This is the only example with a minimap and grades along the top-right, this is because the levels in the game are procedurally generated, and the player needs to be able to see quickly where they are and where they need to go. The map also shows enemy placements, and the player is given an indicator of when a projectile is about to hit them off screen. Because healing is harder to do compared to the other games, taking a hit is far more punishing and the player is given more information to compensate.

The reticule itself shows the accuracy of the weapon, but surrounding it are details for the class's special weapons, and the recharge time for their additional movement abilities. The bottom of the screen show the character's power, and the player is given an audio cue when it's fully charge. What artifacts are available are on the bottom-right along with the weapons equipped, and chosen perks along the upper-left. Health is along the bottom-left along with character level and experience. This is a good GUI with the only thing I would add to the middle would be a better indicator for running out of ammo in the equipped weapon.

Here is the general UI for shooters for keyboard and mouse and gamepads:

| Command | Keyboard and Mouse | Gamepad |
|---|---|---|
| Movement | WASD Keys | Left analog stick |
| Jumping | Spacebar | South face button |
| Primary fire | Left mouse click | Right trigger |
| Alt fire | Right mouse click | Left trigger or right button |
| Reload | R | Right button, west face button |
| Use/interact | E | West face button |
| Secondary attack/Melee | Q or Z | East face button |
| Dash/dodge | Shift | Left trigger or left button |
| Bring up menu | Tab or escape | Start or select |

8. Advanced Shooter Design

These are just the most basic commands and the most popular ones to be featured in a shooter, and there are always exceptions and games with more commands depending on the gameplay loop.

One universal point regardless of the game you are making is understanding the notion of the "neutral position" that someone is holding a gamepad or using a keyboard and mouse. For a gamepad, outside of people with physical disabilities who may require a specific controller or peripheral, they will rest their left thumb on the left analog stick, the right thumb on the right analog stick or use it for the face buttons, and their index fingers will be resting on the back of the controller to hit the trigger and shoulder buttons, while the rest of their hands hold the gamepad.

For the keyboard, most games are centered around using WSAD for movement or the primary commands that someone will use their left hand for, and the right hand will be responsible for the mouse. In this position, the left hand can usually hit keys that are one to two away from WSAD easily, and the thumb will be responsible for hitting the spacebar. Putting important keys and commands further away from the neutral position can lead to players having to constantly readjust their hands or keep them in an awkward position on either the gamepad or keyboard. When it comes to the UI of your game, this is one area where you don't want to try and reinvent the wheel. At this point, there are thousands of games in every genre out there that you can look at when building the UI. A point I bring up in every deep dive is the importance of affordances – ways people can associate a command or input to something else. Like I said earlier in the book, every shooter will always use the triggers for shooting, because the player can instantly associate pushing a trigger to firing a weapon.

One aspect that is unique to shooters that you need to be aware of is how to swap between different weapons. In most shooters on the PC, the player can hit any of the number keys to switch between weapons or use the mouse wheel for quick scrolling. Some may categorize them by different types that correspond to the keys: 2 for all pistol and handguns, 3 for shotguns, etc. A popular GUI element that has become standard in any shooter with multiple weapons is the "weapon wheel" (Figure 8.6) By holding down a button, the game will bring up a wheel that shows all weapons, their available ammo and equipable items. During this time, many games will either slow down the rest of the game or just pause it outright to enable players time to think about what weapon they want to use. If you're building a game with a lot of weapons with different rules and use cases for them, this is an essential feature for people who don't have fast reactions. In terms of placement on the gamepad or keyboard, you want this button to be easily accessible, and something that the player can hold down comfortably while keeping their other fingers on the normal keys or buttons.

Being able to quickly swap to weapons also opens the discussion of the technique known as "quick swapping." Because the weapon's rate of fire is also dependent on the downtime and animation frames after the gun is fired, if the game allows it, by swapping weapons fast enough, it is possible to swap the second the firing animation is done to another weapon, removing the recovery frames and

Figure 8.6

The weapon wheel doesn't sound all that useful for expert players, but it is important from an approachability standpoint to allow people who aren't good at rapid hotkey switching to be able to swap to different weapons comfortably.

allowing the player to fire again almost immediately with their other weapon. Both *Doom Eternal* and *Ultrakill*'s high-level play make extensive use of this. In *Doom* Eternal, it is considered customary to finish off marauders by quick swapping between the super shotgun and the arbalist, two weapons with long recovery animations, while they are stunned for a very quick kill. Ultrakill goes as far as rewarding the player with a better score for swapping between weapons while fighting instead of just using the same weapon, and there are several weapon combo attacks that require quick swapping to perform them. If quick swapping is in your game and intended to be used, you should inform the player about it during the tutorial or somewhere in the game's documentation. From a UI perspective, many shooters feature a shortcut that allow players to swap quickly between their current and previous weapon to make it easier to use specific combos.

Returning to the aesthetics of your weapon, there are several other reasons why having unique-looking guns can make your game better. For games built on personalization, you want the player to be able to personalize the looks of their weapons in terms of coloring, decals, or any other effects to stand out from other players. From a gameplay point of view, visible clarity is an important aspect of fast-paced gameplay. When someone is busy focusing on enemies or dodging projectiles, they're not going to have the time to look away from the main screen to examine small details. Being able to instantly recognize what weapon they are using by the outline and general look is vital because of this. From a marketing standpoint, good weapon variety in terms of what they do and how they look

Figure 8.7

With the different screenshots in this section, look at how each game shows the secondary information that's associated to it. This one is from the game *Battle Shapers* by Metric Empire that is still in development while writing this. The GUI here keeps all information focused on the bottom of the screen as opposed to focusing on a different corner. Remember, every game is going to be different, but you can use other examples to see what has been done and if it could be used in some way in your game.

can be a great selling point for your game. Returning to *Gunfire Reborn*, every weapon type is completely original from one another – there are no two guns that visibly or aesthetically look alike.

Besides the GUI of how someone shoots and moves in your game, you also need to make sure that other aspects of your design are easy to process (Figure 8.7). Regarding enemies, if your game has special rules for how enemies behave or how to deal with them, the GUI needs to make that abundantly clear to the player. Returning to *Doom Eternal*, the marauders will always flash to indicate that this is the perfect time to hit them to stun them. For many shooters where health is hard to come by, such as action roguelikes, enemies may flash, or the player will hear an audio alert when someone is about to attack them.

Another point about clarity is that if your game features different conditional warnings, you want to make sure that they are distinguishable from one another. Many action games that have attacks that cannot be blocked or parry will come with an additional warning when the enemy is about to perform them to let the player know that the next attack needs to be avoided at all cost.

The amount of visual and audio cues in your game is going to be dependent on any advanced rules or game mechanics you want to include. However, this is not a case where more equals better – the more elements outside of shooting and your core gameplay loop the player needs to focus on, the harder it's going to be to concentrate on the game at hand. Part of good UI/UX design is figuring out the easiest and clearest way to explain your game to the player. This is where playtesting and user feedback is king for a developer. If people are constantly getting confused by a specific rule in your game, not following an on-screen element right, or simply making mistakes due to unclear rules, these are points you need to adjust.

## 8.3 Shooter-Filled Progression

Progression in shooters varies wildly depending on the game and the kind of core gameplay loop you are building. In most boomer shooters, the only upgrades and carryover the player gets is being able to keep their weapons from one level to the next. In boomer shooters that are framed around an episodic structure, the player's weapons will be reset back to the starting ones at the beginning of a new episode.

For games built around roguelike and roguelite design, they can have persistent elements and unlockables (for more on those systems, please read *Game Design Deep Dive: Roguelikes*). Part of what I discussed in the last chapter was how level, enemy, and weapon design needed to be in sync if you want your shooter to work, and the same can be said about progression.

As you introduce new elements in your game – new weapons, new hazards, new enemies, etc. – everything that comes after must integrate those elements in. It is poor form to give the player a new weapon and then tell them that it won't be used again for another ten levels.

Another aspect of progression is with permanent upgrades. Again, roguelike/ lite games will introduce them as a form of the run-based progression, but other shooters over the 2010s have made use of abstracted progression (Figure 8.8). Returning to role-playing shooters, the entire system of leveling up your character to unlock new skills or find better weapons. Letting the player upgrade their core attributes in *Doom 2016* and *Doom Eternal* is a lighter version of this.

With this kind of progression, you need to decide how important these systems are in relation to the reflex-driven gameplay. Some games will scale content and drops based on the player's level, while others will flatly state that certain areas are meant for specific level ranges. The problem with stat-based progression in reflex-driven games is that they will always dilute the actual run-and-gun mechanics to some extent. The joy of playing games like *Doom* is that every level, every enemy, and every weapon are balanced for one state. When playing games like *Destiny, The Division, Warframe,* etc., even if the player is skilled at shooting, if their character is under-level, they won't be able to fight as effectively. If your game does feature optional rewards that permanently boost the character's attributes, the rest of your game, at least on the normal difficulty, should not be balanced around having those boosts turned on. Many games will treat health upgrades, ammo upgrades, etc., as something to help the player with the normal difficulties and be a requirement if someone wants to play the game at the highest setting.

Figure 8.8

The main difference between meta progression or persistent elements in a rogue-like/lite, and what we see in games like *Doom*, is that the meta progression is some-thing that can keep being applied while the player is going on runs, and future runs aren't being altered or balanced around continued it, unless we're talking about having progressive difficulty. In *Doom* here, the upgrades are tied to fixed points within the levels – so there is a limit on what the player can get based on where they are at in the campaign. The persistent upgrades do have a limit as well, but it will take far longer, and many runs, before the player will reach it.

As I mentioned along with level design in the last chapter, any kind of per-manent progression that changes how someone plays the game must be factored into the level design and pacing going forward. For every new ability you intro-duce to the game, the level design should accommodate it going forward. Part of metroidvania design is the act of replaying/revisiting areas with new upgrades and powers to find secrets and alternate routes. For shooters and action-driven design, replaying levels with exception for score challenges or mastery is not really done. While you can have secrets and collectibles for the player to hunt down, they should all be accessible on the initial play of that level. The end of the game in terms of challenges, arenas, and level design, should be noticeably differ-ent compared to what was introduced at the start.

Returning to enemy and level design, a lot of your focus on progression will be upping the challenge and depth of your enemy encounters and level design as the game goes on. As I've previously stated, it's not a case of just raising the difficulty ever higher but creating new and interesting ways of testing the player (Figure 8.9). *Ultrakill* is a good example to study of this – the game is split into acts which are further split into different layers with each layer ending with a boss fight. While the layers are all built on specific themes, each level will do something different with it. The fifth layer involves water, and the first level has

Figure 8.9

You remember the Cerberus from *Ultrakill*? This is the first fight in the level P-2, that is one of the hardest levels in the game. Fighting four of them in close range, with additional enemies that you can't see in this shot. This level features some of the hardest arrangements of enemies and arenas and shows off just how hard this game can go.

the player using water physics to fight enemies, the second level has them crossing over a massive sea to reach a boat, and the third level involves exploring the boat and having it capsize while the player is in it with the fourth level being a boss fight with a giant sea creature.

Part of the progression model you need to decide on is the overall structure of your game. Is your game about completing different episodes of content like in the boomer shooters, is it just clearing a campaign of levels like modern shooting, or do you want the player to reach a specific level with the abstraction like in live service and RPG-based shooting? As I'll elaborate with the differences in multiplayer shooters, multiplayer design is not about having an intended end, so the progression is different there.

Regarding the depth of your game, one other aspect of progression you need to be aware of is the intended skill curve of your gameplay. This includes the skill floor that is the minimum skill someone should have to beat it, and the **skill ceiling** which is what is required to see the game through to the end. Every reflex-driven game has a baseline skill level that they expect people to have going into it and what the general play will be balanced on. In *Doom Eternal*, the different difficulties do not change the base stats or attributes of the player, their weapons, or the enemies. Instead, they impact the overall aggressiveness. What this means from a player's perspective is if someone can master how the gunplay works on normal (or in Eternal's case "Hurt me Plenty") it is quite possible for them to attempt

Ultra-Violent or Nightmare (hard or very hard). As I talked about before, having advanced or master-level challenges in your games is a great reward for players who want to seek them out, but you do want to make sure that the average player knows this content is optional and not required to beat the game.

One kind of shooter that lends itself more toward RPG and open-world design is the appropriately named open-world shooter. In these games, the player is exploring a massive area or areas and can find upgrades, new weapons and abilities on and off the beaten path. This kind of design is different than the shooters I've talked about. In this respect, you are building an open world or ARPG, but the main gameplay is about shooting and gunplay (Figure 8.10). Open-world design is its own unique beast when it comes to building a game and will be most likely discussed in full in a future deep dive.

However, a lot of the general aspects of progression and pacing do fit. Where and when you introduce new enemies, new challenges, etc. needs to be balanced with what the player has available at the given moment. Linear or nonlinear, you want to avoid putting the player into purposely bad situations to fix it later with some power or ability. One of the few points that I'm not a fan of with *Doom Eternal* is that the game waits until the second level to introduce the dash ability which becomes your main defensive option to avoid damage. This makes the first level feel slow, at least by *Doom Eternal's* standards, by comparison. Just remember this point – most players

Figure 8.10

Open-world shooters like the upcoming *S.T.A.L.K.E.R. 2* (as of the time I'm writing this) are different from the other games I've talked about. Progression is often tied to what equipment the player can buy/find. For you reading this, if you are building an open-world shooter, be sure to understand that you are not designing a game for the same market as the other games mentioned throughout this book.

are not going to wait around for you to "fix" an issue they with your game at a later level or area, they're going to quit and be frustrated by your design.

Due to shooters being reflex-driven, it means that story progression is going to be secondary in most cases for keeping someone invested. A good story does help your game, but with shooters, this is not going to distract someone if they don't like the gameplay. And for the final point in this section, your first level is going to be what most consumers will judge your game on, and why you want to make sure that it is the best example of what your game is going to be about.

## 8.4 Single vs. Multiplayer Design

This book has been dedicated to single player design when it comes to shooters, but it's important to discuss how things are different when players are fighting each other rather than the AI (Figure 8.11). Multiplayer design is its own topic that touches on elements of shooters and live service. For more about live service design, you can find that in *Game Design Deep Dive: Free to Play*. Also note, the differences that I'm talking about in this section pertain to competitive multiplayer; there are a variety of coop-focused multiplayer games that would lean more toward the style of single player design.

Earlier in the book I mentioned the differences between hitscan and projectile attacks, and I wanted to reiterate that multiplayer shooters tend to focus on hitscan

Figure 8.11

Multiplayer design could easily fit an entire design book and does require a different philosophy compared to building a single player or cooperative game. Gunplay and feel are still important, but you are now balancing that against human opponents.

due to technical issues and playability. Projectile-based attacks are often saved for stronger attacks, or ones that are less frequently used like someone's ultimate move. In a single player game, the player is only worrying about the projectiles they use and that of enemies; each one is designed to be very explicit in terms of its visual design. Returning to the original *Doom*s, the player can tell immediately if an imp fireball, cacodemon blast, or reverent shot, is coming at them. In a multiplayer setting, when you can have at minimum four to eight players, battle royale notwithstanding, in an area firing at each other with different weapons, which can easily obscure the screen and make it almost impossible to tell what is going on.

Another reason why hitscan weapons are preferred is the very fact that players move and react faster than an enemy AI. If you've watched any competitive shooter play online, you will see players jumping, diving, sliding, crouching; doing anything within their power to keep the enemy's reticule off them. Without hitscans, a lot of casual and average players may not be able to even hit an expert player who knows all the movement tech with projectile attacks.

Part of having a good UX when it comes to shooters is providing clarity to the player about what is happening. The more players, with their own guns, powers, and characters on screen, will all impact that. Another specific detail about UI design with multiplayer games is providing the player with information about what is happening with their team and the match itself. Besides having GUI information on health, ammo, and special abilities, you also need to provide the player with information about the match, if friendly players are dying, and markers or mapping to inform the player about the current objective(s). If your matches are about competing for points or controlling the map, then there must be GUI elements to let the teams know who is ahead (Figure 8.12).

From a pacing standpoint, multiplayer shooters are not paced the same as a single player game. A level in a single player shooter could take a few minutes if it's a boomer shooter, or 15–30 minutes in a campaign structure. Multiplayer design is about creating "matches" – said match can have different time limits based on the overall design, but you as the designer need to figure out a baseline for it. The reason is that the longer a match is, the more of a time commitment players will need to see it through. It is also possible depending on the skill levels that a match can go on for far longer or far shorter if there is a disparity between the teams.

Long matches are generally frowned upon for several reasons. In games that track if players are quitting early and banning them for frequent drops, being tied to a match for a long time or risk punishment doesn't sit well with people who must budget their spare time. In a competitively driven game, the extreme focus needed to play these games can wear on someone if they're doing it for 30+ minutes at a time.

It's because of these points that multiplayer design today has been shifting toward ways of limiting just how long a match can go. In a MOBA like *League of Legends*, because the punishment for dying goes up as characters become higher level, one big mistake 30–40 minutes in can easily cost a team the match. The use of killstreaks in the *Call of Duties* allows a team to massively increase their score or wipe out the opposing team if done correctly. Even asymmetrical games have

Figure 8.12

Any and every piece of information you provide the player during a match is going to dictate the flow of the game. In *Hunt: Showdown* once again, the game will alert every player on the map once someone has one of the boss bounties, this is done to accelerate the end of the match and provide tension for the player with the prize. As the designer, you need to determine what information every player should have access to play the game correctly.

seen these changes; as I'm writing this in 2024, *Dead by Daylight* changed how "stalling tactics" work to prevent matches from going too long or someone keeping everyone stuck in one match. Long matches should be the exception and not the norm if you want to build a competitive game.

Perhaps the strongest and most explicit example of match limiting is from battle royales. Because the map shrinks at a fixed rate every few minutes, there is nowhere for players to hide or prolong matches – at some point, every player who is still alive is going to be forced to fight each other at close range. Figuring out match length is going to be dependent on the design you are making and the number of players that are part of a "regular match." The reason for the air quotes is that some games allow players to set up custom games or have modded servers that can feature wildly different rules than the normal matches.

It's because of this speed of play that certain weapon types and powers that would work for a single player game won't be as effective in multiplayer. Time is the biggest factor, multiplayer games are by their nature faster than single player, and any move, special power, or weapon that takes a long time to perform is generally worthless. Also note, when I just wrote "long time," that could be as long as 30 seconds to a minute. Anything that is slow moving is an easy dodge by players who are running, jumping, or flying away from danger.

To get around this, designers will build ultimates and special abilities that once the opposing player is caught by them, they are susceptible to the whole thing, and may make the casting player invulnerable while the effect is going on to prevent the enemy from stopping it prematurely. The other option is that the power is to be used in conjunction with your teammates. Having an ultimate that stuns the opposing team may not sound that useful if you're alone, but this can be absolutely devastating if you coordinate with your teammates who are ready to take them out easily once the skill is up.

Speaking of stuns, hit stuns is an important aspect of single player shooters to stop the enemy from attacking. In multiplayer games, since the opposition is another player, being able to stop them from doing anything would mean that whoever gets the first shot off automatically wins. Therefore, multiplayer shooters will not have any impact like that when someone is being hit by a weapon. This also makes these games more challenging to play – as the player must be constantly adjusting their shot to hit a moving target, and why console shooters feature soft lock-ons to compensate against keyboard and mouse players.

Both single and multiplayer designs make use of locational-based damage, but in a competitive game where a few milliseconds can mean the difference between winning and losing, these "sweet spots" matter a lot. Part of the balancing between single-shot and rapid-fire weapons is their impact when hitting a player in the head or chest (Figure 8.13). One heavy shot to an enemy in their

Figure 8.13

Locational-based damage matters in any shooter released today, but it plays a vital role for balancing and weapon design in multiplayer. Part of what makes sniper-class weapons so dangerous, and so rewarding, is that they are a high-damaging single-shot weapon on top of hitting someone in a critical location. Rapid-fire weapons can work with shots in the body and arms if the player can hit enough times, but weak spots provide rewards for people who are good at aiming and gives slower, but stronger, weapons a chance to shine.

head is often enough to kill them or put them close to death; while rapid-fire shots have less control and stability, but a player can put many more rounds in the enemy in the same time frame as one heavy shot. But again, due to the faster speed and movement of players vs. AI opponents, it's far harder to use slower rate of fire weapons compared to faster ones.

Health and healing is something that has changed a lot with multiplayer design over the past 30 years. With the early multiplayer games that were designed around boomer shooter gameplay, health pickups would be placed on maps for players to find, and they would respawn after a few seconds so that other players could use them. In games with very quick matches like *CS: GO* there is no healing at all, with the point being that matches are made to be fast and decisive. In hero shooters, specific classes and characters may have the ability to heal themselves and their teammates.

For games with healing systems, there are three popular options used today. The first is a per character auto heal – the player can either activate it or it will go on after being out of combat for a few seconds. The intention like the *Halo* shield is that players can't just take potshots at one another and expect to down someone, they must finish them off before they fully recover. In hero shooters, one of the roles someone can play will be a healer of some sort. Perhaps the most famous example at this point is the medic of *Team Fortress 2* who also could make one character invincible using their "ÜberCharge." Lastly, for battle royale, extraction shooters, or any shooter that also involves finding items in the world, players can find consumable healing items that they can use to recover health. There is also the option to find armor of some kind that once again acts as a second health bar to give players a greater chance of surviving fights.

Team size is another factor that is unique to multiplayer shooting. There are shooters that go as small as 1v1 matches, to 4v4, 32v32, and even more if we talk about battle royale and experimental multiplayer games. Your team size will also impact the size of maps and again: the balance of your weapons and skills. For hero shooters where each character is unique unto themselves, the team size will also affect how hero combinations can work. Part of the never-ending balancing of these games is figuring out how different powers can work together that can lead to game breaking strategies. For the sake of your own sanity as a developer, the more unique your characters are and their abilities, the smaller your match sizes should be to keep things easier for balancing. For example, *Apex Legends* matches are built on 60 players at one time split into 20 teams of 3. As an easy determination, if your game is made up of characters who are categorized by unique roles/classes, having a team that can include one of each class is a good starting point. You also need to factor in if players can pick the same character on a team or are they locked. This is an important consideration if you have ranked modes and the option for each side to ban specific characters they don't want the other team using. Banning only works if your game features a huge pool of characters within each class/role.

Level design specifically for multiplayer shooters is its own field of design and is different from designing a campaign or single player structured game. A good single player map is about creating unique situations, worrying about enemy placements and resources. For multiplayer, your focus is on creating maps that can provide multiple areas for players to engage with each other, while still making it readable and easy to learn. Single player content is something that most players will not return to once they win; in multiplayer, these maps can be played daily for years. Every object, doorway, and even corner of a room will be scrutinized by your player base to figure out the best ways to approach every encounter.

You want to design areas specifically where players will be fighting each other and have enough environmental obstacles to hide and move around through. However, you want to avoid designing areas where whoever is the first team to reach it will be able to become so entrenched that the other team has no way of breaking through. Because level design like in single player games is going to be contingent on what abilities and gameplay are in your game, there are very few universal approaches to it. "Memorable" for a multiplayer map is about creating an interesting space where matches between players and teams can occur. And if you do build your shooter around collecting pickups around the map, their placement will also need to be factored into the design. You don't want one side of the map to have better access to stronger weapons than the other, as that would favor one team more.

One last detail before I move on regarding verticality. You need to be aware of how players can interact with the world in terms of moving around. Some games explicitly give players the ability to transverse areas using movement abilities, while other games due to how the geometry is set up, could let players get on top of buildings, walls, or just hide in areas you wouldn't think possible. Due to the importance of learning the map layouts, you'll need to balance where players can go to hide or sneak around a player. Rewarding an agile player who gets the drop on the opposing team is one thing; getting into a spot where there is no way for someone to engage with the player is another.

Game modes are another point that distinguishes multiplayer-focused shooters from single player. The more modes you have in your game mean the more variety of matches. However, this also comes at the price of splitting your consumer base depending on which modes people prefer. Part of designing a multiplayer game is that you must have a community big enough to support your matches (Figure 8.14). A sign when a game is dying/dead is when it becomes difficult to find enough players for a general play. If you are building a competitive shooter, or any game that has competitive/rank play, you should always include a casual mode where players can enjoy themselves without worrying about matchmaking and rankings. There is more about the infrastructure of building an online game, and one that is centered on live service design, which is beyond the scope of this book's topic. One important point about game modes in multiplayer shooters, if you're going to feature completely different modes of play, you want to make sure that each mode is balanced separately from one another. In the *Call of Duty* games,

Figure 8.14

Asymmetrical multiplayer presents an additional hurdle for communities – how do you convince people to play two different playstyles? With *Evolve* on the left, players got frustrated if they weren't on a good team of hunters or if they were up against a better monster player, and when it became hard to get a full match filled, people stopped playing. *Dead by Daylight* has a similar problem with people preferring all survivor or all killer playstyles, and they will incentivize people to play one with additional rewards when the server notices a lack of one player type.

how someone plays warzone is completely different from the other multiplayer modes, and the single player campaign is separate from the other options.

If you are building a live service or progression-based multiplayer shooter, you do need to be mindful of how players of higher levels interact with everyone else. Some games simply give the player more options as they level up, while others will flat out give players weapons that are better than the starting guns. You want to make sure that players of higher ranks are playing against comparable players. Some developers have tried to use their matchmaking services to put lower ranked players, or those that haven't bought better weapons, against higher ranked ones to drive the former to spending. This is considered an unethical design practice and can get you in trouble with your fanbase if you try it. In reflex-driven games, any and every advantage can be looked at under a microscope by your players to determine if your game is fair or not. Early live service games could get away with literally selling power to players in the form of weapons only available with real money, but the market has shifted away from that.

In terms of weapons in competitive shooters, you will either design a generic pool of weapons that can show up in a match or be bought during play, or each character has their own unique "weapon" that could be anything that represents that character. If your game is built around roles/classes, weapons should have some relation to the class itself – if your medic has a gun that is more accurate than a sniper rifle, does more damage than your offensive class, and heals every-one around them instantly, then there might be an imbalance going on. However, weapons still need to be able to compete by the obvious point that you are build-ing a shooter and if a character or weapon doesn't feel good to play, they're not going to be used.

Multiplayer balance is also fundamentally different compared to single player. You are not only having to balance weapons and skills in relation to one another, but also how this relates to casual, core, and hardcore players. One of the worst things you can do for the longevity of a game is only cater to one group. If your game is viewed as too simple, then core and hardcore players aren't going to keep playing. If it's too easy to solve or play the game one way, then the hardcore play-ers won't invest their time and people won't want to play a "boring" game. And if you only cater to the hardcore with complicated and challenging gameplay with a high skill ceiling, casual players will be put off by it and core players won't want to play a game that only has one method of winning. You also need to be aware of how much your game experience can change through balance patches and new characters/mechanics introduced.

As I've said in my *Free to Play* book, if you are intending on building a multi-player game in today's market, shooter notwithstanding, you are also inherently building a live service title. That means you not only need to think about how your game is being played currently, but what new content will be added over the days, weeks, months, and years of its lifespan. Introducing a new character or weapon that is better than anything else in the game can create an arms race that leads to players dropping out if they feel the only way to keep playing is to spend money on the newest stuff.

There are specific Quality of Life (QOL) features and issues unique to any multiplayer-based game that you need to be aware of. First, you should have tools and systems in place for reporting players and limiting someone's ability to talk to someone – such as blocking voice and text chat. The reason why is that there are plenty of people who will take trash talking to extreme levels of vitriol, and if people are forced to listen to this because there aren't preventive systems in place, they will quit your game. You will also need people who can handle the reporting of players for conduct that violates your terms of service.

Speaking of, unfortunately for multiplayer games today, especially those with a competitive following, you will most likely need to have some kind of anti-cheat software in your game. There will be people who will try to use cheats to either pad their records, or even use them to win official tournaments. Without having measures in place to stop and punish cheaters, regular players will not want to play if they have no hope of competing against them.

Multiplayer shooters can be a hard market to get into now, with many live ser-vice games that aren't massive successes failing, and the major names continue to dominate. The most important lesson, and something I will come back to in the next chapter, is that you cannot build your game just like the other ones on the market. No matter how good your game is, or you think your game is, trying

Figure 8.15

Multiplayer games is the big time for any studio and why this market has been chased by many developers and publishers over the years. If you want to succeed today, you can't just make "Game X, but shinier," you need to be able to show people that your game is legitimately different than those other games, as you're never going to be able to directly compete with the likes of *Fortnite* or *Call of Duty* with the same exact gameplay.

to directly compete with any of the major names will not end up working well for you (Figure 8.15). Fans of popular games become entrenched, and they will not switch to your game unless you give them a very compelling reason to do so. The reason why the multiplayer shooters that succeeded in Chapter 6 worked was that they each provided something new that hasn't been seen before. This is why multiplayer games are such high risk/high reward – when they work, you basically corner the market on that specific kind of gameplay; when they don't, it can be a studio closer for some.

## 8.5 The Contextualizing of Shooting

One aspect of shooting and FPS design that I haven't spoken about in this book is the idea of taking the mechanics of a shooter and doing something different with them. When most people think about "shooting" or "shooters," their minds will obviously go toward games built on violence. However, part of the growth of game development has been the realization that different genres can be depicted in any kind of way. Mechanics in a vacuum do not create the tone or aesthetics of your game.

Shooting in of itself is simply aiming something at something else, and those "somethings" can literally be anything your mind can think of. Instead of firing guns, you could be a chef tossing food at hunger customers, throwing musical

　　　　　　　　　　　　　8. Advanced Shooter Design

notes at people to get them to dance, and many more. One of the first examples of this concept was the game *Chex Quest* released in 1996 by Digital Café. A total conversion from *Doom* that was centered on fighting aliens and used as a promotional tie-in for the Chex cereal. Instead of killing enemies, the player was simply teleporting evil aliens back to their home planet.

One of the most popular games that did just this was *Power Wash Simulator* by FuturLab released in 2022 (Figure 8.16). In it, your sole job is to use your power washer and clean up a variety of environments and objects throughout the neighborhood. The gameplay is done in the style of an FPS, but instead of running around shooting monsters, killing demons, and being violent, you are just cleaning up buildings, vehicles, and playground equipment. The game is not anywhere close to being a difficult or hard game to play, but it is the perfect vehicle for a casual experience where consumers can lose hours relaxing and cleaning up. With estimates from Steam Spy putting it at between 1 and 2 million copies sold. This is again why part of the game development process is coming up with who the audience is for your game and understanding what they want out of a game.

Could the developers have created content that is high stakes like fighting mud monsters or putting out giant fires? Of course, but that would go against the theme and the aesthetics they were aiming for. With aesthetics, you always want a unified theme to your game, unless you are purposely trying to make something unnerving or out of place.

Figure 8.16

You may not think a game like *PowerWash Simulator* would be something people played, but the game took the act of shooting and transformed it into a low stakes, relaxing experience that delivered a kind of game that no one had played quite like that before.

Shooters have also gone in the way of not being about a character running around with a gun. There is an incalculable number at this point of games where vehicles are shooting at each other, and when I say "vehicle," I mean any kind of vehicle – boats, spaceships, cars, tanks, planes, anything you can think of. For vehicle-based combat, this does take us to the subject of simulating physics beyond just how a character moves. There are games that try to accurately simulate what a fighter ship in space would feel like, just as it could be 100% arcade-like. One of the most popular online games is *World of Tanks* by Wargaming (first released in 2010), that is all about teams of players fighting each other in tanks modeled after their real-world versions. Talking about simulating different vehicles is beyond the scope of this book.

Just as you can go serious and very realistic, you could build a shooter on an absurd and comedic premise. *Fashion Police Squad* by Mopeful Games (released in 2022) turns the idea of the fashion police into a shooter. Instead of shooting guns at bad guys, you are using weapons designed to fix fashion faux pas and make everyone stylish. Sales are estimated between 20 and 50k according to Steam Spy.

The point of this section is to get you to think about FPS design beyond just focusing on guns. Not every game needs to be grim and dark, and you can make a name for yourself by taking the aesthetics of a genre and going somewhere completely different with them. No matter how you design the tone of your game, you still need to think about gunplay and feel. Just because someone is using a whoopie cushion or throwing a pie instead of a pistol, it still must feel good to do (Figure 8.17). This is another trap that is easy to fall into as a new designer

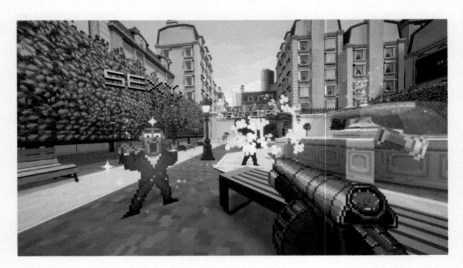

Figure 8.17

*Fashion Police Squad* does play like other shooters that came before it, but the entire tone is more comical than violent. All the weapon designs fit within the style of other shooters, but are made to fit the theme of the game.

8. Advanced Shooter Design

when trying to stand out – there are some parts of your design that you don't want to try and fix that weren't broken in the first place. For any gameplay loop in your title, it must feel good to interact with. For developers who combine genre mechanics and systems into something original, there is a tendency to only focus on one element and leave the other one not feeling right. As I said earlier in the book, when you combine different elements of games together, you are creating a title specifically for someone looking for that combination and not the sum total of fans of each. If your game is both about high speed shooting and crafting different weapons, you don't want the crafting angle to be hard to do or cumbersome. As I said in the last chapter, it is better to have one complete concept than having multiple ones that don't feel equal to each other.

And if you don't want to focus on making a refined and polished shooter with gunplay, you can always go for something that is unique and plays like nothing else. For example, there is *Cruelty Squad* (released in 2021 by Consumer Softproducts), a game that its entire mission statement was to be, look, and play like nothing else on the market. The game went viral thanks to its unusual design and aesthetics and has an estimated 1–2 million copies sold according to Steam Spy. If you are going to go the route of being different, you still must convey that and what someone must do to play your game.

There are already an infinite number of games that play like the original *Doom*, just as there are as many *Super Mario World*-likes thanks to modders. No one wants to play your version of these classic games; they want to see something new and original.

## 8.6 The Philosophy of Powers and Push-Forward Combat

For this last section, I want to discuss two aspects of shooter design that aren't just about guns. As I've talked about in previous chapters, the 2010s came with it a change of shooter design to integrate more abstraction and character diversity into their design. For these games, it's not only about providing solid gunplay, but also giving the player abilities that are unique to them to give them an edge over their enemies.

Building a shooter, single or multiplayer, around unique powers is a way to make your game stand out from everyone else on the market – there have been many shooters from indie developers who went viral thanks to just one GIF showing off what makes their game different from everyone else. With shooters, or any reflex-driven game, if you can't get people excited about your game through a GIF showing combat or your gunplay, then you don't have something marketable (Figure 8.18).

If you're hoping for a step-by-step breakdown of how to build "uniqueness" into your shooter, even beyond your gunplay, that is not going to happen here, as there is no repeatable checklist for originality. The first thing you need to decide is the "power" or powers of the main character and the player – how strong are they compared to the rest of your game? In shooters like *Severed Steel*, the player

Figure 8.18

Your job with any genre as the game designer is to be able to show someone "the cool" of your game. The shorter and to the point you can, the better. Arkane Studios who have made games like *Dishonored* and *Deathloop* use unique visuals and combat to catch the attention of consumers.

is more powerful than any enemy on the field, but this is compensated for by the fact that they can only take one hit and are always going to be outnumbered. If your enemies have unique powers like teleporting, summoning minions, etc., can the player do that? And if not, what do they have to counter it? Ideally, you want your unique selling point or ability in your game to be as far away from "gun" as you can. The point isn't to give the player more guns to stand out, but to give them something that they won't find in any other shooter.

This is also where world building and story design can help you with your gameplay. In *The Darkness 2* by Digital Extremes, released in 2012, the entire game is built off a comic series where the main character has the literal power of darkness in him thanks to a demon. In it, the player is powerful whenever the main character is in the dark, but this comes with the weakness to light that the enemies make use of. Levels are full of spotlights and other light sources set up by the enemies to weaken the player; requiring them to destroy them to make full use of their powers.

The balancing act when it comes to power and uniqueness is that if the player is never in any danger, is completely in control over the situation, and the enemies have no way of responding to the player, then you end up with a shooter, or any game that becomes boring to play. To add to that, the world itself must "respond" in some way to the player's abilities (Figure 8.19). If for example you are building a shooter where the player can literally create fire and lightning out

8. Advanced Shooter Design

Figure 8.19

*The Darkness 2* does a great job of not only presenting a protagonist who is pound-for-pound stronger than any enemy on the field, but also building the world and gameplay around what enemies can do to try and fight them. From earlier in the book, giving the player cool powers, unique abilities, etc., only feel good when the world and enemies react to it. This also opens up the option to create enemies built to mess with the player's ability and turn combat on its head.

of their fingertips at will, the player is going to want to use that in some fashion for the main gameplay loop. Remember this point – if you are building your game as an FPS, anything that is unique about your game must be attached to that gameplay loop.

Returning to *Portal* and *Portal 2*, both games' design and puzzle philosophy begin and end with the player's portal gun – every enemy, every new environmental obstacle, every new "invention," or puzzle mechanic can be used in some way by the portal gun, which is the player's form of interacting with the world. This also has the added benefit of allowing you more flexibility in terms of designing content related to new elements. The more ways that something in your game can be used or repurpose will give you more options with designing new areas and situations. The worst thing to do is to create something unique that took months of time, money, and resources, for it to only matter for about 10 seconds of actual playtime in your game, or it has nothing to do with the core gameplay loop.

Uniqueness for the sake of uniqueness is an easy trap I've seen developers fall into with any genre. There must be a point to your mechanics, to your rules, and to your design, if you want people to resonate with your game. As an example of doing this right, the shooter *Hellscreen* that is in early access at the time of me writing this by Mixtape Games UK is built off the entire idea that the player can

Figure 8.20

*Cruelty Squad* is a game where there is not one screenshot I could show you that would make it clear why people enjoyed playing it. And I don't have the space in this caption to go into detail about it either.

fight enemies behind them using a rearview mirror. This not only gives the player a complete field of vison all around them but is necessary to find and fight invisible enemies in the level. Once again, *Cruelty Squad* was a game that was not designed to be the next *Doom Eternal*, but to be as weird and original as one can be, and those decisions resonate through the entire game (Figure 8.20).

And I want to stress the point that making either your enemies or your character behave differently than in other shooters must be balanced. To go back to my earlier example about rate of fire and gunplay, if every enemy in your game is super-fast and moves and reacts several times faster than the character and the player can, there needs to be some balancing element for what the player can do to get around that. If you want enemies to be fast and the player must rely on slower weapons, then those weapons could be balanced to one shot an enemy to go with the downside of taking a longer time to fire again.

With that said, let's talk more about push-forward combat and what it means from a game design standpoint. As I discussed earlier, the point of this philosophy is that the player should always be engaging with the combat or core gameplay loop. In games that use this, it is made quite explicitly that aggression and offense is the name of the game. Returning to *Ultrakill*, the game's rating system was updated after launch along with the game's use of "hard damage." Hard damage builds up as the player gets hit and prevents a certain percentage of the health bar from being recovered by doing close-ranged combat. This was meant to punish players who tried to tank hits and just relied on rushing in and hitting

Figure 8.21

*Meatgrinder*'s entire M.O. is the more over-the-top the better. But it still has that weird feeling when the player is technically punished for standing still, although by the design of the game, that doesn't happen too often.

the enemy to gain it all back. With the style system, the higher the player's style meter is at any time will affect the rate that hard damage is removed. If someone is at S or higher, hard damage disappears very quickly.

Some games make this ***very explicit***, such as *Meatgrinder* (released in 2023 by Vampire Squid). In it, the player literally cannot stop moving, because adrenaline equals health and health recovery (Figure 8.21). Stand still for too long, and the character will die; keep moving and shooting, and they will recover health. The downside of this approach is that it takes the reflex-driven design into overdrive and can become tiring to play for long stretches.

What you are trying to achieve is a game where the player should always be "on." Returning to cover-based shooting in the 2000s, due to the high risk of getting hit and the longer downtimes, a popular strategy was to try and snipe every enemy as far away from the arena or battle as possible before engaging. Or in boomer shooters: open a door, fire a bullet, run to the side of the door to let it close, and rinse and repeat. While these strategies worked, they also made the games boring to play, or frustrating if the player chose not to do it due to getting consistently hit. Push-forward design is all about keeping the player in action whenever possible.

A detail that you will always have to balance with anything unique in your game, push forward or otherwise is the player's resources around those elements. Giving the player some kind of super powerful attack, but it can only be used with incredibly rare ammo, means that they will hoard that option. The more you want someone to use something in your game, the easier it should be to use it. If your game is built heavily on special powers, either make their use on a cooldown, or allow the player to recharge those resources through play. However, the cooldown needs to be balanced based on the pacing of the gameplay. There are games where the cooldown before someone can use their powers is so high that the player can only use these abilities once maybe every other encounter. If you are designing an ability that is meant to be overpowered, like freezing every enemy in the area, then you obviously don't want the player to use it every 5 seconds. But the player should never feel like they're being punished for a lengthy period for wanting to do something in your game. This is why many games, not just shooters, have moved away from lengthy cooldowns and instead tie its use to a conditional event – kill X enemies, pick up ammo, take damage, etc. This way, while the skill still is powerful and can't be immediately used, but the means of replenishing it will naturally occur during the general play. Again, this is the major functionality of push-forward combat, by allowing the player to recharge essential resources through combat, it means that the player is never punished due to a lack of supply in any given encounter.

That last point is something that has represented some of the major shifts of action and abstracted design over the 2010s. Traditionally, the player's ability to recover resources is always limited – by money or the number of supplies on the map. If the player is too aggressive in the short term, or takes too much damage, it can punish them long term or even cause them to become **soft-lock** and unable to continue due to a lack of supplies. By keeping essential resources easily recoverable, it means the player may be punished short term for using too much ammo, taking too much damage, etc., but they will be able to recover for the long-term play.

Uniqueness does sell any kind of game, but it only works if the rest of your design is solid. As I said further up, just making something unique to say your game is unique doesn't translate into more sales. The games that make this work take their unique selling points and fully integrate them into the rest of the design. If you are making something that seems cool but doesn't relate to anything else that's in your game or your core gameplay loop, you may want to question whether it's worth it to keep working on it (Figure 8.22).

As one final point about uniqueness and pacing, games that are built on unique or specific mechanics are often shorter than other ones. The reason is that even with those unique elements, you still need to make sure that there is progression happening in some way, shape, or form, in your game. It's a lot harder to keep coming up with different use cases for an ability that isn't easily definable. Returning to *Portal*, both games are on the shorter side compared to other titles, as each puzzle and situation was designed to specifically fit with the use of the portal gun and the unique rules of each new element. This is why being smart with how you add new content to your game matters – if you can work on something that affords you more chances to build new content vs. something that only works one time, the former is a better investment. There are exceptions if that one specific thing is a major set piece or a defining moment in your game, but it all comes back to how all this relates to the playing of your game.

Figure 8.22

Immersive sims are built around having all their abilities and tools be usable in almost any circumstance. With *Prey* (released in 2017 by Arkane Studios), there are multiple ways of approaching any situation based on what skills the player has available, and it is even possible to play the game without any of them as a challenge.

No matter how unique or generic your gameplay is, just remember that more doesn't equal better in the eyes of the consumer. If you can create 100 hours of entirely original, never-before-seen, and fantastic gameplay, more power to you. Consumers today want a quality experience – whether that's 20 hours, 10 hours, or 40 minutes, it doesn't matter. As I tell designers, your first goal should be simply creating 30 minutes of amazing gameplay; if you can't manage that, then no amount of unique features, gripping storylines, or amazing graphics is going to save your game. And if you can do that, you should be able to build off of that to create more amazing content.

# 9

# The Future of Shooters

## 9.1 Old vs. New Shooter Design

Shooters, like all game genres, have seen a massive change and shift in their approach and gameplay over the 2010s. For the market, we are seeing a resurgence of boomer and arcade shooting, and in an odd turn a decline in modern shooting. While the heavyweights like *Call of Duty*, *Valorant*, and Destiny *2* continue to do well, there is a malaise being felt with regard to live service design and shooting.

Much like the mobile market, there is this point where the already established games are locked in with regard to their success, but new games are facing an uphill battle of courting consumers without having the name recognition or trust built up over years of support and success. There is no doubt that *Call of Duty* as a mega franchise is going to be doing well, but like the push for battle royale games, anyone else trying to break into that specific space is going to find challenge (Figure 9.1).

Consumers are becoming tired of having every game wanting to be their "everyday game," and when you throw in the competitive aspect of shooting on top of that, it becomes a shrinking market of people willing to shoot and spend

DOI: 10.1201/9781003449959-9

Figure 9.1

A similar point I mentioned with live service games is that you should not be distracted by the amount of profit the makers of these games report or how much they've made in the past. As a developer, you should not be attempting to compete for the same market as them unless you can make something different. And other than *The Finals*, I could not find any other new multiplayer shooters released at the end of 23 or into 24 who is doing their own thing.

in these games. Part of this is trying to connect competitive shooters to eSports, with all the major names in the space having backings from eSports teams and brands to go with them. However, creating a great game and creating a great competitive game are two different goals, and trying to force one onto the other has led to many games crashing and burning.

As I was writing the ending of this book, a new competitive shooter hit the scene in the form of *The Finals* by Embark Studios. A quick look does show that they are trying to do something different in terms of gunplay and general mechanics, but there is one important detail about any live service game regardless of its genre – the true measure of the longevity of live service is if a game can survive at minimum 1 year from launch.

If you want to attempt to build a live service shooter, you cannot just recreate *Call of Duty* or *Fortnite* but with a different aesthetic. And if you want to chase after the likes of *Destiny 2* or *Warframe*, you are really going to need to do something that neither one of those games are doing/have done, and that is a tall order.

On the flip side of the coin, arcade-based shooting has seen more growth and movement since the success of *Dusk*. There has always been a market for arcade shooting and popular mods being made, but they're now getting more mainstream recognition. Despite the success of *Doom 2016* and *Doom Eternal*, there

Figure 9.2

Even with the newfound appreciation of boomer shooters, consumers don't want to keep playing the same games with the same design, and they don't want to play yet another battle royale or military shooter clone. For shooters coming out that are doing something different, there is the immersive sim stealth game *Gloomwood* with the tagline "*Thief* with guns." And the horror shooter *Paperclip* where drawings become alive and are out to get the player. Both games are not out at the time of writing this book.

hasn't been another push-forward/arcade shooter from a AAA studio, instead we have been seeing more innovations and titles from the indie space. However, more interest from consumers also means these games are being judged harder than they were 5 years ago. For any shooter developer or modder wanting to take that next step and build their own original boomer shooter now, they are going to be in for the same rude awakening that platformer and RPG designers had over the 2010s – consumers don't want to just keep replaying the classics. There needs to be something special about your game, something that hasn't been seen before if you want more people to check it out.

With so many shooters being released on top of every other genre, just making a "good" example is not enough if you want your game to reach people beyond just the hardcore fans (Figure 9.2). The advantage of reflex-driven design is that every game can feel differently to the consumers – just because you've played one FPS it doesn't mean you now know how to play all of them. However, that puts everything on designers to go above and beyond if they expect their games to meet or beat the previous best example.

To prove that point, *Dusk* at the time of writing this sits at just over 18k reviews on Steam with an estimate ranging between 1 and 2 million copies bought according to Steam Spy.[1] Of the other boomer-shooter-specific FPSs that have

9. The Future of Shooters

come out since, not one has managed to outdo it numbers-wise. With every genre that I've covered so far, there is this assumption that once a genre or subgenre goes mainstream thanks to one big-selling game, then everyone else in that space can then make games with similar sales. However, that is not the case, and for your game to then stand out, you must go even bigger than the last hit. And for some genres and hits, "going bigger" may not literally be possible, which means doing something different that may not bring in the same numbers but will still earn you a fanbase and a piece of the market.

That said, if your goal isn't to dominate the shooter market with your title and just make an appealing game to the hardcore fans, then you are certainly free to do that. Sometimes a successful game is one that just manages to "stick the landing" at the end of the day. But no matter what genre you are working in, understanding the market, and keeping your budget under control are essential lessons for surviving long term in the industry.

I always hate giving predictions when it comes to the game industry, as things can move so fast that by the time this book is printed, I may either be completely right, or some new trend has upended the entire conversation and invalided my prediction.

There is one aspect of predicting the future that I am curious to see – will another AAA-level studio try to compete in the single player shooter market that isn't id Software? This is tougher than it looks to answer. AAA studios have the budget to create high-fidelity shooting that is beyond the scope of an indie. However, that fidelity will always come at the cost of performance and hardware requirements. The current aesthetic trend for many indie studios today has been a return to early 3D/PlayStation 1 or PlayStation 2 graphics. While this look is not going to be as impressive, it does allow them to focus on the gameplay and an easier time making sure their games run properly. Pushing hardware requirements will always leave out consumers who don't have the money to upgrade. On the console side, typing this at the start of 2024, it remains to be seen when there will be the next generation of consoles that will push the hardware from that side even further.

Shooters and the FPS design have seen a boom period beyond the live service multiplayer shooters. Many indie developers have released or are working on fantastic takes on the genre. However, this is both the best and worst time to create an FPS – the recognition in the space is at its highest that we've seen since the 90s and early 2000s, but it has also created a sense of fatigue that we have seen previously with deck builders that even the best examples of them still struggle to stand out in a market full of them. On the live service side, it's going to become harder to convince someone to dedicate time to your game compared to the major names, and why so many battle royale games have come and went with exception to the already established ones. While that side has become harder, that doesn't mean that multiplayer shooters are completely close to you, *The Finals* notwithstanding.

## 9.2 Where Can Multiplayer Design Go?

For as long as people are going to have online friends, there will be a market for multiplayer games that aren't as live service-focused compared to the bigger names. People are always looking for games that they can play in quick bursts of time on their schedule, and that leaves the door open for designers who want to capture that market without the overwhelming design of live service with daily play, loot boxes, monetization, and more. Returning to *World War Z*, the game became a surprise hit and lasted much longer than anyone could have anticipated by being a well-made spiritual follow-up to *Left 4 Dead*. Monetization was focused on quality with new expansions and DLC as opposed to quantity with trying to capitalize on every aspect of the design.

With any multiplayer game that is expected to last for years, you must have a plan for monetization and long-term growth, which doesn't mean you need to focus on the same aggressive schedule as live service games go. *Deep Rock Galactic* is another success that has been going on for years at the time of writing this with a more relaxed schedule for content, because the gameplay itself is unique and good enough to keep people invested.

Examining the multiplayer shooters released in the 2010s that have survived and thrived, each one was designed to be different and occupy its own specific space in the market. If your plan as a studio is to just rip off *Battlefield, Valorant, Fortnite, Apex Legends, Destiny,* or *Rainbow Six: Siege*, your game is not going to make any waves in the market. And people are getting tired of games all trying to copy the monetization model (Figure 9.3).

As I mentioned earlier with *Lethal Company*, this is an example of a game that came out of nowhere, offered something different, and resonated with a lot of people. Part of growing as a game designer is trying to understand what people are looking for in a game. Trying to build the "every game" is never going to work; you must figure out what you can offer to consumers that they either want, or don't know that they want. Who knows, by the time you're reading these very words, there may be yet another game that has blown up and has once again changed the state of the market.

As I was finishing this book, news was breaking that many studios are going all in with live service games going forward in 2024 and into 2025. Consumer fatigue is real when it comes to games that are being designed to take over their free time. And like I said at the end of my live service book, it's perfectly fine to go into a game with the intention of making money; but if your goal is to try to make all the money with live service practices and build your whole studio around that, you're going to find that people have gotten tired of being told they need to invest hours daily into a game to keep up. The industry has reached a point where there are now literally more games being released than anyone has the time to play them all. In 2023, I played over 1,000 different games, and even that wasn't enough to keep up with everything. Multiplayer design lives or dies

Figure 9.3

Being the top dog of a specific kind of game can be just as good as dominating the market. *Dead by Daylight* continues to be the undisputed king of its 4v1 gameplay, and has outlived each major competitor to date. *The Finals* has been standing out by once again doing something purposely different than the other shooters, and it will be telling to see where the game is at by the end of 2024.

based on keeping people around to play – all the lootboxes and daily rewards are not going to hold people hostage to a game they don't feel like playing anymore. With so many live service games and studios being closed in 2023 and 2024, I personally feel that the market is shrinking for the traditional live service model developers have been using for years now. The major game success released in 2024 for cooperative shooting was *Helldivers 2* by Arrowhead Game Studios, and it succeeded by being different from any other cooperative shooter on the market today. Will that success follow for years to come? It's hard to say, but just copying what everyone else has done is not going to work anymore.

## Note

1 https://steamspy.com/app/519860

# 10

# Conclusion

## 10.1 Summing Up the Shooter Genre

As I've ping-ponged between genres with this series, I find it interesting to look at the parallels between the ones I've covered. Shooters and platformers are both similar in that it's easy to think that because people still hold the likes of *Doom* (or *Mario* with platformers) in high regard, that the genre is simple to make a good game in (Figure 10.1). As you've read over 70k words in this book, I think you know as well as I do that's not accurate at all. With shooters and RPGs, both genres have seen a fundamental split in terms of what people expect out of them today, and how making a "shooter" and making an "RPG" can mean vastly different things depending on the designer.

What is unique to this genre is how quickly these games can rise or fall due to their gunplay and gameplay. Depending on the RPG design, gamers may need a few minutes or more to see if the systems work for them, but here fighting one enemy may be all someone needs to decide whether your game is worth playing.

This is a good genre to test your abilities when it comes to game feel, and this is something that is incredibly hard to describe, but when it's right or wrong the consumer can just tell. In a way, it makes the genre easier to build a game around

DOI: 10.1201/9781003449959-10

Figure 10.1

Congratulations on finishing this book, while I don't have an energy sword to present to you, just imagine that all the information you've learned in this book is like a sword and your muscles should be just as big as the Doom Slayer. Rip and tear, until it is done (your game that is).

as you'll know quickly whether you have something or not, but that also means that standing out is going to be harder if you don't know what you're doing.

My biggest advice for you in terms of starting to make a shooter and marketing one is this – can you show someone 5 seconds of amazing and original gameplay? Shooters by their very design are easy to market and show off, but, if you can't even get this right, then you don't have a game that people are going to be interested in. For marketing purposes, look at the social media for any FPS designer and watch the GIFs they put out. Many of these games blew up simply because they showed off 5 seconds of "awesome" that highlights what makes their game special. And if you don't want to make a game about guns, strangely enough, that's also fine thanks to the games we've talked about, among many others, that use shooter mechanics in a different way.

You may not be interested in making the goriest and most violent shooter, but maybe you want to make the ultimate pie throwing simulator the world has ever seen. A point that keeps coming up in these deep dives is that, while feel and UX matter, don't look at specific mechanics of a genre as being set in stone. Just like with RPGs, so many now famous examples came about thanks to a developer saying, "what if I make my game with/without X?" And if you're not comfortable with trying to make an original game for an idea, there is a bevy of modding tools and software for you to experiment with.

Once you get it right, it is something that you can keep doing and improving on no matter if your game is about the highest detail a game engine can produce or just highly detailed pixels shooting at one another.

For you reading this, if you have a weird or original idea for a shooter that you haven't seen before, try it out. Make a prototype or a quick GIF and show it to people. Fans and developers of shooters are always looking for something cool and different to show to everyone else, and many games have been given life simply by showing people that new idea. And if it doesn't work, that's perfectly fine as well. Not every idea is meant to be the next billion dollar earner, but if you want to improve as a designer, you need to keep building and improving your skills. And if you do end up making that ultimate pie throwing simulator, be sure to mention my name.

# Glossary

**Aesthetics:** The emotion or mood you are trying to convey in your game using the gameplay and the visual and audio design.

**Diegetic:** For video games, having either music or in-game GUI elements represented within the world itself.

**DLC:** Stands for downloadable content and is a catch-all term for anything and everything that developers sell as purchases beyond the base game.

**eSports:** Playing competitive games at the professional level with teams, sponsorships, and big money and recognition on the line.

**GUI:** Stands for Graphical User Interface and represents all on-screen elements that someone will be looking at in order to play a game.

**Hitbox:** An invisible wireframe around a character or projectile that is used by the game engine to determine whether the model has collided with something. For shooters, the character's hitbox when struck by a projectile will register as a hit and will cause damage to that character.

**Lootbox:** A monetization practice of allowing the player to open a box using real or in-game currency for a randomly selected reward from a fixed pool, with some items rarer than the others.

**Metroidvania:** A genre of game that focuses on exploration and combat with the player able to upgrade their character with new ways of moving around to better explore the world.

**MMOGs:** Short for massively multiplayer online games and is a genre of game known for having large numbers of players interacting with each other at the same time.

| | |
|---|---|
| MOBA: | Short for multiplayer online battle arena and is a genre where every player in a team controls one unique character and they must work together to beat the opposing team. |
| Mods: | Custom content created by fans either using a software development kit (or SDK) or creating their own custom tools. Mods can come in all shapes, sizes, and variety of changes to the base game. |
| Roguelike: | A genre built on replaying the game with each run resetting the player's progress and the entire world, providing a fresh experience for each play. |
| Roguelite: | A variation of a roguelike where there is carryover or persistence across runs allowing players to grow in power whether they win or lose the previous run. |
| Skill Ceiling: | A way to describe the overall skill level someone will need to see a game from start to finish. |
| Skill Curve: | Used to describe the general progression of the game from the point of view of the player, and how fast or slow the game will expect more out of someone to keep making progress. |
| Skill Floor: | Used to describe the skill or knowledge someone should have when beginning a game to be able to understand what is going on and start making progress. |
| Soft-lock: | A situation where the player is unable to keep playing the game or make any progress, but the game itself has not crashed. |
| Spawn: | Used to describe enemies appearing in a level after an event trigger has been activated. Can also be referred to as "respawning" when a player's character comes back after being killed in a multiplayer game. |
| UI: | Stands for User Interface and is a catch-all term for all the different physical interactions someone has for playing a game. |
| UX: | Stands for User Experience and is used to describe what it feels like to play a game and any positives or negatives about interacting with it. |

# Index

Note: *Italic* page numbers refer to figures.